"When it comes to growing up, our modern culture acts as if we are all amateurs. Rites and Responsibilities stands on the ancestral wisdom that is in the bones of all people and all generations. We've lost our way in these trying times, but this book shows it's all accessible. Our young people must be seen, heard, guided, and cared for on their journey toward adulthood. We know how to do this. Using modern techniques of research and inquiry, and her own extensive lived experiences as well as stories of many young people, Darcy proves it's never a lost art."

–Luis J. Rodriguez, author of the memoirs Always Running, La Vida Loca, Gang Days in L.A. and It Calls You Back: An Odyssey Through Love, Addiction, Revolutions & Healing

☾

"As a formerly lost young person, it wasn't until rock bottom experiences that I realized that I could afford myself the love of finding guides that actually cared. Darcy and community are among those teachers, with this book delivering much of the knowledge and understanding gained through the school of life that has desperately needed to be documented for the collective to behold. It will serve as a pillar in youth education and emergent strategies that will carry us through paradigm transitions and emerging shifts to come..."

–j. nyla "ink" mcneill, Owner, Mx. Lifestyling and Steward, School for the Ecocene

☾

"This robust and passionate book points towards becoming ever more human in an increasingly inhuman time. Filled with stories and insight, Darcy has diligently gathered all kinds of gifts here. It rehydrates wonder."

–Martin Shaw, author of Courting the Wild Twin

"Rites and Responsibilities is going to help a lot of young people and adults, empowering them with tools to serve them on their journey toward healing for themselves and their communities: body, mind, heart, and spirit. Through sharing her own life experiences and the experiences of a number of young people, Darcy helps readers connect with the earth and all the healing that can come through this connection. At its core, that's what this book is all about."

–Sharon Blackwolf, Indigenous elder and former educator in the school system

☾

"Finally, an intelligent and comprehensive book that not only teaches, but guides young people, and adults, into the important understanding of the necessity of rites of passage for our youth today. It artfully bridges the many thousands of years in which most every culture offered this ceremony for the balance and health of their communities ... into our world today and its many serious challenges and cultural adjustments. Our youth are hurting, and struggling to find their place. We need to return this time honored earth-based wisdom to its place in human society."

–Meredith Little, author of The School of Lost Borders: A Love Story and Co-Founder, School of Lost Borders

☾

"I have met few white two-leggeds walking a more dedicated, humble and generous path, in service of healed relationships with ourselves, each other and our ecosystem, than Darcy Ottey. She is a perpetual student, making for the best kind of teacher, both in theory and by example. This book is one of many brilliant offerings from Darcy that embody her walking of her talk. Her deep hope in, as well as care and respect for young people come through in every word. Young people and the adults who love them, all have something to gain by reading this book."

–J. Miakoda Taylor, Lead Steward of Fierce Allies

"In this timely and accessible guide to navigating youth rites of passage, Darcy Ottey brings a depth of cultural awareness, a pragmatic and inviting approach to crafting ritual, and a spirit of kindness and embodied care. Her work is tempered by years of experience weaving rites of passage in ancestrally diverse communities and a keen understanding of the tender, complex, and necessary work of cultural recovery and Earth reconnection."

–Daniel Foor, author of Ancestral Medicine: Rituals for Personal and Family Healing

☾

"Darcy Ottey authored a remarkable book of life's passages, relevant for our contemporary minds and hearts. It encourages us to trust the inner being that is the child and the child is us, the one that emerges from these journeys to tell the truths of the inner world and the one who finds the confidence to stand in the midst of global changes and give their gifts. We will be reminded that the pathways are always around us with old and new ways of returning to a higher shared purpose through the gifts of being in community. Rites and Responsibilities: A Guide to Growing Up is also a guide to growing into ever deeper belongings with the greater life."

–Orland Bishop, author of The Seventh Shrine: Meditations on the African Spiritual Journey From the Middle Passage to the Mountaintop and Founder of Shadetree Multicultural Foundation

☾

"Darcy does an incredible job at exploring rites of passage, healing, purpose and sharing her experience with initiatory practices in this book. The healing practices found in this book have the capacity to not only change lives but even save lives. This is an incredible self healing and growth resource for anyone seeking to find purpose in their own lives and looking to connect deeper with the power that lies within them."

–Arturo Quiros, Producer and Social Justice Advocate, Soul Felony Productions

"The intelligence of nature acts in the interest of planetary life through Darcy Ottey. This book is an expression of the ancient memory that we as human beings are, in fact, both scientifically and spiritually related to all creation. Page by page we are initiated into the recollection of our belonging in a divine order, and to the rights and responsibilities we have thereby been entrusted with. Generations of wisdom are given a unique voice here, making a way for the healthy cultivation of wisdom by many more, over generations to come. May you also receive the benefit of this offering and may it bring forth more of your own personal medicine for the greater good of all our relations."

–Seth Lennon Weiner, Director of Life Comes From It and once initiated youth

☾

"To Whom Much is Given, Much Will Be Required"

The adage "the apple does not fall far from the tree" could not be more appropriate than for what Darcy Ottey has contributed through "Rites and Responsibilities: A Guide To Growing Up".

This timely youth development handbook is a product of ordeals, challenges, nurturing, guidance, and calling. There is no better time for this handbook than during this "moment of truth." It serves as an introduction for young people to rites of passage, their birthright and social and ecological responsibility. What Darcy has provided is a guide for the cultivation of a "new harvest" that can assume responsibility for themselves, community and planet—the living and unborn!

–Elder Paul Hill, Jr, National Rites of Passage Institute, East Cleveland, Ohio

☾

"I am full of gratitude for the emergence of Rites and Responsibilities: A Guide to Growing Up in our time! Cultural visionary Darcy Ottey offers us a template for significant rites of passage – and what it means to be a true adult – in this monumental book. At the epicenter of the movement for many years, her passion, dedication, warmth and care shine through on every page. Written for a diverse audience of young people, organizations serving youth, rites of passage practitioners, nature immersion guides, educators, social justice activists, and seekers from every stage of life, Rites and Responsibilities is a brilliant resource. Including examples from her own life and the stories of others, Darcy outlines the human developmental process, how trauma and displacement happen from a lack of rites of passage, and how to uncolonize from the western worldview. As both a spiritual guide and practical workbook, R&R includes exercises for knowing the self, essential mindsets for initiation, new possibilities for cultural identity, tools for mentoring and other supports, creating personal rituals, the importance of ancestral connection, and facing the complexities of late-stage capitalism. With an emphasis on bonding to nature and learning from First Nations, this guidebook weaves the values of cross-cultural protocols and collective liberation with finding our special roles and skills, and embracing healthy relationships, both with people and the land. To step through the gateway into adulthood requires the preparations as outlined in this important book, and this transition can happen even in our later years. True adulthood means taking on a path of service, adopting the practices of the authentic, or initiated life, and holding a deep understanding of our connectivity to Beloved Community, both human and other-than-human. Embodying the ancestral wisdom of rites of passage is essential in this era of massive change, and Rites and Responsibilities: A Guide to Growing Up will take us on that journey of transformation."

–Pegi Eyers, author of Ancient Spirit Rising: Reclaiming Your Roots & Restoring Earth Community www.stonecirclepress.com

☾

"I wish I had access to the wisdom offered in this book when I was an adolescent. It guides the reader on a path toward a healthy, whole adulthood filled with a strong sense of identity, purpose, and belonging. No matter your age, this book offers important insights and suggestions for how each of us can play a role in repairing a society and world that can feel irrevocably broken. At its core, this book is about making connections and taking steps that will bring us closer to revealing the magic lying within us. Following its recommended exercises will usher in the potential for a deeper relationship with yourself, the people in your life, your wider community, unseen guidance, and the natural world."

–Shelly Tochluk, Author of Witnessing Whiteness: The Journey into Racial Awareness and Anti Racist Action and Living in the Tension: The Quest for a Spiritualized Racial Justice

☾

"Rites and Responsibilities is a significant contribution to the world of rites of passage for young people. As one with great passion and heart, a truth-teller who has dedicated her life to the essential nature of this work, Darcy's experiences with rites of passage began at a young age and now, she is a true "middler," bridging the worlds of youth and elders in ways too often missing. She makes relevant the practices of our times, contributing to the needed healing in our world. This book is truly relevant for all ages, helping readers have a hand and heart at the center of what is on fire and needs tending today."

–Gigi Coyle, Co-Founder of Youth Passageways, Beyond Boundaries and Walking Water

☾

"Darcy Ottey has created a detailed roadmap for restoring rites of passage. Her generous, compassionate perspective offers essential and well-considered nuances for the journey. Rites and Responsibilities makes space for people of all identities to be initiated in safe and authentic ways.

–Hilary Giovale, 9th generation American settler, reparationist, and mother, goodrelative.com.

☾

"Darcy is a leader helping young people and the field of contemporary youth rites of passage come of age in a healing, just and transformative way. We are blessed to sit by her fire, to learn from her wisdom, and to journey with her toward a future that is calling to us all."

–Joshua Gorman, Youth & Community Organizer, Founder of Generation Waking Up

☾

"Rites and Responsibilities is a blessing. So much used to be oral history. Now it needs to be written and recorded for our young ones and future generations. Much has been lost as our librarians, our elders, were taken from us. Our rites of passage, protocols, and ceremonies, share the importance of where you come from, and what your ancestors went through for you to be here today. All cultures and traditions have these teachings, and Darcy helps young people access them so all youth can grow up connected, knowing who they are, where they came from, and what they came here to do."

–Becky Chief Eagle, Founder of All Nations Gathering Center

RITES AND RESPONSIBILITIES
A Guide to Growing Up

by Darcy Ottey

Forward by Ramon Gabrieloff-Parish and M. Kalani Souza
Illustrations by Smo Sienkiewicz
Cover art and additional graphics by Derya Albayrak

LOST BORDERS PRESS
BIG PINE, CALIFORNIA

Lost Borders Press
PO Box 55
Big Pine, CA 93513

© 2022 Darcy Jane Ottey. All rights reserved. Please contact the author for permission to reproduce in any form, save in short quotations.

Please read this warning before using this book:
Rites of passage present emotional, mental, physical, and spiritual risks, which may result in emotional and physical injury or even death. Difficult and sensitive topics are discussed in this book. Some of this content may cause anxiety, confusion, or activate unwanted memories. Please engage in this content to the extent that feels healthy. Based on your unique personal needs, practices and activities in this book may not be helpful, and may even be harmful. Please seek advice from qualified health professionals or trusted mentos regarding your personal conditions and needs.

No expressed or implied guarantee as to the effects of the use of the recommendations can be given or liability taken by the author for your use of this material. Please do not depend solely on information in this book for your personal safety and do not allow this book to take the place of proper guidance and support. Employ a trained guide or a trusted mentor if you are unsure of your ability to handle any circumstances that may arise while engaging in these practices.

Cover & Text Design and layout by Derya Albayrak
Illustrations by Smo Sienkiewicz

Antonio Machado, Proverbs and Songs #29: ["Walker, your footsteps"] from *Border of a Dream: Selected Poems*, translated by Willis Barnstone. Copyright © 2004 by the Heirs of Antonio Machado. English translation copyright © 2004 by Willis Barnstone. Reprinted with the permission of The Permissions Company, LLC on behalf of Copper Canyon Press, www.coppercanyonpress.org.

Excerpt from "What to Remember When Waking" in *The House of Belonging* by David Whyte, copyright ©Many Rivers Press. Reprinted by printed with permission from Many Rivers Press, www.davidwhyte.com Langley, WA USA.

ISBN 978-1-7333123-0-1
Printed in the United States of America

A minimum of 10% of the proceeds go to Black and Indigenous-led efforts to reclaim land and lifeways.

For Zachary, Xavier, Jean, Emma, Maya, Jackson, Sage, Khalil, Lucia, and Kian. You all have been, and continue to be, my most brilliant teachers. May this book serve you, and may you fully embody the gifts you have to bring.

TABLE OF CONTENTS

Acknowledgements III

Forward by Kalani Souza and Ramon Parish IX

Introduction 1

PART I: GETTING STARTED 29

CHAPTER 1:
Packing a Bag for the Journey. 31

CHAPTER TWO:
No Longer a Child, Not Yet an Adult 75

CHAPTER THREE:
Restoring Cultural Habitat: Rites of Passage for
Justice and Healing. 101

CHAPTER FOUR:
Sex, Drugs, and Rites of Passage. 129

PART II: CULTIVATING IDENTITY,
BELONGING, AND PURPOSE. 167

CHAPTER FIVE:
Who Am I? 169

CHAPTER SIX:
Who are My People and Where Do I Come From? 209

CHAPTER SEVEN:
Where Am I Going and How Do I Get There? 243

**PART III: CROSSING THE THRESHOLD
TO ADULTHOOD** 269

CHAPTER EIGHT:
Initiation 271

CHAPTER NINE:
Return 293

CHAPTER TEN:
Living an Initiating Life. 309

APPENDIX I: BIOGRAPHIES OF YOUNG PEOPLE. 333
APPENDIX II: WORKSHEET FOR A SELF-DESIGNED RITE OF
PASSAGE INTO ADULTHOOD. 341
APPENDIX III: YOUTH PASSAGEWAYS' CROSS CULTURAL
PROTOCOLS IN RITES OF PASSAGE. 345
ENDNOTES. 353
INDEX 371
LINK TO ONLINE RESOURCES FOR FURTHER STUDY . . . 388

LIST OF ILLUSTRATIONS, CHARTS, AND FIGURES

Solo Vigil in the Rain. 4
A (Very Incomplete) List of Ways People Self-Initiate 16
Triple Rite of Passage. 19
Ten Essentials for a Rite of Passage 35
Cultural Iceberg. 37
A Few Differences between Indigenous and Western Worldviews 40
Four Doorways for Connecting with Nature. 49
Short List of Sensations. 59
Short List of Emotions 60
The Four Shields 78
The ESSENCE of Adolescence 88
Three Types of Power. 106
Social (in)Justice Framework 109
Ways People Engage Across Cultures 122
Map of Exploration 137
Following the Pleasure Goddess in the Forest. 149
Risk Management Inventory 156
Johari Window Chart 177
Johari Window Illustration. 178
Pod Map Exercise 217
Our Ancestors are at Our Backs. 221
Ways to Connect with Your Ancestors 227
Observing the Unfolding Universe. .236
Word Cloud of Intents from Young People, 2013-2016. 251
An Altar in the Forest. 259
Steps in Designing Ritual. 260
Archetypal Ritual Actions adapted from Virginia Hine. 262

Threshold within a Threshold within a Threshold 275
A Few Benefits of Guided and Self-Designed Rite of Passage
Ceremonies 281
Four Elements of A Rite of Passage. 282
An Initiate Returns 299
Practices for Living an Initiating Life 315
Cross Cultural Protocols in Rites of Passage 325
Worksheet for a Self-Designed Rite of Passage into
Adulthood. 341

ACKNOWLEDGEMENTS

So much gratitude to the places that brought forth the stories in these pages: the rocky coastline of Cape Alava, the black lava rock and wild waves of Ka'u and Puna, the open savannah of the Okavango Delta, the teak forests of Mendha Lekha—not to mention Payahuunadü, Red Amphitheater, the Carpathian Mountains, the West Midlands, Wales, Cornwall, Devon, Lypa. And especially the Methow River watershed, home.

Humble gratitude to the Indigenous stewards of these lands and waters since time immemorial, who have fought to preserve their lives, their cultures, and their ability to protect these lands for future generations. This book exists due to the extraordinary courage and resilience of generations of Indigenous activists, teachers, and medicine people who faced persecution, genocide, and exploitation to uphold the lifeways of their peoples.

Gratitude to People of the Global Majority that have woven resilient families and communities in the face of violence and oppression, and held a mirror up against the injustices that they face. My work is indebted to generations of activists, healers, cultural workers, educators, and organizers who have fought back oppression, worked to restore ancestral cultural practices and built emergent healing practices to meet the needs facing their people. A special shout out to the Black women and queer and trans folks who have birthed so much beauty, dignity, and power in the world, and whose work is too often belittled, ignored, and stolen.

Mom, you have truly been my biggest teacher. For better or worse, you have shaped my worldview and given me language to articulate what I have experienced over the course of my life. I hope that as you read, you can see your imprints on my mind and heart. Also, thank you for your careful, encouraging, and quick read of the text.

Stan, I am continually reminded how blessed I am to have had a mentor like you. I hope that this book does justice to your legacy. It was your belief in me that allowed me to take risks and find what I believed, and I know you gave this to countless other people. May I be half the mentor to others that you were to me.

Dave, your steadfast belief in me, and the worthiness of this effort, may be the penultimate reason this book will make it to print. Your support—financial, emotional, intellectual, energetic—allowed me to keep going even when it seemed a hopeless task. I know the sacrifices you have made; thank you.

Mike, this book is what it is because of you. You knew what it wanted to be before I did. Your companionship on this journey was an immeasurable gift. May it serve Asher, too, one day.

Thank you to my family of origin: my father David Ottey, my stepmom Elinor Ottey, my brother Sean Ottey, and my sister-cousin Sasha Kusnic, all of whom have shaped and supported me.

Topher Stephens, Mads Deshazo, Laura Brady and Grae Gerlach, thank you for your support tending to the details, editing the text in varying stages, and holding my hand along the way! The four of you served as a sort of relay team of book-doulas, each bringing your own gifts and helping me move the project forward. Your wisdom and insights pepper this book throughout.

Jess Magnan and Smo Sienkiewicz, thank you for your artistic talents that made this book better and brought it to life. Derya Albayrak, thank you for going so far above and beyond, and loving this project patiently alongside me.

Will Scott and Sobey Wing, thank you for your careful and critical reads of the text, and many years of grappling with the concepts with me. Thank you Melissa Michaels, Michael McGee, Clement Wilson, J. Miakoda Taylor, Steve Smith, Lizz Randall for your careful review of particular chapters and sections related to your areas of expertise, helping me to "stay in my lane."

Steve Costa and Gigi Coyle, thanks for your ongoing support, encouragement, and advice at especially critical moments.

Thank you to all the young people (some now not so young) that gifted me with your words, thoughts, and stories, some of which made it into this book and some of which didn't. I hope I did justice to your experiences and ideas. Gratitude in particular to Militza Tapia, Vianey Moreno, Atlakatl Ce Tochtli Orozco, Dayvon Williams, Khalil Parekh-Richardon, J Nyla "ink" McNeill, Shlomo Pesach, Zachary Ottey, Xavier Young, Emma Ottey, Jean Young Sage Schrager, Maya Schrager, Jackson Riley, and Lucia Riley.

Thank you to everyone that contributed financially to this project! The outpouring of support came at just the right time practically and emotionally; feeling my community at my back was critical in the final weeks of editing. Special thanks to the generosity of Grant Abert, Aidoneus Bishop, Teresa Castner, Tracy Cutchlow, Nancy Farr & Dale Sekijima, Steve Costa & Kate Levinson, Gigi Coyle & Win Phelps, Johanna Goldfarb, Amy Higgins & Joanna Fitzhugh, Grae Kindel, Marianne Moskowitz, Abraham Lateiner, Mary Jane Marcus, Mike McGee, Roger & Margot Milliken, Ralph Moskowitz, Carol Olson, David & Elinor Ottey, Dan Roller, Patsy

Sellars & Carter McBride, and Shay Sloan & Brendan Clarke. Each person who contributed (too many to name here!): I saw, appreciated, and put to work each of your gifts. Teena Pugliese, thanks for sharing your gifts with camera and film with me.

Thank you to the friends and guides that welcomed me to my ancestral homelands and helped me find my way, especially Natalie Vickers, Anastacia Khromova, Kataryna Babenko, Andriy Klymyshyn, and Svetlana Leshenko. I learned so much about what it is to protect ancestral homelands, language, and culture from each of you.

Pınar & So Sinopolous Lloyd, Ramon and Michelle Gabrieloff Parish, Kruti Parekh, Marisa & Cameron Withey Byrne, Sobey Wing, Shay Sloan, J. Miakoda Taylor, Brendan Clarke, Meagan Chandler, Siri Gunnarson, Jett Cazeaux, Dane Zahorsky, Ashanti Branch, Katheryne Lewis, Tarek Kutay, Tree Willard, Teena Pugliese, Scott Davidson, Clement Wilson and Joshua Gorman, Kevin and Liz Riley thank you for being my accomplices in this work. Each of you stretch and strengthen me, influence my thinking and teaching, and help me to be a better person. You know intimately my weaknesses but appear to love me anyway. I am so grateful to be in collaboration with each of you.

Speaking of peers, my deepest gratitude to my fellow Earthlinks, guides, supporters: Spesh, Uwe, Rebekka, David, Will, Christi, Gillian, Lucy, Lance, George, Scotch, Noah, Kent, Farion, James, Beau…it was with you that in many ways this journey began, sitting and praying on this earth alone together, healing ourselves, each other, our ancestors, and generations to come. This book is part of the mantle that I have been carrying, doing my best, and I pray it serves you also.

Thank you to the following elders and olders for your patient and generous mentorship. I sincerely hope that this book does justice to what you have taught me. Both the path you carved through your work, as well as your direct guidance for me, have shaped my work immeasureably. Elder Paul Hill, thank you for blessings, support, and willing phone calls, nudges, and lessons about the cultural specificity of rites of passage and their role in movements for justice. Gigi Coyle, thank you for your incredible investment of time and energy in me; I learn so much from your fierce, courageous, and transparent presence. Luis Rodriguez, thank you for your guidance with language, for your powerful wisdom, and being a living example of the power of healing. Orland Bishop, thank you for helping me to see beyond culture and expanding and elevating my imaginal capacity. Melissa Michaels, thank you for introducing me to the dance, helping me ground rites of passage in my body, and your continued support and care even when things get hard. David Blumenkrantz, thank you for helping me see beyond the "program paradigm" and teaching me about the central role of community in rites of passage. Meredith Foster, thank you for seeing me, and for your humble, steadfast commitment to the ceremony. Rebecca & Dallas Chief Eagle, thank you for teaching me about what it means to be spirit-led, and love each other more than our mistakes and limitations. Sharon & Hubert Blackwolf, thank you for opening your hearts and lives to me, and teaching me about family, spirit, and culture. Joseph Lazenka, Patricia McCabe, Selah Martha, Lizz Randall, Bill Plotkin, and Kalani Souza, gratitude to each of you for your guidance, mentorship, and trailblazing. Each of you has shaped and influenced me (and continue to) in unique and different ways. Nancy Jane, Munro Sickafoose, and Christopher Quiseng, thank you for helping me wrestle with the ideas and experiences that informed early drafts of this book.

Gratitude to Youth Passageways and Beyond Boundaries, for being communities of belonging for me.

Jennifer Wilhoit, thank you for your patient partnership and companionship in the first years of writing this manuscript. Laura Schrager, thank you for your diligent proofread(s) and loving support.

Lost Borders Press and Meredith Foster, thank you for believing in this project unreservedly and giving it a home.

There are so many more people, places, and beings that I could name; may each of you that contributed to this book feel my gratitude.

Thank you to the ancestors who have set me on my path, and continually give me my next tasks. While I don't always understand, every once in a while I can catch a glimmer of the bigger picture. I hope this book is close enough to what you asked for.

FORWARD

By Ramon Gabrieloff Parish, Assistant Professor of Interdisciplinary Studies, Naropa University and rite of passage educator. Ramon teaches foundations in ceremonial arts, embodiment, conflict transformation and environmental and food justice through an evolving Afrofuturist praxis.

and

M. Kalani Souza, University of Hawaii National Disaster Preparedness Training Center, and Olohana Foundation Founding Director. Kalani is a gifted storyteller, singer, songwriter, musician, performer, poet, philosopher, priest, political satirist, and peacemaker.

The worldview, which is to say the world, of the last 500 years is ending. Assumptions, paradigms, and systems that have governed the last several centuries are not adequate to take us into the future. As former Los Angeles Poet Laureate and Elder Luis Rodriguez put it, the house is burning and everyone knows it. Nation-states cannot contain, nor prevent, the flow of distressed peoples running from political, economic and climate instability. Economic systems cannot keep up or ever hope to pay off the debt they generate. Pandemics and the smoke of burning forests do not respect municipal, state and national borders. Police cannot keep the peace when they themselves are the perpetrators of violence. Politicians cannot distinguish themselves from entertainers and demagogues. Billionaires keep trying to act as saviors, but offer boyish visions. And we cannot even agree on the terms of what constitutes truth or how to arrive at it. Is the world spherical or flat or what? 2020 severed us from the leftovers of the last century and we saw our way of life change within weeks. Yet in significant ways, it also showed us the more things change, the more they stay in place. The beginnings of the pandemic highlighted the centuries of the marginalization and targeting of whole groups for slow and swift violence by way of skin color, hair texture, body size, cognitive style, immigration status, nationality, Indigeneity, social class, age and more.

It also highlighted that we can clear air if we all agree to relax driving our cars and taking airline flights—if we can kick our addiction to cheap energy. The Black Liberation Movement made a renewed and potent claim on national and planetary imagination, garnering allies in every major city in the US and from nations as widespread as France and New Zealand. Maori peoples recognized their common struggle with the peoples of the African diaspora. Transnational corporations were forced to change the terms of their language and speak the tongue of equity, even if only to throw off the movement's attention for long enough to resume the status quo. Our proximity and dependence on technological mediation and the interconnectivity of our lives has increased with the zoomification of the world. Meanwhile, mental health has reached epidemic lows in nations around the world.

Call it the Anthropocene. The Colonialcene. The Ecozoic. The Rapture. The Sixth Sun. The advent of the Age of Aquarius.... Call it what you will. But clearly a transformation of planetary significance has gone critical and the youth of today, Gen Z as some call them, must become adults, while the adult world is crumbling.

WHY THIS BOOK IS IMPORTANT RIGHT NOW

In many ways our time is the same as any other time. Each generation grows up, each young person gains the stature of adulthood, and the heart and soul wonder why? For what? For whom? Who shall I offer my love, my energy, my mind and heart to? And how shall I give it? And what or who holds me when I can't hold myself? What called me into being and what supports me on my journey? The perennial questions. Yet the historical and even evolutionary setting of these questions shifts, perhaps intensifies.

As Darcy says in the pages to follow, "it's never easy growing up, but now might be harder than any point in history." What does it mean to come of age *now*, when agelong assumptions and the structures that are built around them are falling down? What does it mean to come of age, when patterns of male domination are withering? When the notion that the few can own the resources of the many is going the way of the divine right of kings? What does it mean to come of age when whiteness is understood to be just another shade of brown, rather than the pinnacle of human culture and beauty?

Across the world and across centuries, youth have been faced with rites of passage and initiation that steer them toward meaningful engagement with these questions. This book asks readers why so many people around the earth lost memory or access to their traditional rites of passage. Why do so many communities, of all colors and classes, experience so much brokenness and alienation? Has it always been this way? What can we do about it? How might we shape our rites of passage if we feel at home in the mainstream of dominant culture? How might we re-shape or reclaim them if we feel disaffected, excluded, or oppressed by that culture?

This book also addresses questions that present themselves to youth in this decade with renewed urgency. How might youth develop a sense of cultural pride, to love or at least make peace with where and who they come from? How can they relate to families or to larger institutions that have both offered gifts and perpetrated harms? As they reach toward adulthood, rather than side step (or "transcend") the histories of violence and stigma that are attached to our skin color, our sex, our privileges, how might they reframe these as the casting of our fates at this time, and integral clues to our destiny?

This book cannot answer all of the questions it raises. But it can serve as a spur, a map and guide for young people coming of age at this time. It can serve as a resource for rite of passage practitioners, nature connection guides, educators, youth workers and activists that often have the responsibility of leading youth toward embodied, historically informed, politicized, ecologically awake spiritualities.

Darcy Ottey has dedicated her life energy to creating transformational processes for youth, reweaving webs of community life shredded by colonization and capitalism, and reviving earth based ceremony and ancestral tradition. We know her as a nose to the grindstone fireball, willing to learn from her mistakes, share her findings and take the next steps. We know her as a peer and a sister in the work of our generation. And we look to her for the energy, integrity and persistence that she consistently shows.

We met in 2008 on the island of Hawai'i as part of a painful and instructive conference on rites of passage. Ramon, a young Black man who had come as part of the organizing team. Kalani, a middle-aged Hawaiian cultural practitioner and mediator between cultural worlds commissioned to record the gathering. Darcy, a young white conference attendee who did her best just to stay out of the way. Our experience on The Big Island was a volcanic wakeup call, full of conflict and missteps. What transpired at that event bound us together, with others, over the past years in the painful work of bringing forth justice and healing for all our peoples through rites of passage.

Since that time Darcy Ottey has done the difficult and continuous work to transform privileged embodiments and positions into a sacrament of reconciliation, an offering on the altar of a just and healed future. Because of her commitment to this, the book might feel most relevant to others walking with considerable privilege--and especially those born into middle-class, white bodies. But she has also worked hard to share stories and quotes from young people with very different life experiences than hers. There's been a lot of damage done by white authors attempting to universalize their experiences and assuming they are relevant for everyone. Darcy acknowledges the limitations of her experience while also stretching to increase the accessibility of these truly life-saving, culture-renewing practices.

In spite of our lofty intro, this book is practical. It poses powerful inquiries to young readers seeking initiatory experiences, guides them in the direction of healthy practices, and helps them to navigate difficult questions that were unseen even a decade or two ago. Readers should enter this book if they are ready to engage in practice and begin or continue a transformational journey.

Ultimately, this book is a resource for the curious, for the intense, for those consciously moving toward earth, healing, justice, service. You will find exercises, reflective and contemplative questions and most of all illustrative biographic moments that can serve to hearten, inspire, challenge, and (as needed) check sincere seekers. This is not a book to be read in one sitting, but one to be worked with over time and in various settings, in the woods, on the bus, in the airport, at the shore. This book will call you into deeper practice and into rituals or healing or reflection which will help you discover a more profound relationship to self, community, the more than human, and your own personal power. If you are already on that path, or curious about it, read on.

RITES AND RESPONSIBILITIES

INTRODUCTION

When I was thirteen, I came across a brochure sitting on my mom's desk talking about a "rite of passage journey." I didn't know what a rite of passage was, but something about that brochure caught my attention. Maybe it was the sense of adventure that inspired me. Whatever it was, when my mom came home that night I told her that I wanted to take part.

"Oh, honey," she said. "We can't afford it. You'll need a scholarship." The trip cost $895, a lot of money in our family.

Despite the costs, I was determined to participate. It's still hard for me, today, to pinpoint exactly why. Was I attracted to it as a spiritual journey? Spirituality was something that drew me in as a child, an unfulfilled longing since it wasn't a very big part of my family. Was it the time in nature? I had always loved being outside and was just beginning to explore this in a bigger way with school camping trips. Perhaps it was both of those things, and more. One thing I definitely didn't know at the time, but I can see now, is that my destiny was on the journey, and something sparked in me that I was aware enough to follow.

The next day, I called the man who ran the program, Stan Crow. He was friendly and kind to me, and told me we would figure it out. If I could come up with $750, there'd be a spot for me on the trip. I immediately set to fundraising—babysitting, cleaning houses, asking family friends to donate to the cause. I would do whatever I could to make it happen.

I have a vivid memory of stopping at the bank on our drive to the start of the program. Before they handed me a cashier's check, representing all the money in my bank account, I asked them if I could hold the cash. Seven crisp hundred-dollar bills, and one fifty: more money than I had ever seen in my life. And I had earned it.

I was determined to get everything I possibly could out of the experience, and though it was difficult, I loved it. From the first moment I arrived at the forested basecamp on nine acres just outside of Seattle, where Stan, his family, and several other families made their home, I knew this was the place for me. The four counselors were a fun, kind-hearted bunch, ranging in age from mid-twenties to mid-fifties. The other eight kids were from all over the United States, and two lived overseas. We quickly became a tight-knit group. We spent three weeks backpacking throughout Washington State, in the mountains and on the coast.

By far the most significant part of the program for me was a "solo vigil." By myself, without food, I was asked to stay awake and keep a fire going for 24 hours. As a kid who had grown up in the city, even starting the fire was a huge challenge. I remember gathering big driftwood sticks that were far too large for kindling, and trying to light them with the firestarter I had been given: cardboard inside of wax inside a tin can.

Despite my poor firemaking skills, I was able to get the fire going in four matches. And it was a good thing I did! That night, it rained the hardest it did all summer long. I kept my fire going by covering my wood with my tarp so it would stay dry. I sat on a log next to the fire all night long in the pouring down rain, dressed in all my layers beneath a ripped plastic poncho, utterly determined to keep my fire going.

The night was ferociously black. At some point, a raccoon made its way across the tree limb above my fire, all shadowy and looking very hungry to me. As it stared down at me with beady yellow eyes, all I could think was, "if my fire goes out, that racoon will eat me." This kept me attentive to my fire throughout the darkness.

But I was cold, and the night was really long! Sometime before dawn, I fell asleep. Next thing I remember, my mentor Louise was gently shaking me awake. Still disoriented from sleep, I began sobbing, telling her I couldn't make it, it was too hard. "Darcy, look around," she said. "You already have made it. The night is over." I glanced around, and saw it was full daylight. What's more, the rain had passed, and the sun was beginning to peak out from behind the clouds.

After she left, and I finished fully waking up, I felt a tremendous feeling of joy. "I have never felt like I felt right then," I said in a letter I wrote a couple of weeks later. "I felt invincible."

That one night had a powerful and long-lasting impact on my life. I knew at the time the experience had been potent, but exactly how significant the experience was for me wasn't clear until years later, when I went to college across the country from my family and far away from the only world I had ever known.

Going to a small, East Coast women's college was a very different world than growing up in urban Seattle, going to public school and community college. I felt like I didn't belong. Academics were much harder than I had experienced before. The wealth of many of my peers overwhelmed me, and I quickly

Solo Vigil in the Rain

went into credit card debt trying to keep up. The New England winters were brutal.

Through it all, I kept a picture of myself at my vigil site by my bed, taken by my mentor Louise that final morning. Each night, I would look at it, and say to myself, "If I could do that when I was 13, I can do this now."

Realizing how much I counted on that experience to give me courage in college made me very appreciative that I had been given such an opportunity. I began to study rites of passage both in school and by apprenticing and participating in existing programs.

As I learned more about them, I began to understand how key rites of passage are to healthy human development, and what the consequences are for our whole society when young people don't have access to them. I began to see that not only was I deeply affected by my coming of age experience, but the same thing happened to many other young people who had similar experiences to mine. This made me strongly committed to doing whatever I could do to help bring rites of passage to other young people and my community.

It's been many years now since I made that commitment. Over that time, I've supported hundreds of people, from pre-teens to folks well into their elder years, through transformational experiences in their lives. I've seen how powerful rites of passage can be. And, I've also seen how they can fall short, be incomplete, and simply be inaccessible for many people.

This book is my attempt to share rites of passage in ways that are accessible and relevant, and give you the tools you need to take responsibility for your own passage into adulthood.

If you're reading this, chances are you're 5, 10, 15, maybe even 20 years older (or more!) than I was when I had my coming of age experience at age 13. That's fine, it's never too late! My coming of age at 13 was just the beginning for me. It was not the experience that made me an adult; it was the experience that opened a doorway to a path I've followed ever since. As this book talks about, the path toward adulthood is long, and many folks in our society never seem to reach it (even if they have well-paying jobs, families, and the other trappings of so-called "adulthood").

But it must be said right up front: rites of passage don't make the road through life easy. That road is still fraught with hazards, pitfalls, and mistakes. But easy is not the goal! In these pages, you will find a roadmap of growth and change, a way of stepping forward in your life that is filled with meaning, purpose, and a sense of how you fit into the whole of community.

> ⚘EXERCISE: Get yourself a brand-new journal to accompany you as you're reading this book. Choose something big enough to allow your creativity to flow, small enough to be a companion to your daily life.

WHO I AM

Before we get any further, please allow me to introduce myself. My name is Darcy Jane Ottey. I was born in Tacoma, Washington, on lands that I have since learned is the territory of the Puyallup Tribe. My ancestors came to the United States from Europe, and include early Quaker settlers, British coal miners, and Ukrainian peasants that immigrated in the last century. They made possible the lives of my parents, Edith Jane Kusnic and David Pennel Ottey, two Baby Boomers who came of age in the 1960's and spent their working lives in education and social services. They divorced when I was about 10. Both of them are still alive, for which I am profoundly grateful. You'll hear more about my mom a little further along in the book; my experience with rites of passage started a journey for her, too. Over many years, she became a participant, guide, and trainer for the program I had done myself as a youth, and a lot of her writings and reflections have informed my own.

I am a white cisgender woman. I come from a mixed class background, and I'm always understanding more about how this impacts me. I am able-bodied and neurotypical, meaning my brain and body generally function in ways that the society I live in is set up for, though I have struggled with depression on and off since my teen years. I identify as a recovering alcoholic. You'll hear more about the people I come from a little later on, both the good and the bad, and more about how I relate to different parts of myself.

I live in the Methow Valley, a rural community in north central Washington state, in the traditional territory of the Methow people whose lands were forcibly taken from them less than 150 years ago. I am married to a man named Dave; we have been together since I was 19. We have a non-monogamous and complex relationship based on supporting each other to be our full selves, even when that's scary. Even at age 44, I'm still not sure how to define my sexual identity; pansexual or queer are the terms that feel most true for me. I don't have any children or any pets.

I work as Co-Director of Youth Passageways, a global network of individuals, communities, and organizations helping to regenerate healthy passages in today's world, which means I get to meet lots of folks doing amazing work in their communities, all looking for how we can care for ourselves, our families, and our communities in these complex times. You'll hear more about Youth Passageways later, too.

It's important for me to share a little about myself right at the outset because I want you to know where I'm coming from. There's a good chance that you're younger than me if you're reading this, and perhaps we don't share gender, race, ethnicity, class, family background, nationality and more. In the ten plus years I've been working on this book, I've debated a lot about how much to share about my own personal experience, especially since it's been a long time since I was young! In the end, I do share a lot of my own story, mostly because it's the story I know best, the only one I'm really an authority on. So I'll keep coming back to it as an example of how the themes in this book all weave together, how complex and interrelated they all are, and how long the path to true adulthood really is.

Throughout the book, you'll also get to read dozens of stories of other young people navigating the path to adulthood; many of their biographies are in an appendix in the back. I wish that I had been able to include many more voices than I was able. While I sought to include voices from a variety of ages, genders, races, classes, nationalities, sexual orientations, geographies, abilities, and more, many voices from the full spectrum of experiences and identities are missing. Still, my hope is that you'll be able to relate to some of the young people included in this book, and some of them might open your mind to entirely different experiences growing up in the world today.

CHALLENGES YOUNG PEOPLE FACE TODAY

"One challenge of being a young man today is to not fail. It's a lot of pressure today, especially for Black men and the society I live in. Society expects me to fail. They expect me to drop out of school, they expect me to not be something in the future. I don't want to be nothing. I wanna make an impact on everyone's lives. I wanna change the world."
–Deshun, age 16

I'm sure I don't have to tell you that it's hard growing up today; you know far better than I do! The truth is that it's never easy to be a young person, too old to be considered a child but not-yet-fully-an adult. It's an inherently awkward, uncomfortable time. Young people are both learning the way the world has worked, while simultaneously carrying the seeds of the future and creating a new world as they go. This is a tricky tension in which to live. Young people throughout time have thrown up their hands and said, "Adults don't understand!" and the truth is, this is completely true!

Still, although it's never easy to be in this adolescent stage, it is quite possible that it's harder now than it has ever been, and the difficulties are compounded by factors like race, class, gender and more. Today's young people face unprecedented challenges on their path to adulthood, including climate change, growing inequality, rapid technological innovation, and increasingly globally interconnected economic systems. Social norms and demographics are quickly changing. And this was all true before COVID!

The pace of change makes it difficult, if not impossible, to keep up. As Cameron, age 29, says, "Looking at my nephew who's 13, even I can't understand the world that he lives in to some extent. It's different. It's not that adults don't understand, it's that they *can't* understand unless they really take the time to ask and be with and observe, and loosen their assumptions about life. I feel like a curmudgeonly adult already with the younger ones!"

Here are a few key challenges common among young people today. As you read through these examples, notice which ones you can relate to:

- *Mental health issues:* Young people today face unprecedented, alarming rates of mental health struggles, far more severe than any previous generation. Spiking rates of suicide, anxiety, depression, and other psychological issues have become the norm for today's young people, leading this generation to be the most pharmaceutically medicated generation in the history of the planet. Experiencing a global pandemic and the resulting social isolation significantly worsened this frightening trend.

- *Technological connectedness:* Young people today experience a level of technological engagement and connectedness that is also unparalleled in the history of humans on the planet, with both positive and negative consequences. Studies are finding that the widespread use of cell phones leads to depression, weakened ability to "self-regulate" (the ability to take care of yourself under stress or difficulty), and can impact the development of imagination, hope, and resiliency. Screen addiction is common. At the same time, technology also allows a level of global connectedness and access to information that no previous generation has experienced either.

- *Social isolation and bullying:* Bullying is a pervasive part of the lives of far too many young people. This has been an issue for generations, yet has gotten significantly more acute and pervasive since cyber-bullying came on the scene, reducing the ability of victims to remove themselves from bullying situations.

- *Substance use and abuse:* By no means a new challenge for this generation, substance use and abuse remains a critical challenge facing young people today. Substances alter our way of seeing the world and evoke new states of being, which can be a wonderful gift in certain circumstances. Yet they also have the power to negatively impact the ways young brains are forming and can lead to all sorts of negative results.

- *Conflicting messages about sexuality:* Sex is a huge part of our lives as humans. We are sexual beings, biologically designed to seek pleasure and connection. Yet we live in a strange culture that is both sex-obsessed and sex-repressed. Constant, sexualized images throughout all forms of media, not to mention widespread exposure to pornography from a young age, creates a difficult landscape in which to develop a healthy sexual identity, and understand consent, desire, pleasure, and boundaries. For young people of all genders, this can be very confusing.

- *Student loan debt and financial insecurity:* Young adults face a staggering $1 trillion among them in student loan debt, and are coming of age in an uncertain economy with rapidly changing social systems. As Jess, age 22, says, "Paying my bills - honestly, that is my priority at all times. Money is always in your brain."

- *Concern about the future:* According to a recent study by Harvard University, the majority of young people today are fearful about the future of America. As humans across the planet grow more and more interconnected, our shared environmental, political, and economic futures feel increasingly uncertain. The weight of this uncertainty falls most heavily on the shoulders of young people. Kay, age 17, puts it this way: "We are expected to solve all the world's problems that older people left behind for us. We're expected to go out and change the world and fix everybody else's messes, which I guess is a lot of work, but we have to do it!"

> ✿ EXERCISE: In your journal, reflect on the biggest challenges you're facing in your life at this time. Are they similar to the issues raised here, or are you facing different challenges? With this and all the journal entries, you may choose to write your

reflections, or to draw them, paint them, collage them, audio or video record them, or otherwise express them in a way that works for you.

ENTER: RITES OF PASSAGE

With all of these challenges facing young people, growing up can seem pretty daunting. Meanwhile, the lives of many adults may be uninspiring. Zachary, age 22, puts it this way: "A big challenge I face and I think a lot of people face is figuring out the path that I'm going to take in life—if I'm going to go ahead and follow that cut-out path for me. You know, go to school, graduate from high school, go to college, graduate college, get a job, and then just work my ass off for like 40 years or whatever. Figuring out how much I'm going to adhere to the social norms of what it means to be an adult, that's been the struggle. Trying to figure out how much I want to commit to what feels like a robotic sort of path, but at the same time that path almost feels necessary to sustain living and how crucial it is to the functioning of this country and a lot of the world."

Why on earth would someone want to grow up, when being an adult means, like Zachary says, that you "work your ass off for like 40 years or more"?

We'll get into this further in Chapter Two, but for now, let's leave it at two simple reasons. One, change is inevitable, so we might as well do change well rather than fighting it every step of the way. As Micaela, age 25, says, "I'm the first to say that I struggle with transitions. I dread them. I muddle through them. But simply knowing that about myself has led to less anxiety around them. It is also easier to find the opportunity in transition and see how it is good for me rather than planting my feet and staying where I am."

The second reason for growing up is simple: all we have to do is turn on the news for five minutes to see the consequences of a world where people refuse to grow up and take responsibility for themselves, much less contribute to their communities.

But how do you do it? How do you move forward toward adulthood in a healthy, positive, inspiring way? Rites of passage provide a roadmap.

WHAT IS A "RITE OF PASSAGE?"

The term *rites of passage* was first used in 1908 by Belgian anthropologist Arnold van Gennep. He used the term to refer to the rituals that mark an individual's changes in social status or position in his or her community*. Nowadays, "rite of passage" is a phrase used in all sorts of ways, and there are many different definitions. When I use the term, here's what I mean: *an intentional, meaningful marker of transition from one state of being to another.*

By *intentional*, I mean that it's a conscious, deliberate process. White American storyteller Michael Meade, drawing on an African proverb, says "If the fires that innately burn inside youths are not intentionally and lovingly added to the hearth of community, they will burn down the structures of culture, just to feel the warmth."** There is a fundamental need of young people to test themselves, go through challenges, receive blessings and be welcomed by a broader community. And when such experiences are not provided for them, young people will create their own forms of self-initiation, often in dangerous and destructive ways. School shootings, drug overdoses, falling down the rabbit hole of online extremist ideology, cyber-bullying—these are all the inevitable byproduct of the unmet impulse toward initiation.

By *meaningful*, I mean that rites of passage must be significant. They must include challenging ordeals that have been overcome *that are worth overcoming*. Afterwards, things need to be different for the young person, and for those who surround them: parents, peers, school, and broader society. Someone who

---

*I'm not a big fan of using the term "rites of passage." The term grows out of the legacy of the Western scientific tradition of the turn of the last century, a tradition that served as an instrument of colonialism worldwide and caused immeasurable harm to Indigenous cultures. But shared language to describe the same or very similar things is helpful, and so far "rites of passage" seems to be the most generally recognized term to describe practices for navigating life transitions. My hope is that in coming years, shared language and definitions will emerge to replace the term "rites of passage" as well as other terms imposed on cultural traditions from outside.

**Meade doesn't provide a more specific attribution than "African." As we collectively strive for specific acknowledgement of traditional cultural knowledge, hopefully a more precise acknowledgement of this quote will be readily available in the future.

has undergone a transition needs to be seen and treated differently, held to new standards, given new responsibilities and at times new privileges.

The next part of the phrase is *marker of transition*. A rite is a ritual. We engage in rituals all the time: blowing out the birthday candles, honoring the dead with funerals and memorials, high school graduation ceremonies. Ritual is an important way we create shared meaning. It transforms change from an intellectual process to an actual bodily memory, complete with sights, smells, and emotions. We can talk about how things are different in a family when a child hits puberty, but this hits home in a different way when a ribbon connecting parent to child is ceremonially cut, and the child is pulled away into the forest to undergo initiation. Ritual connects us with the larger world: the earth, the cosmos, the traditions of our ancestors, in ways that may feel foreign to many of us now but are actually lodged in our DNA, having been a part of our evolution since our earliest human beginnings.

Finally, a rite of passage is a *transition from one state of being to another*. Of course, there are many passages, big and small, in a human's life. Each of these transitions is a confusing, risky time in our lives, a time when old ways of being no longer meet our needs or the needs of those around us. I reserve the term "rites of passage" for massive life transitions, those occasions when things change and can never return. It's like when Harry Potter found out he was a wizard—he couldn't just go back to being a regular person after that!

While there are other significant transitions, each human experiences three primary transitions in their lifetime, the ones most defined by biology. Birth and death are two of these. And there's the passage between childhood and adulthood, called in Western culture, adolescence, in which we grow through the massive physiological changes we call puberty, marked by sexual development, hormonal shifts, and changes in our brain chemistry.

My passion centers on this last transition, from childhood to adulthood, through adolescence. It is the only one of the three primary life transitions in which we have consciousness as we understand it on both sides of the transition. This makes it unique in the course of a human lifetime, as the transition through which we can experientially learn how to navigate all the others that follow in our lives. It offers a roadmap to take forward into the crisis moments that each young person will face in their lifetime.

WHY ARE RITES OF PASSAGE IMPORTANT?

Rites of passage have been around since our earliest human ancestors. Please pause for a moment to think about this. For tens of thousands of years, humans have honored the critical transition from childhood to adulthood through ceremony and testing. Yet over the last several hundred years, we have experimented (mostly unwillingly, as we'll see later in the book) with removing them from the center of community life. The results of this massive social experiment have been far-reaching and powerful.

There are so many benefits of rites of passage I could talk about them for months, but three in particular feel critically lacking in our world today. First, rites of passage instill a *sense of belonging*, a basic human need like food and shelter. Generations of cultural disruption and overt efforts to destroy cultures took with them many traditional rites of passage that helped young people to understand where they come from, and their place in their community and the more-than-human world. Many of us don't even realize that there are rites of passage in our lineage, or think that this is important. Yet many of the social issues we face today, from individual isolation to the rise of white nationalist hate groups and other forms of extremism, have their roots in this loss.

Whether we are made up of one, two, or twenty ethnic lines, by connecting with our roots, rites of passage push us to see our lives and communities in a larger context, and begin to see our role in the circle of life. Each of us carries our own story, threads of the past that are there to help weave our collective future.

Rites of passage are uniquely suited to help us find our particular place within a community, no matter who we are or where we come from. As people understand how they fit into the whole, an interlocking web of mutual support develops in which it is no longer acceptable for individuals to be out for their own gain at the expense of others. In this web, it simply isn't possible for individuals to be caught in feelings of social isolation without those around them noticing and providing support.

On the individual psychological level, rites of passage instill a sense of confidence and purpose. They affirm one's gifts, talents, and skills, and provide an opportunity to be recognized and celebrated as one moves forward through life's stages. Being recognized and celebrated is not just a "nice thing." It's actually essential for mental health and well-being. Elder Paul Hill, Jr., founder of National Rites of Passage Institute, says, "rites of passage are a cultural antihistamine to a socially toxic culture." We need to know that we are loved, important, and that we belong. This serves the broader social good, preventing alienation that can lead to things like self-harm, violence, crime, and dangerous risk-taking.

We learn not only do we belong, we belong to something *worth belonging to*. Rites of passage are an essential tool to help transmit, affirm, celebrate, renew, and evolve the values and practices of a community or culture. This in turn can provide a sense of pride in who and where one comes from. This is available to all of us, regardless of our background. While the idea of pride in one's culture continues to be warped time and time again in white nationalist and other insular, extremist communities, nonetheless culturally-based solutions for addressing our needs as humans navigating a complex, interconnected world are essential. How we build this sense of cultural pride—a sense of belonging to something worthy of our belonging— in a way that creates welcoming, inclusive, equitable, and truly just communities is the heart of what this book is all about.

A second major benefit of rites of passage is the road map for survival they offer: a sort of *"transition literacy."* Transition literacy—the ability to read, understand, and navigate change—is an essential skill in these times of fast-paced technological, environmental, and social changes, more important than most, if not all, of the subjects taught in school! Rites of passage prepare us to navigate the inevitable losses and transitions that will occur throughout our lives by increasing our comfort with ambiguity and giving us tools to adapt and thrive. For example, when COVID hit and everything felt profoundly uncertain, my background in rites of passage helped me orient myself to what was happening, and learn how to respond.

Third, rites of passage *call forth the unique gifts of young people in service to wider and wider communities.* I'm not talking about resurrecting old forms that aren't relevant in our lives today. Cultural traditions have always morphed, finding ways to serve changing needs. Young people are usually the ones ushering in change. You have the seeds of our future inside you. Ideally, you would be surrounded by adults and elders with the ability to nurture your creative life, help you find and make sense of your gifts, and help you learn the things you want and need to grow. Rites of passage prepare young people to inherit the world that *you* will live in, in a fascinating dance between your unique gifts and passions and the needs of the community.

A (VERY INCOMPLETE) LIST OF WAYS PEOPLE SELF-INITIATE

- Substance use
- Sexual activity
- Coming out (as gay, transgender, etc)
- Travel
- Running away from home and/or moving
- Body art such as tattooing and/or piercing
- Spending time outdoors
- Self-harm
- Fighting
- Law breaking
- Attempting suicide

Rites of passage are a natural and essential part of the human experience. When adults and elders don't provide them for us, we find ways to provide them for ourselves. Luis Rodriguez, writer, founder of Tia Chuchas Centro Cultural and Bookstore, and activist/healer among troubled youth, incarcerated people, and the dispossessed, talks about the "echoes" of rites of passage that remain in practices like hazing, street and school violence, and risky sexual encounters. Like the sound of a human voice echoing off a canyon wall, these forms of rite of passage bear some resemblance to the original, but they lack fullness, character, and substance. "How," Rodriguez asks, "does the psyche get pulled through?"

Say, for example, you decide to join a fraternity, sorority, street gang, or similar insular group of young people. As part of joining this group, you'll go through a hazing, meant to test your resolve and commitment, perhaps also physical capacities, and more. As many authors have pointed out, this form of initiation has much in common with traditional rites of passage. Yet ultimately, these forms of initiation are fragmented rites of passage. While some are harmful outright, others are simply less whole than they could be—maybe completely unseen by family, not providing a roadmap for future transitions, or not providing an enduring sense of unique gifts and talents. They don't provide a place in a broader, multi-generational community; they only give you a place in a subculture which can attend to some, but not all, of your needs. As we will talk about in Chapter Three, they don't help you cross into true adulthood.

⚘ EXERCISE: In your journal or in conversation with someone you care about, reflect on these questions:

- In this section, we explored how when rites of passage aren't provided for people by the culture, they will often find ways to "initiate themselves." In what ways have you tried to self-initiate, or experienced a "fragmented rite of passage"? What was helpful for you about these experiences, and what was harmful? What was the impact of these experiences on your community?
- Can you think of a time when you had a transition that was supported by your community, in your life so far? What did the experience offer for you? What was missing? If you can't think of anything, what feelings or thoughts does that bring up? Throughout the rest of the book, you'll be introduced to examples of rites of passage that will likely shed a new light on your experiences so far.

"A TRIPLE RITE OF PASSAGE"

"Only collapse as initiation can illumine, at the deepest levels of our being, the choices we make as we attempt to transform a devastated civilization. The transition is utterly dependent on inner transformation." –American Author Carolyn Baker

Even as we talk about rites of passage and what they offer to you as an individual, the truth is that this is a secondary benefit to what they offer to the community. One thing that feels important to say at the outset of this book is that anyone undergoing a rite of passage today is doing so as a microcosm of larger planetary forces. Your own individual journey, on the road toward adulthood, is a mirror of what's happening for our species as humans, and for planet Earth as a whole.

In this era of climate catastrophe, we are undergoing a "rite of passage" where we are forced to find a new way of being as humans. Mythologist Michael Meade says, "there may be no time more suited to the study of rites of passage than the threshold between the end of modernity and the uncertain future of humanity."

Yet it does not end there—this is not "just" the story of our species. If we zoom out even wider—perhaps taking the image of our planet viewed from space—we see that what is happening is that industrial societies have spurred a change to the entire globe, where all of life on our planet is undergoing a time of unprecedented transformation, caused by our impacts. This is a "triple rite of passage," as youth and community organizer Joshua Gorman refers to it, where a young person in the midst of life transition (youth initiation) is a microcosm of our species-wide rite of passage (humanity's initiation), is a microcosm of our planetary rite of passage (Earth's initiation). All of these layers are playing out at the same time. And all of these layers, it seems, are making a sort of transition through adolescence: that shifting, uncomfortable time where the innocence and carefree nature of childhood is gone yet the responsibility and maturity of adulthood are not yet fully claimed.

Triple Rite of Passage

HOW THIS BOOK WORKS

My journey with rites of passage began when I was 13, alone in the dark and rain. Over the years, I've followed this path many places, including teak forests in India, black rock coastlines in Hawai'i, open savannah in Botswana, and the bustling city of Los Angeles, trying to understand the role of rites of passage in the lives of young people today, and what rites of passage can do for our human species as a whole.

On my journey, I have come to recognize that initiation is the birthright of every human being that inhabits this planet, a fundamental right as essential to community vitality as clean water and clean air. Time and time again, the huge barriers to meaningful initiation in Western culture have made themselves readily apparent.

Everyone, including you, has the right to be taught and tested, to prove yourself, and to have a meaningful welcome into adulthood. You have a right to be offered skills and guidance that will allow your unique gifts to shine. You have a right to confidence in yourself and confidence that the community around you will care for you. You have a right to a culture that is vibrant and life-affirming, imbued with meaning, one that defines you not as a prospective consumer or a threat or a naïve idealist, but as an absolutely essential piece of the greater whole. You have a right to know that your life is imperative for the survival of the collective, and you have a responsibility to make your life as full, rich, and meaningful as you possibly can—for reasons we will get into soon.

Yet, we as a society haven't yet gotten our act together so that you can have these things. You may be lucky and have caregivers that tried hard and were able to provide access to all sorts of creative or cultural opportunities. You may have had a pretty hard go of it and be clawing your way into some healthier sense of what it means to be alive than what you had access to growing up. You may feel totally burned out, apathetic, and hopeless about the whole thing. No matter your upbringing so far, the truth is, you have been failed by the broader culture.

Regardless of your background, this book is for you. Some of this book will be outdated by the time you even read it, because you're inheriting a world that is moving so fast and you, yourself, are bringing in new directions. But it offers some of the wisdom previous generations have struggled to learn and preserve, and that you may be able to carry forward.

In the rite of passage tradition in which I was raised, someone goes out seeking insight not for themselves alone, but for their people, and the story they bring back is not just theirs but belongs to their community. So it is with this book. It is my offering to my community. Specifically, I offer it to my younger siblings hungry for meaning in their lives, yet surrounded by a culture that offers them little substance but lots of empty calories. As I wrote the manuscript, I kept my nephew in mind, as he navigated his late teens and early twenties. Older readers have shared that the book is relevant for them also. Parents, educators, and youth workers will find the tools, frameworks, and exercises useful, as well.

Spoiler alert: I definitely don't have it all figured out! In fact, writing this book has made me realize how much I don't know. But in sharing this book with the world, I trust that those that read it will challenge me where I've fallen short, and that this is part of us all learning and growing so that future generations can grow up held in a richer, more just fabric of culture, living in partnership with the other beings that call this planet home.

One comment about language: throughout this book, I make liberal use of the word *we*. "We" is kind of a troublesome word; it makes all sorts of assumptions. When I use the words "we" and "our" throughout this text, I'm referring to experiences typically shared by those raised in or heavily influenced by

"Western culture"* in general, and dominant culture in the United States in particular. These experiences are by no means universal, and the impacts of the dominant culture differ amongst us all.

Parts of the book will likely feel more relevant to readers living on Turtle Island, a name for the lands often referred to as North and Central America. The name *Turtle Island* comes from some Indigenous origin stories, like those of the Haudenosaunee and Anishinaabe peoples, that tell of how the land was formed on the back of a turtle, and is a non-colonial way of describing the continent. I apologize in advance for this geographical bias.

In addition to the stories of young people that I share, I reference scholars, philosophers, wisdom keepers, cultural practitioners, writers, activists, and more. Describing people and their work in just a few identifying words and phrases proved challenging. Where was someone's race, gender, nationality, cultural background, or other aspect of identity important to highlight? What aspects of their work were relevant and make sense in a few brief words? Where I could, I asked people how they'd like to be identified, and include their descriptions of themselves when I share their words and ideas. For others, I did my best based on publicly available information. As you read, I encourage you to get curious about the sources I reference, look them up, and reflect on their words, ideas, and research in light of what you discover.

Some of the people and works I reference in this book are controversial, and have caused harm. I've gone back and forth about what and who to include and what and who not to, and ultimately I included ideas and insights that felt essential to the whole story I needed to tell. I also tried to uplift voices often erased in many conversations. Over the course of writing this book,

---

*Wikipedia defines Western Culture as "the heritage of social norms, ethical values, traditional customs, belief systems, political systems, artifacts and technologies of the Western (i.e. Western European) world. The term also applies beyond Europe to countries and cultures whose histories are strongly connected to Europe by immigration, colonization, or influence." Western culture is also associated with capitalism, scientific rationalism, hierarchy, and domination. This term "western culture" is imperfect (West of what? Is there only one "Western culture"?), but I'm using it here and will throughout the book because it is a broadly used, somewhat accessible, and somewhat accurate term. We'll be exploring culture more deeply in the coming chapters, and getting more specific about what Western culture is all about.

monuments have fallen and powerful public figures have been held accountable for their actions. With actions like these, new possibilities emerge for a world free of violence, where those who have been silenced and ignored can shine and be celebrated. At the same time, making room for the wholeness and imperfections of each of us and the ideas we put forth is part of the world I want to live in. Inclusion of someone's ideas or work is not a wholesale endorsement; nor are the critiques I make a wholesale rejection.

One of the tricky things for me has been balancing the complexity and nuanced nature of the topics with the desire to make it readable and accessible. I also wanted to provide proper references without overwhelming you with millions of footnotes. To balance these aims, I've provided endnotes at the back with page numbers and language cues so you can see and access original sources for references in the book. You might have noticed already I also provide in-text asterisks for more substantive comments. This is clunky I know! Hopefully it doesn't get in your way too much as you read.

This book, organized into three sections, was written to be read slowly, from front to back. In Part I, *Getting Started*, you'll be introduced to tools and ideas to orient and prepare you for the work ahead. In Part II, *Guiding Questions for the Journey*, you'll dive deeply into explorations of identity, place, belonging, and purpose, getting yourself ready for an initiation. In Part III, *Crossing the Threshold into Adulthood*, you'll create a community-supported rite of passage for yourself, and then return back to your life and explore what this means for you going forward.

At times, you may wish to speed ahead, to get to the juicy, more exciting stuff. Please be patient! There are no shortcuts to initiation. There are lots of exercises and of course you don't need to do them all, but be mindful of giving this journey the rigor and attention needed to do it well. What is contained in these pages is a step-by-step approach to a process that typically takes years, supported by a community providing clear guidance and preparation. This is difficult, dangerous work. Please tread carefully, slowly, and humbly.

Each of the topics brought forward in this book are whole worlds of study. At the end of the book you'll find a QR code that will take you to an online collection of resources for further exploration, organized by chapter.

And so we begin! Safe travels on this journey.

☾

The edge of things is a liminal space. The edge is a holy place, or as the Celts called it, "a thin place" and you have to be taught how to live there. To take your position on the spiritual edge of things is to learn how to move safely in and out, back and forth, across and return. It is a prophetic position...When you live on the edge of anything with respect and honor, you are in a very auspicious position.

–Franciscan priest and author Richard Rohr

There are three ways to travel in unknown terrain:

1. *Learn the language first. Become fluent in it.*

2. *Find trustworthy guides to interpret and lead you.*

3. *Flail your way through with a series of missteps and dead ends.*

The first is hard to sustain without the inspiration of the journey. The second risks dependence and puts much power in the hands of another. The third is frustrating and at times demoralizing. The path to adulthood requires all three. What can anchor them all, and provide ease through the hardship, is community.

—personal journal, 2017

PART I:
GETTING STARTED

Chapter 1:

PACKING A BAG FOR THE JOURNEY

"No journey carries one far unless, as it extends into the world around you, it goes an equal distance into the world within."
–Lillian Smith, white Southern Author and Social Critic.

My mom, an educator and historian, frequently references the story of Yup'ik (Alaska Native) Harold Napoleon, as he tells it in his essay entitled *Yuuyaraq, the Way of the Human Being*. The essay begins with Napoleon explaining to the reader that he's writing from prison, where he's been held for many years since his son's death, "due directly to my own abuse of and addiction to alcohol." Prior to his incarceration, Napoleon served in different leadership capacities, with great promise as one of the next generation of leadership for his people.

Trying to understand what has happened to him, Napoleon listens to the stories of other prisoners. He discovers that his story is shared by many. This leads him to explore the forces creating the conditions where many people of his generation lost themselves on paths of personal destruction that ultimately, he saw, were killing his culture.

Napoleon saw a pattern as he looked at the history of his people for help in understanding the cultural phenomenon of which he was a part. Where the story of his people began to go wrong, he saw, was at the turn of the 20th Century, at the time of what he calls *The Great Death*, the 1900 world-wide flu epidemic. The Great Death happened while white Christian missionaries were moving into Alaska to convert Native peoples. The convergence of these two events was culturally catastrophic. Not only were missionaries telling the people that their beliefs were wrong, but people were dying in huge numbers. It was hard to resist the impulse to connect the deaths with the story being told by the missionaries that their culture was to blame.

Napoleon describes a generation of survivors in post-traumatic stress. With so much death and loss, doubts sown deeply about their beliefs, and their leadership discredited, these survivors did the only thing they could figure out to do: they became silent. They stopped teaching their ways and traditions. They stopped telling their stories. They no longer had authority over the education of their children; instead their young were educated by missionaries and teachers. They watched as their children were punished for speaking their native language. The shame and confusion they felt kept them from passing on the knowledge of their culture to their descendants. Instead, it was the shame they passed on, though they did not speak of it, or speak of their grief. During this time, Yupi'k children grew up with little connection to their past, set adrift in a white world that had little respect for them.

And with that, the circle of community was broken.

Napoleon's story goes on: he traces the progress of this cultural dislocation working its way into succeeding generations, leading to his own plight and that of his fellow prisoners. Napoleon ends his story with a very simple prescription for healing: to re-weave the circle of community by creating opportunities for the stories of people's experiences to be told, to make spaces for the truth to be spoken. By mending the circle of community, generations find their rightful place in the wheel of life, and gradually *yuuyaraq* (the Yupik law of living in this spiritual universe) is restored.

When she read it, this story spoke to my mom across a vast cultural divide. As she looked around at contemporary American culture and reflected on her own experiences growing up as a middle-class white woman in post-World War II United States, she saw broken circles everywhere. She saw Napoleon's work as a balm for collective repair, in addition to individual healing.

Years later, after my mom was introduced to rites of passage more fully through my coming of age experience, she began to see the link between what Napoleon was saying in *Yuuyaraq* and what she saw happening through rites of passage. "When we engage in the work of bringing rite of passage experiences to our people," she wrote in a training manual she created for Rite of Passage Journeys, "we are doing that healing work; we are reweaving the circle of community. We are restoring the role of generations in carrying the culture forward through time and we are cultivating the inner resources of individuals to renew and revitalize our culture."

The need to mend broken circles remains strong today. Like we talked about in the last chapter, teens and young adults often feel isolated. I frequently hear young people describe their struggles as personal weaknesses or failures. This is reinforced through a culture that emphasizes individualistic strategies to deal with young people's challenges like mood-altering medication, private psychotherapy, and incarceration and surveillance while not prioritizing healing or care on a community level*.

---

*I'm not suggesting that private psychotherapy, mood-altering medications, and other interventions are not useful and necessary tools for many young people (and adults). If you have sought help through these tools, as I have, I applaud your courage in doing what you need to take care of yourself. Modern therapy and medical practices can (and often should) be part of one's path to adulthood. However, they should not replace rites of passage and will not fulfill the basic human need for healthy initiatory processes. The youth mental health epidemic is a symptom of a larger cultural sickness, and until we deal with these underlying issues, things will keep getting worse for successive generations.

It's important to me that you, and every young person, understand that your individual struggles are not your own unique burden. You are not broken! Your challenges do not reflect your own, individual pathology. Instead, you are a mirror of a much wider, cultural pathology, and, as you heal yourself, you help to heal the communities of which you are a part.

Rites of passage are a path to this sort of individual and cultural healing. Yet, it's a long and sometimes hazardous journey! So you'll want some provisions to help you along your path.

When I was learning how to backpack, I was taught about the Ten Essentials: items of equipment, like a water bottle, map and compass, and raingear, that are important to always have in your backpack, just in case. As you prepare for this journey into adulthood, here is a list of ten essentials that you too will want to gather for your (metaphorical) backpack. These are tools, practices, and ways of thinking that can help you when the road seems long and lonely, and when it feels like you have perhaps lost your way.

1ST ESSENTIAL: UNDERSTANDING CULTURE AND UNLEARNING FALSE NARRATIVES

"I think of culture as what's around me and what I'm supposed to be doing and how I'm supposed to be educated. I also think of counter-culture. In my community, we don't have friendships that way, we don't buy clothes that way, we don't have jobs the way the culture encourages us to." –Dante, age 21

Culture is defined as "the sum total of ways of living built up by a group of human beings and transmitted from one generation to another." It includes all of the material things which unite a group, like food, technology, and clothing, as well as language, expectations of behavior, religion, and more. Culture shapes the way we see the world. I recently heard the definition, "Culture is what we think of as normal."

Likely, there are many different subcultures that you have been exposed to in your life. For example, think of high school cliques, like band kids, jocks, honor students, etc. Each subculture has their ways of dressing, behaving, and interacting with each

Ten Essentials for a Rite of Passage into Adulthood

other. You might be able to relate to these subgroups more easily than relating to culture on the big scale, like American culture or Western culture. But exploring how we are impacted by these larger cultural influences is important in developing the ability to make choices.

Culture can be very difficult to understand from within, especially when systems don't require us to step out of our cultural context in order to get needs met. For example, if all of the doctors who serve you come from the same cultural background as you, you might get a sense that all doctors behave in very specific ways. Yet if you receive medical care from doctors from a range of cultural backgrounds, you'd likely notice a variety of ways that doctors treat patients.

One way to look at culture is as an iceberg. Above the waterline are the elements of culture readily seen. Imagine visiting a new culture. What are the things you would notice, without needing any background information? Likely, you'd notice things like food, language, and how people dress. These are the things we generally experience when we visit a new place without a guide or interpreter.

A guide or interpreter, however, can often explain *why* things are the way they are and point out more subtle things happening that we might otherwise miss. These are often what is going on below the waterline of the cultural iceberg. The vast majority of what comprises a culture lives below the waterline, including values, beliefs, assumptions and attitudes.

Assumptions or misunderstandings about what's happening below the waterline can lead to all sorts of conflict and confusion.

For example, a few years ago I gathered with a large, culturally diverse group of people with different cultural understandings of the value of time. Some folks felt that following an agreed-upon schedule set in linear time was an important value. Within the cultural context of the Indigenous hosts, however, this was a far less important value than taking time for honoring, acknowledgements and addressing what was arising in any given moment. As a group, we ramrodded our collective ship straight into this cultural iceberg and suffered some damage as a result. It wasn't just that different values around time collided. Part of the

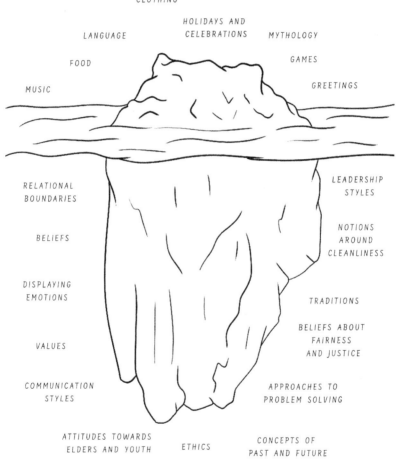

Cultural Iceberg

HISTORY AND LANGUAGE

Imagine our early ancestors as they first developed the capacity for speech. The ability to verbally communicate with one another allowed humans to create new forms of shared understanding, grounded not only in the immediate present and physical reality, but also in reference to the past, future, and geographic locations. It also allowed them to explore and describe conceptual abstractions. How exciting it must have been to find that they could communicate with one another in this way!

Language offers us the power to name and define. Our worldview is shaped by the words we use and the words we don't. Jeannette Armstrong, a Syilx Okanagan author and educator, shares that in her language, "our place on the land" is the same word as "our language." This means that among her people, they actually understand their language and their homeland to be the same thing. If this feels foreign to you, imagine the impact of having your language taken away from you, as so many Native cultures have (including, likely, your own ancestors at some point in the past, wherever they came from). How might this shape you?

The words that we use to describe our history—and the words that we don't use—are particularly important for understanding and unlearning the narratives of the dominant society. All versions of history depend on your perspective, and they impact our political understanding of the world around us. We grow used to the versions we hear over and over again, desensitized to or unaware of the biases they may contain. Many of us are not used to words like genocide, murder, and imperialism—except when these words are being used to describe those whom we fight against. Yet, these words are central to many of our family histories.

To engage in our own rite of passage in its deepest, fullest sense, requires that we understand our own life within this historical context and be thoughtful about how we describe it. These stories open the door for our liberation from fear, scarcity, and division. As Black liberationist and political exile Assata Shakur said, "No one is going to give you the education you need to overthrow them. Nobody is going to teach you your true history, teach you your true heroes, if they know that that knowledge will help set you free."

problem was that for many of us Westerners (particularly white attendees) we didn't recognize that following a set time schedule was a culturally-specific value; we just thought it was the *right way to do things.*

To step into your power as an adult, you'll need the capacity to step outside of Western cultural conditioning and take an observer's role. Like anything, this is a skill that requires practice! Throughout this book, you will be asked to question Western ways of understanding how the world works—understandings that often come to us through formative experiences in schooling, media, family and other forces.

You may already be practiced at stepping out of Western worldviews because you've grown up as part of another cultural background, as well. Perhaps you are Indigenous to the lands where you live or your family arrived just recently and is maintaining cultural traditions from different lands. Perhaps you are part of a marginalized group in broader society, and your community works hard to maintain or re-enliven traditions beyond what consumerist culture provides. Some of this book may affirm what you already know; please have patience if I sometimes share things that seem patently obvious to you!

On the other hand, perhaps you've fully lived on the Western cultural iceberg your whole life. Your ancestors may have left their lands generations ago, and actively discarded their traditional cultural ways seeking access to jobs and the ability to fit in as quickly as possible. For those in this second camp, please try to be patient, supportive, and kind to yourself as you encounter new ways of thinking. The chart in this section can give you a place to start in considering common elements of Western worldviews in contrast to Indigenous perspectives.

Part of stepping out of Western ways of looking at things is being able to unlearn what you've been taught: letting go of old understandings of how the world works, so we can engage in critical inquiry and use our minds to explore new ideas. One of the benefits of being younger is that you have less to unlearn, but society has been sending certain false messages to you since the moment you were born. Martin Luther King, Jr., talking about how to live in a society sick with the disease of racism, suggested

A FEW DIFFERENCES BETWEEN INDIGENOUS AND WESTERN WORLDVIEWS

"There is no single Indigenous or Western way of knowing. It is easy to fall into the traps of 'homogenizing' and 'othering' by reducing vast and varied traditions to simplistic and general terms. However, it is important to offer some starting point...to bring Indigenous and Western perspectives into conversation with one another." –Jane Stinson, "What are Indigenous and Western Ways of Knowing?"

INDIGENOUS WORLDVIEWS	WESTERN WORLDVIEWS
Time is cyclical in nature, and measured based on cyclical events like the seasons.	Time is linearly structured and future oriented, connected to clocks and calendars.
Holistic and interconnected. Emphasis on spectrums, multiplicity, and diversity. Capacity to hold many truths at once.	Compartmentalized and specialized. Emphasis on dualism, hierarchy, and competition of ideas: good/bad, mind/body, true/false.
Emphasis on extended kinship ties.	Individual and nuclear-family oriented.
Everything and everyone is related. Humans are an equal part of a vibrant, interconnected whole. Individuals are related as part of kinship-based ecosystems.	Everything on earth is ranked, with humans at the top. Society is made up of self-interested individuals, competing with each other for limited resources.
Economy is interdependent, decentralized, and resources are intensively used to minimize waste. Health of the economy is measured by the health of the whole. Beliefs	Economy is accumulation-oriented, oriented around centralized production, and driven by an assumption of scarce resources. Health of the economy is measured by high

A FEW DIFFERENCES BETWEEN INDIGENOUS AND WESTERN WORLDVIEWS CONTINUED

INDIGENOUS WORLDVIEWS	WESTERN WORLDVIEWS
that there is enough for everyone encourage kinship and sharing.	production and consumption. Amassing wealth is for personal gain.
Land and resources are sacred and sovereign beings, usually given by a creator or supreme being. The needs of future generations are as important as present-day needs.	Land and resources should be available for development and extraction for the benefit of humans. The needs of humans today are more important than future considerations.
Culture is rooted in the land.	Culture is transferable.
Success and well-being are measured by the quality of relationships. Identity comes from connections.	Success and well-being are measured by goal achievement. Identity comes from distinguishing oneself.
All people learn from everyone and everything. All life stages are honored and respected. Emphasis on intergenerational contact and mutual respect.	Generations are segmented. Value to others is measured through productivity, power, and wealth. The knowledge of children and old people tend to be devalued.

that we need to practice "creative maladjustment" with the society we live in. We need to remain unadjusted to a life of severe injustice, he said, incapable of fitting in, always finding creative ways to challenge systems that seek to exploit the many for the sake of the few. In order to practice this, we need to understand the ways we've been socialized, and the ways that we've been taught to live in boxes that deny our true nature.

Serena, age 25, doesn't pause when asked what he's working to unlearn. "Definitely the tough love thing…Love does not have to be tough. If anyone ever says that to you, that's bullshit. The people, especially, that should take care of you and hold you and things like that, their love does not have to be tough. It can be gentle and it should be." Serena connects this with growing up in a mixed-race Indigenous Maori household, struggling with the effects of colonization: "Especially as Indigenous youth, the people who look over us should cultivate that more for us so that we don't grow up to be hard, which I think a lot of us are forced to do. Then we have to grow up and decolonize from that. There's nothing wrong with being strong, but there is something kind of damaging about just being rough all the time."

Dante, age 21, who grew up in a white, middle-class household, expresses a different concern with trying to unlearn false narratives: "No matter how much I know about how destructive it is, my productivity is still my number one concern at all times. The thing that motivates me to be well and be good to myself is how productive I will be…The thing that motivates me to not get addicted to drugs is, 'Oh, then I can't do the work I need to do.' That doesn't sit right with me. It's like my life is still about work and there's so much more to love about my life and beauty to see than just what work I can contribute."

⚘ EXERCISE: Think about a culture of which you are part (could be as large as a nation-state, or as small as a town or school). Looking at the cultural iceberg graphic, jot down notes on what you notice about the culture, making note of things you're not sure about.

⚘ EXERCISE: Go back through the list, and consider a culture with very different components in each of these areas; it can be a foreign culture with which you are familiar, or an imaginary one. How does it feel to imagine something different?

🌱 **EXERCISE**: Having the ability to move between different worldviews, and recognize their gifts and limitations, is important for cultivating mental flexibility and cultural humility. Review chart of the Differences Between Indigenous and Western Worldviews. What do you think are the benefits and drawbacks of each one?

🌱 **EXERCISE**: In your journal, write a list of societal messages you've received that you don't necessarily agree with. Think about messages you've received about what is and isn't valued, or ideas you've been taught about how the world works. They could relate to beauty, sex, money, power, drugs, family, media—anything you can think of. For each one, reflect on how this shared societal message influences you, even if you don't agree with it.

2ND ESSENTIAL: EXPLORING THE PHASES OF A RITE OF PASSAGE

Navigating transition is hard, whether it is a transition we are choosing or one that life thrusts upon us. As you prepare to venture into the unknown, there is a simple framework that can help you make sense of the journey and act much like a compass for helping you to get your bearings. This framework is the Phases of a Rite of Passage.

These phases were first written about by Belgian anthropologist Arnold van Gennep, the person who coined the term *rites of passage.** Based on his research on initiatory practices from around the globe, he claimed that initiatory rites of passage (that of stepping into a new status or role in the community) involve three important stages. The first is *severance*, in which an individual sheds their old identity. This is generally marked by an abrupt departure from the old status and role. The second stage is *transition*, sometimes called the *liminal* phase. He likened this stage to a threshold: the strip of wood, metal, or stone you cross over when you go through a doorway. In this stage, an individual has no status; they are "no longer/not yet." This stage is an uncomfortable time because one has no fixed identity or role. The last stage is *incorporation*, in which an individual returns and assumes their new role, typically with great celebration.

There are many problems with van Gennep's model (see the footnote), but it is still highly valuable for individuals navigating times of transition. I have found many people (young people especially) are particularly comforted by the concept of severance: the need to let go of some part of themselves or their life. In the early days of the COVID pandemic, understanding what was happening as a cultural severance, and a step into a collective liminal phase, helped me find my footing in a quickly-changing world. You'll find that we draw upon the helpful simplicity of the framework throughout this book.

> ⚘EXERCISE: Think back to a transition that you have navigated in your life—perhaps the one you reflected on in the last chapter. What did each of

---

*Van Gennep's work has been criticized over the years, dismissed as gender-biased, overly simplistic, and (as were many anthropological analyses of his day) culturally-biased. The most important criticism was that his three-part model was not uncovered through his research, but was the lens through which he looked at rites around the world. More modern scholars have found that what's going on is far more complicated and nuanced than his model indicates. There are other important models of rites of passage, which offer a more complete picture. Yet van Gennep's work remains important today, in large part because his three-fold scheme underpins many, if not most, rites of passage that have arisen in Western communities over the last 50 years. His work underlies countless books and articles on the subject of rites of passage in contemporary Western society. His model is perhaps the primary organizing system for how to go about creating rites of passage within a Western cultural context. And its simplicity is valuable—I think of it like training wheels for rites of passage.

the stages of severance, transition, and incorporation look like in that rite of passage (and perhaps what was missing or incomplete)?

3RD ESSENTIAL: CULTIVATING INTUITION AND THE ABILITY TO LISTEN

"I think my intuition has to do with my stomach. My mom always told me to listen to my stomach, or gut. In Hawaiian, or in 'Olelo, that's called na'au, and that literally means your intestines. And that's a place that's thinking, a place of knowledge and sensing." –Serena, age 25

As is probably becoming clear, this is a journey of all parts of you, not just your intellect. The mind is only helpful to a point and at times can even get in the way. An essential tool to carry in your backpack is the ability to listen to your intuition. While navigating the road to adulthood, you need access to information from beyond the logical and rational.

Intuition means different things for different people. Some people, like Serena in the quote at the beginning of this section, locate this sense of knowing in the stomach, or describe "gut instinct." For others, it means "listening to your heart," with all of its longings, passions and wounds. Still others describe intuition as a "sixth sense," or a "knowing in the bones." Over time, I've come to realize that for me, my gut, my heart, my bones, my "sixth sense"—they each describe something slightly different, and provide me with different information. But they are all part of what makes up my intuition.

People receive intuitive information in different ways: sounds, visual images, emotions, sensations, even smells or tastes. It can take a while to notice what way of accessing intuition works for you.

Personally, I access my intuition primarily in two different ways. One is to connect with different parts of my body: What *feels* right physically? This can mean I pay attention to whatever sensations or insights come, or intentionally tune in to certain parts, like my heart or my belly. Another way of accessing intuition is listening for the words that come: asking my heart, or my ancestors, or my inner guidance for direction, and then listening for any messages they may offer.

We can access intuition by tracking our inner world through meditation, prayer, working with our dreams, and more. We can access intuition in the outside world, as well. We can look for signs and omens in nature, and even in the human world. We can use "oracles" like cards, runes, and the dozens of tools available. While these are often seen as hocus-pocus, for many people oracle devices are an invaluable tool for accessing information that lives beyond the intellect. It's not about "fortune telling," it's about tapping into ancient currents of wisdom and knowing, and making use of the tools available to us. No matter whether you access intuition through meditation, prayer, time in nature, oracle devices, the arts, or other practices, quieting down and listening is the key to hearing what it is telling you.

In his book, *Gift of Fear*, author and "Bodyguard-to-the-Stars" Gavin de Becker talks about the intuitive knowing that survivors of violence often report having experienced before they were harmed. He believes that there is some sort of physical cue that our conscious mind simply hasn't picked up on. Wherever intuition comes from doesn't matter much to me, to tell the truth. What matters is that when I quiet down, pay attention, and listen, I receive a lot of information of value about myself, and the world around me.

⚜ EXERCISE: Find a quiet space. Sit comfortably and take a few deep breaths and consciously relax your body. Leaving your eyes open or closing them, whatever is most comfortable with you, invite your intuition to share with you a little about how it works. You can speak aloud or in your mind. As you continue to sit and breathe for a few minutes track what you notice. What physical sensations do you experience in your body, and where are they located? Slowly bring your attention to different parts of your body, inviting them to share with you anything about how they are part of your intuition.

Keeping your attention on your inner world, slowly bring to your awareness each of your senses, inviting them to share in their language of sound, taste, touch, sight, and smell anything they want to tell you about how intuition works for you. Take at least 5-10 minutes for this exercise. When you are complete, thank your intuition for being with you, even if the voice is still quiet and you can't yet access it. Try this exercise daily for a week and see what happens.

4TH ESSENTIAL: CONNECTING WITH NATURE

"I feel truest and like I belong when I am in nature." –Chandi, age 26

Learning how to be in nature, and find comfort and connection with the many beings of the land, was perhaps the greatest gift of my coming of age at 13. Over the last several decades, an unbelievable amount of time, energy, and resources have gone into scientifically proving what is obvious: time in nature is good for our brains and bodies. This can be big-N- Nature or little-n- nature: a 1,000 mile hike or putting our hands in the dirt of the potted plant on our windowsill.

If you're new to connecting with nature, welcome to a wide open world of possibility! Whether nature is the plant on your window sill, the grass growing up between the cracks in the sidewalk, or a roadless mountain range, here are a few strategies for building a relationship with the world around you. If this doesn't interest you – or if it makes you feel a little nervous — I encourage you still to give it a try.

First, it's essential to take care of your physical safety and well-being. If you don't have safe places in nature to go in your neighborhood, or your body doesn't allow you to access them, consider what you can do to bring nature to you. Can you plant a seed in a cup on your window sill? Do you have a pet, or does your neighbor have a pet that you can observe? My friend Lucy suffers from a chronic, debilitating illness. Several years ago, when her illness left her bed-ridden in her apartment in London for months, her companion was a squirrel that would come to her window each day. This squirrel brought her solace and connection with the world during a very painful, inwardly-focused time.

Second, connecting with nature can often be uncomfortable for people. It is not always inspiring and awe-inducing! Sometimes, it brings up feelings of inadequacy, grief, fear, discomfort and more. If you have any of these feelings, please know that this is a normal part of the process and it doesn't mean you're doing anything wrong. It just means you're exercising new muscles, and those muscles need time to strengthen. Please stick with it! Access to nature is our birthright.

Whether your access to nature is big or small, here are Four Doorways for Connecting with Nature.

First, you can develop a relationship with nature through learning natural history. By observing and learning about specific flora and fauna, you can become grounded in the landscape. Witnessing the natural forces—wind, rain, the passing of seasons, the pathways cut by the sun, the ecological webs—you are drawn into natural cycles, and learn more about your place in them. Learning the history of what forces created the mountains, valleys, and waterways gives a sense of the power of geologic forces. In an urban landscape, researching the traditional paths of water can help you to see what lies beneath the concrete.

Second, you can develop a connection with the land through practical engagement. Gardening, making medicinal teas, building fires: all of these deepen connection to the natural world in an interactive way. A relationship with nature is forged through mutual interdependence. When I need to make a fire, I pay much more attention to the qualities of different woods, and what is good to burn. Engaging actively, I am impacting the world around me and being physically impacted myself.

Connecting to the earth also means learning from the natural elements as a mirror, through the language of metaphor. This is a third way to connect with the natural world. As I observe a squirrel busily collecting acorns, I am reminded that I must attend to all of the details in my life. These metaphors can become richer and richer the more I attend to the first two ways, learning about nature and engaging with it in a practical way.

Four Doorways for Connecting with Nature

Direct communication is a fourth doorway to connecting with nature. As humans, we communicate readily through language, so this may mean speaking to a place, being in dialogue with it—sharing our stories, longings, fears, and listening to the responses we get back. This may mean communicating in other ways as well: through using our senses, noticing our feelings, relating through body language, song, gestures, stillness and more. All of these ways of relating assume that nature is animate, alive, and we can communicate directly. The owl that hovers around my house, that I see occasionally in the darkness—we can communicate with each other.

If you are new to connecting with nature, don't worry. All four of these ways of engaging with nature are lifelong pursuits. And, all four are equally essential elements of a relationship with, as American ecologist and philosopher David Abram says, "the more-than-human world." When we look to nature as a mirror but don't have a naturalist's eye, there is so much information that we lack. When we harvest willow to make a basket, but we don't ask the willow for permission, we cut ourselves off from a reciprocal relationship. Yet when we incorporate all of these ways of being in relationship we gain access to one of Life's ultimate truths: we belong to the Earth. There are some resources in the back of the book to support you in deepening your relationship with nature in different ways.

> ⚘EXERCISE: One foundational practice to connect with nature is the practice of a sit spot.* Each day for a week, visit the same place in nature for a minimum of 10 minutes (a place in nature can be by a window if that's what's accessible to you). Take a few breaths to quiet your mind, and begin to observe what's around you, noticing with each of your senses.

---

*I first learned this practice through the Wilderness Awareness School. Along with other nature connection lineages, Wilderness Awareness School is undergoing a process of reflection/reckoning on the ways that their programs and teachings have inadvertently upheld systems of oppression. For more on this topic see Chapter 3.

❦EXERCISE: For one month, pay attention to the moon. Notice what phase they are in. Day after day and night after night, see if you can catch a glimpse of them.

5TH ESSENTIAL: LEARNING TO BE ALONE

"Most of my teenage years and my youth was spent solo, and not being around or having a lot of friends. It sucked, but I do think that that kind of afforded me a lot more opportunities to learn more about myself."
–Serena, age 25

When I was growing up, I thought of myself as a total extrovert. I was very social, perhaps extremely so, always trying to keep connected and wanting to be part of things. Every once in a while, though, it would become too much. I'd hit a wall, and get completely overwhelmed until I fell apart.

As I look back, I realize I was afraid to be alone. I was scared of what would happen when I was surrounded by emptiness, when I had no distractions or attention from my peers. I had the gift of my coming of age experience, so I had known the beauty and magic of solitude. But I found it difficult to strike the proper balance and still do today.

What is your relationship with alone time? Are you like I was growing up, or is solitude your default and being around others more challenging? Or is there a different way that you relate to both? Whether you find being alone easy, or like me you struggle with it, developing comfort with being alone is an essential item for your backpack.

This doesn't mean just being alone in the sense of not being with other humans. It also means letting go of distractions, like screens and other habits. Letting go of distractions opens up our awareness and allows us to connect with parts of ourselves that might feel awkward or uncomfortable but are part of who we are in the world. It can help us become more aware of what's happening inside our bodies, which also means that unexpected feelings may come up that we'd rather ignore or push to the side. We might feel scared, sad, or lonely.

In addition to opening up our awareness and helping us move through difficult feelings, learning to be alone helps prepare us for one of life's inevitable truths: sometimes we have to navigate hardship without support from other people coming the way we might like.

One of the most intense moments I've ever had came when I was just a few months sober, when I was having a hard time with a person I was romantically involved with. He wanted space from me and was taking it in a way that felt really scary for me. One night, things came to a head. I knew that no matter what I did, he was not going to talk to me and help me feel safe. It was late at night, and I felt all alone. I lay on my floor in the moonlight and sobbed for what felt like hours. I learned a lot that night about what it is to be alone and navigate hardship.

One of the things I learned is that I'm never really alone. I might not have other people, but I always have the more-than-human world to turn to for support and solace. It was the moon that got me through that night, that helped me know I'd be okay.

This book is going to ask a lot of you, and that's going to take time and the ability to be present and focused. Investing energy in creating alone time will be part of what allows this to happen.

> ⚘EXERCISE: If solitude doesn't come naturally for you, start small and simple. For the next week, take 15 minutes with no screens, no people, and no tasks each day. You can choose to meditate or engage in other activities which are truly nourishing for you like writing, drawing, making crafts or music, but keep this time separate from the chores you need to do and if you notice yourself getting into "productivity mind," stop your activity! The intention here is to be with what it feels like to be alone. Observe how this feels and what comes up for you. Over time, gradually build up to longer, trying even a day or two. See what emerges in the still and quiet spaces.

6TH ESSENTIAL: THE HEALING POWER OF THE ARTS

"The easiest way to talk about myself is through poetry." –Serena, age 25

I was in a workshop a few years ago, playing an icebreaker game called "Step into the Circle." The teacher called out different prompts: "Step into the circle if you have a sibling," "Step into the circle if you had eggs for breakfast this morning," and so on. At one point she said, "Step into the circle if you're an artist." I froze.

I thought back to when I was in fourth grade and learned that I definitely was not an artist. I got straight A's in school that year—except in two subjects, art and PE. When I saw that line of A's, and those two C's sticking out like sore thumbs, I internalized something about myself that I've been trying to unlearn ever since. I learned that I was good at academics, and mediocre at physical and creative engagement. This story has burdened me ever since.

In Western culture, we've allowed the arts to be separated out, commodified, and codified. No longer are most of us taught to create things with our hands that are beautiful or shown that craftsmanship is as valuable as mental pursuits. In those limited arenas where we do learn the arts, we are often asked to fit into limited frames of what "good" and "bad" look like, rather than being encouraged to messily explore our own inner muse and unique creative genius. Dante, age 21, puts it this way: "I have had a lifelong love and sometimes heartbreaking relationship with music. It's a medium I need to express myself through, but the way I was raised and taught to create was so distorted that it completely killed my creativity."

Asked to describe what it was like being trained as a musician, Dante goes on to say, "I was taught to think about music as a competition, as about being better than other people, about it being a job or profession; something I have to make money off of and therefore have to market. I didn't know anything better until I met musicians for whom it wasn't about their personal success as musicians. They were making music for larger goals."

Now, Dante is in a process of unlearning the messages they received about being a musician. "I long for it to be something that is just about creating beautiful things for myself and so that other people could hear stories. I really had to fight to find ways to be creative that weren't stifling. And now I'm like, 'Oh, it wasn't me, it wasn't my fault. I was never given any tools to be a creative person."

Dante's story illustrates two key pieces of healing through the arts. First, unleashing your creativity means letting go of what you've been taught about what things should look, sound, or be like. This doesn't happen all at once—it's an ongoing process. Second, any difficulty you experience in letting go of that conditioning doesn't come from your personal failings. You came into this world an endlessly creative being, capable of bringing forth unique offerings. Even if this was nurtured in some spheres, it almost definitely was discouraged in others.

The journey offered in these pages is a journey toward wholeness, and restoring health for ourselves and our communities. As you engage with this journey, please pack your tools as an artist—whatever that means for you. It is through our unique creative journey that we can find our soul's calling.

> ⚚ EXERCISE: Think back to when you were a child. What was your favorite artistic medium? Perhaps it was drawing, building forts, playing drums, or dancing. Maybe you have continued to develop this craft, perhaps you laid it down long ago. Either way, try it again, giving yourself complete permission to create something awful. Notice what wants to be expressed, and where you block creativity with expectations or fears. What voices share their judgements, and what do they say? Consider continuing on with the craft throughout this book, as part of the journey.

> ⚚ EXERCISE: Free write about what "art" means to you. Who benefits by keeping the definition of art small and limited? Who suffers as a result?

7TH ESSENTIAL: RESOURCING: WORKING WITH STRESS, TRAUMA, AND CHALLENGING EMOTIONS

"Being happy all the time just is not possible. Yes, I am happy and I am sad and I'm anxious and I am angry...now I don't put so much pressure on myself to feel a certain emotion. All emotions are equally important. Allowing myself to experience emotions without judging myself for being sad, angry, or anxious opened the door to what it is like to truly feel content with the situation. Experiencing more sadness helps me feel more happiness and it also allows me to feel a lot more contentment."
–Alyson, age 30

When Alyson was in eighth grade, her mom died after battling cancer for several years. Immediately, Alyson's whole life changed. Her dad sunk into a deep depression. According to Alyson, sharing her story years later in preparation for a three day solo rite of passage, he "remarried an awful woman, turned to whiskey and vodka, and made several suicide attempts."

Alyson didn't have anywhere to express her grief, fear, or anger, and so she compensated by overperforming. "I went on my merry way," she wrote, describing this formative time in her life. "Straight A student, working 40 hours a week. Anytime I started to feel sad, I would invite a friend over, pick up a shift at work, or go to the library to study. I have never given myself time to be sad. Anytime I feel a 'negative' emotion creep in, I immediately distract myself." By the time I met her when she was 25, Alyson was ready to confront what had happened. "I deserve to mourn," she wrote, "or at least I deserve the opportunity to figure out if I need to mourn."

Alyson carried a lot of trauma into her 20's. When she wrote this, after many years of subconsciously working to create the right conditions, Alyson found herself safe enough to begin to address it.

Trauma is *an experience that overwhelms our capacity to process and respond,* or as I first heard from embodiment educator and Golden Bridge founder Melissa Michaels, it is when something is experienced as "too much, too fast, too soon." It was with Melissa on the dance floor that I first began to learn about trauma: what it is, and how it impacts us physically, emotionally, socially, mentally, and spiritually, and how we can begin to safely unwind the complex and unintegrated energies we carry in our bodies.

Trauma is complex and mysterious. It comes from intense, acute incidents such as abuse, and can also come from more chronic situations where "smaller" impacts stack up to the point where one can no longer process it, as in the case of neglect. We can create situations ourselves that result in trauma, or the situations can be forced upon us. Two people may experience the same situation and one will experience it as trauma and the other won't, based on factors like social support systems in a person's life, other mental or physical health challenges they experience, genetic factors, and more. A person might even experience something as traumatic at one point in their life that they wouldn't at another point. This has to do with the best tools we each have available at any given time.

> "The wound that is not witnessed does not heal."
>
> –Rumi, 13th century Sufi mystic and poet

As a society, we are just beginning to understand how widespread trauma is due to the impacts of chronic stress on our bodies, generations of systemic injustices like colonization, slavery and more. Whether or not we've suffered trauma ourselves, it is important that tools for identifying and working with trauma are in each of our hands, so that we can care for ourselves and become agents of healing for others. An important adage, common among people organizing for social justice, is "Hurt people hurt." More recently, an addition can increasingly be heard: "And healing people heal."

Trauma is caused by a *stress response* that we lack the skills or capacity to integrate. A stress response is a normal, natural response to a perceived threat. We are biologically programmed to react to stress in different ways, primarily fight, flight, and freeze (some people also add "appease"). During times of significant stress, we release hormones that support us to react in these ways, giving us energy surges allowing us to perform physical feats we could not do under normal circumstances. This is part of being human, a great survival strategy.

The challenge comes when the energy build-up from hormonal surges isn't able to be fully discharged. Animals have ways of dealing with this, like a dog shaking off a scary encounter with another dog. Humans do, too. Yet oftentimes in the human cultures today, we are not able to release the energy adequately because of our social conditioning, or because of the chronic nature of stress in a fast-paced world. Stress remains pent up in our bodies and gets stuck.

This causes what's known as *dysregulation,* or the inability to remain grounded, centered, and present in the moment. Some folks get stuck in an on state of hyper-reactivity, which manifests as adrenaline-seeking behavior, anxiety, or rage (fight/flight). Sometimes folks get stuck in an off state, and show signs of depression, dissociation, lethargy and fatigue (freeze). Sometimes, folks fluctuate wildly between these two extremes.

Think for a moment. Have you ever responded to a situation in a way that didn't seem like it at all matched what was happening? Someone said something, perhaps, and it provoked strong anger or fear in a way that surprised you? Or you just checked out completely, even though that's not really what you wanted to do? Have you experienced this happen to someone else, when you said or did something that seemed small, but their reaction was huge?

These are indicators of some sort of inevitable trauma response. Oftentimes when this happens, the person that has the unexpectedly strong reaction may feel embarrassed or ashamed afterwards, or get defensive and blame others to cover up what can be perceived or experienced as an overreaction. They may not remember the incident that led to the trauma response, or quite be able to put their finger on why they reacted the way they did.

But our bodies know. We store our traumas until we are able to fully and thoroughly discharge them through physical and psychological processing. This can impact our actions, feelings, and thoughts in ways that feel overwhelming, distressing, and at times unmanageable.

This is what happens on a personal level, when our own individual traumas are activated.

Layered on top of personal trauma, however, are also collective and ancestral trauma. *Collective trauma* refers to trauma experienced by a group, like a family or even a whole nation. COVID-19 has been a collective trauma affecting all of us (though in varying ways and to varying extents, depending on our situation).

Black lives lost to police violence is a type of trauma that impacts Black communities in particular ways. Racism, xenophobia, colonization, sexism, homophobia, transphobia, and other forms of oppression all result in collective trauma.

Ancestral trauma is related to collective trauma, and refers to the ways that we carry the painful experiences of our ancestors: the accumulation of their life stories as well as our own. Think back over what you know of your parent's life, and their parent's lives before them. As you reflect back through the generations, think of all the wounds that your ancestors carried, lodged in their bodies and unreleased. These traumas came into you through the way you were raised and even through your actual DNA. There is a spiritual component to this, and that spiritual component is backed up by concrete biological evidence. The hereditary nature of addiction is one example. Children of parents with addiction issues are eight times more likely to develop an addiction than those whose parents did not suffer from addiction.* The evidence coming out of the discipline of epigenetics is another example, where scientific researchers like Rachel Yehuda are finding that our DNA is encoded differently based on the life experiences of our parents.

Understanding how trauma works helps me to take my own responses—and the responses of others—less personally. I realize that each personal interaction I have is going through filters of vast accumulations of life experiences. This can make it a little easier to have compassion when I make a mistake or someone else does. When conflict arises, I (often) have the will to navigate through it to healing because I can see it as a larger healing process of my own, and of collective trauma. This inspires me to do the internal work of building resiliency, so that I am able to build connection and intimacy broadly. Part of how to do this is through a set of practices known as *resourcing*.

Resources are things we can draw on or access to meet our needs, and "being resourced" means having access to the things we need to remember that we are, in fact, physically safe and our

---

*Addiction is complex and multi-faceted; I'm not seeking to fully explain it here. My intention in including this statistic is to highlight the ways our lives today are impacted by the people we come from. We'll get more into this, especially in Chapter Six.

survival isn't threatened. According to yoga teacher and author Hala Khouri, ways that we can resource ourselves include:

1. *Orienting in time and place.* To stay or get oriented, notice where you are: colors, textures, play of light and shadow. What's physically happening around you? What sounds can you hear?

2. *Grounding.* Literally feel the ground beneath you, and feel yourself being on the ground. Notice the subtleties: where you feel the most pressure, and the least. Breathe, and help your body relax into the ground.

3. *Centering.* Feeling yourself inside your body. Notice where your center of power is. If it feels outside of your body, begin to draw it inside.

I first learned about resourcing when I began studying with Melissa Michaels. I grew up chronically dysregulated, reliant on caffeine, nicotine, alcohol, and other substances to manage stress and anxiety. Conscious dance offered me an alternative way of resourcing my nervous system and discharging my stress and anxiety. Over time, I find myself more and more aware of what I'm experiencing on a nervous system level, and able to access resourcing to support me.

As you read through the rest of the book, you may get activated. You may disagree with my interpretations, conclusions, and

SHORT LIST OF SENSATIONS

Cold	Tender	Prickly
Hot	Achy	Twitchy
Sweaty	Itchy	Burning
Moist	Sore	Empty
Dry	Tight	Full
Tingly	Nauseous	Energized
Numb	Shaky	Open

sources. There is a lot of collective and ancestral trauma embedded in what I offer. Many of my ancestors would have been killed for saying or believing some of the things you will read, and some of my ancestors would have done the killing.

Tracking our sensations is a critical tool for recognizing dysregulation in our nervous system, and finding ways to resource ourselves. In a breakout box in this section, you'll find a short list of sensations to help you practice identifying what you're experiencing in your body.* As you move through the material, please pay attention to what sensations you experience in your body, and take your time with what you read. Where do you notice excess or uncomfortable energy moving through you, or find your chest tightening, your breath growing stronger and faster? Notice where you gloss over text, and can't seem to absorb the content no matter how many times you read it. These are all clues to your emotional world, and they offer rich exploration and opportunities for growth. They can help you identify when it's time to take a break and go for a walk, listen to some music, or identify sections of the book you may need to take more time or get more support to work through.

Over time, I've learned that particular sensations arise when I'm stressed. For example, I sometimes clench my jaw, usually when I'm anxious about being heard or understood. Now, when I feel my jaw tighten, I can intentionally stretch it to relax my whole

SHORT LIST OF EMOTIONS

Relieved	Resentful	Disconnected
Connected	Proud	Embarrassed
Defensive	Ashamed	Understanding
Grieving	Frustrated	Excited
Curious	Exhausted	Inspired
Afraid	Hopeful	Distrustful
Angry	Isolated	Guilty

*For a more in-depth exploration of this, and a more robust list of sensations, see Melissa Michaels, Youth on Fire, 2016, Chapter Six : Embodying Life's Rhythms.

body, and at the same time make note of the anxiety that's coming up for me. I can then mindfully choose how to respond: maybe to share my concerns, or remind myself that I want to listen, too. Finding ways to be with the sensations in my body, name them, be with them, track them, and allow them to sequence through to release has become an essential survival tool that makes tension and conflict something I need to avoid less often.

This is related to what is often known these days as mindfulness. Recent decades have seen the spread of mindfulness practices, as researchers across academic disciplines have come to uncover many positive benefits the practices yield, including supporting healthier functioning of the body, in the mind, and in relationships. "Science has clearly shown that how we focus our attention will grow our brains in specific ways," says brain researcher Dan Siegel. "People who use their minds to reflect on the inner nature of their mental lives grow circuits in the brain that link widely separated areas to one another...and help avoid rigidity and chaos within self, and between self and other."

⚜ EXERCISE: Review the list of emotions in this section. Which of these emotions do you feel like you experience on a regular basis? Which ones feel more foreign to you? Much of our emotional vocabulary comes from our social conditioning. For example, I have been taught that expressing sadness and fear are totally fine, but anger is not acceptable. This means that when I experience anger (a natural, important human emotion), I often mistake it for something else (typically, sadness or confusion). Begin to track your emotional repertoire, making note of which emotions you do not allow yourself and which ones are ever-present.

⚜ EXERCISE: Like you did with the intuition exercise, find a quiet spot, and sit in a comfortable, relaxed position. Take a few deep breaths and settle your body and mind. Now begin to bring your attention to your physical sensations (not your emotions!). For example, you might observe that you feel sad, but bring yourself back to the physical signs that are telling you that you are sad. "Constricted throat," you might notice, or "achy chest. Continue to track these sensations, starting at your head and moving to your feet, observing them as they arise and then noticing if it's possible to let them go. Following your breath in and out can be a useful tool to help you release the sensations. After you have scanned from head to toes, bring your attention to what emotions you are experiencing. Observe these too as they arise, and notice if you are able to let them pass. After a few minutes of this, make note of your thoughts. What reflections, questions, judgements, or analysis is present for you at this moment? Observe your thoughts, and notice also if you are able to release your thoughts. If you find yourself unable to feel any sensations at all, or your sensations quickly become overwhelming, these are your body's intelligent, self-preserving signals that you may need additional support with this work. If you have a skilled mentor, trusted adult, therapist, or close trusted friend, share your experience with them as you continue on with the book. Move slowly. Please don't push yourself to go faster than what your body can safely move through. If you don't have a trusted adult or peer to speak with, skip ahead to Essential #10 and follow those instructions before continuing further. Having support on this journey is critical.

Practice this exercise a few times in a quiet, solitary space, and then begin to take it out in the world, into your life. Do this practice at work, in the grocery store. Begin to utilize it in more and more uncomfortable situations. You may find that it helps you better understand what's happening inside you, and therefore make more conscious choices about how you want to interact with the world.

⚘EXERCISE: Most of us have received messages about what emotions are acceptable to express, and which ones aren't. This means that many of us have lots of pent-up emotions, waiting to get discharged. How do we discharge these emotions safely, at a rate that we can regulate, so that we don't hurt ourselves or others? Much of psychotherapy, especially somatic (body-based) approaches to psychotherapy, is devoted to this task.

There is so much grief, rage, and terror in our world today, and when we connect with our own emotional fields we run the risk of tapping into a deep cultural reservoir of suffering. So for this exercise, I invite your careful attention and good boundaries! The intention here is to take a small step toward greater awareness and the ability to move stuck energy. The next time you feel a strong emotion (whether this emotion is joy, fear, anger, or whatever), let yourself take the space to express it. Often when you're first getting started, this means quietly and calmly finding a way to remove yourself from the presence of others. Find a personal space—even a bathroom—and let yourself express it through your voice and body. Shake if you need to shake. Go to maybe 75% of intensity—you don't want to hurt yourself, but you want to let it move. Take whatever time you need until you feel the emotion begin to subside. Notice how you feel now.

If this is a new area of exploration for you, you've just discovered a vast world of health and healing! Consider finding a physical practice that creates a safe outlet for moving energy—whether that be dancing, kick-boxing, or whatever practice feels best for your body. Artistic expression can also serve as this outlet.

8TH ESSENTIAL: LEARNING TO EXPLORE SHADOW

A psychological term coined by twentieth century psychologist Carl Jung, *shadow* refers to the parts of us that we hide from ourselves, because there's something threatening about them for our ego. The shadow is beautiful, mysterious terrain, part of what makes us unique in our humanness. There are treasures hidden in your shadow, just waiting to be found. Yet as long as they remain unseen, shadow aspects can't be confronted and consciously incorporated, and we remain unable to reach our fullest potential.

As humans, we frequently project our shadow onto others. Sometimes, it's because the part feels too grotesque for our conscious minds to accept (like selfishness or capacity for cruelty). Sometimes, it's because the part feels too beautiful for us to accept (like our innate charisma or generosity). But the deepest core of us longs to integrate these parts, so we project them onto others as a way to notice them. Strong emotions toward another (like love, hate, fear, and jealousy) are signs that shadow dynamics may be at play.

Sometimes it's not about a quality we want to integrate, but about a life experience that has been traumatic, and we haven't had the skills, time, or support to move what's stuck in us. So we play this pattern out in an attempt to integrate it, projecting our past experiences onto the people that surround us in the present.

Projections are dangerous because they make it hard to actually see real, flesh and blood humans for the complex beings that they are. When the object of our projection fails to live up to our ideal (which they inevitably will), or when we unconsciously project past suffering onto someone in the present, the results can be devastating for everybody.

Unconscious, unacknowledged shadow dynamics lead to all sorts of sideways behaviors. For example, when I was drinking, parts of me (especially aspects of my sense of humor and sexuality) would emerge that I kept totally under control in my daily life.

This drove me to drink to excess because these parts needed to be expressed. Part of my journey towards sobriety was recognizing and integrating these parts of myself and giving them space to express themselves in ways that I can feel good about.

Over the course of this journey, you will be asked to get to know parts of your shadow. You will also be asked to explore parts of the *collective shadow* of Western culture—patterns and projections that impact our behaviors in society-wide ways but are not widely understood, acknowledged, or talked about. As you explore collective shadow, you might consider what lurks in the shadows of your family systems as well.

Delving into this terrain can be yucky, and sometimes even scary. Yet there is gold to be found when we explore this terrain. As you continue forward, I invite you to notice what is in the corner of vision as you look at the world, what flashes on the edge of your awareness. This is often the terrain of the shadow.

⚘ EXERCISE: Think of someone that you have strong feelings about, either positive or negative. Start with someone that you don't know very well, either personally or someone in the media. Make a list of the qualities and attributes that you associate with them. Reflect on your own relationship to these qualities. Are they things that you possess as well?

9TH ESSENTIAL: EXPLORING MYTH AND STORY

"I think stories shape us as people. There's a misconception that our world isn't magical, and when you reach a certain age all of that just goes away. And I think that's fine for some people, but I don't necessarily think it's a healthy way of looking at the world." –Christina, age 17

Stories are among our most precious tools for navigating transitions, providing key information for us to draw on in an entertaining and inspiring fashion. We humans are story creatures: they nourish us and are key to our survival. Stories stir our imaginations, helping us to make sense of the world around us, and also increase our sense of possibility.

Nothing makes more clear how essential stories are than our dream world. Even if we don't remember them, dreams are critical for our survival. Our psyches need the ability to organize our experiences, and make mythological sense of what's happening to us, in order for us to function in our waking lives.

Storyteller Martin Shaw says that dreams are our "personal mythology," whereas myths are a "community dream." Both are stories, and both deserve our tending as part of the way that soul speaks to us.

Tending stories is very different from analyzing them, which can be a form of interrogation, demanding that they perform some psychological trick for us, or give us an answer to solve our problems. Tending to stories means that we let their hidden meanings work their magic on us, revealing themselves slowly as they are ready. Stories do not want to be solved—they want to play and dance with us, to call forth our creativity and our reverence.

Our task is to romance a story as though it's a prospective lover, writing poetry and creating art, dancing with it, whispering our longings and listening closely for any response. Martin Shaw says that the way to really get to know a story is to build an altar to it, and come to it in prayer and contemplation.

Of course, it's easier to communicate with a story if you know its language, and one of the languages stories speak is the language of archetype. Archetypes, defined as a recurrent symbol or motif in art, literature, and mythology, are elements of the "community dream" that rest in our collective imaginations. I can guess that the phrase "jealous lover" immediately conjures an image in your mind, not so different from the one it conjures in mine. It's an archetype. Lover, fighter, warrior, king, queen, servant, orphan—all of these, and many more—are archetypes rooted in our collective psyche, and embedded within our individual dream worlds as well as the fairy tales, legends, and myths we share. Learning to notice archetypes, and develop fluency with them, can help inspire stories to reveal themselves—and similarly, help us to understand that our day to day experiences carry far more meaning and depth than we frequently grant them.

A key part of the work of moving into adulthood is learning to listen to myths and stories, even when they are not neatly packaged for us as such. This means tracking our dream world, and paying attention to the larger story unfolding in the world around us, in our daily lives and through the media we ingest. Ideally, you have guides, elders, and mentors who know how to listen deeply, and mirror back to you the larger themes and precious details, and amplify and uplift the gifts they see in you. Without this, your task is much harder, and lonelier. So this is where we'll turn our attention next, to begin to procure the final item we will need in our backpacks for this journey.

⚕ EXERCISE: Track your dreams for a week, either by writing them down or recording them as voice memos. If you have trouble remembering your dreams, put something next to you to record your dreams when you get in bed at night. Silently offer up an intention to remember your dreams.

It may be helpful to know that some plants suppress dreams while others can be supportive. Research shows that when chronic marijuana use is stopped, dream frequency and intensity usually spikes! On the other hand, mugwort (Artemisia vulgaris) has long been utilized to support dreaming; you can tuck a bit beneath your pillow or sip a cup of mugwort tea before bedtime.

When you remember a dream—even if you only catch a fragment—court these images through drawing, painting, dancing, or enacting them. Or do as Martin Shaw suggests and build an altar to an especially potent dream, by finding or creating objects that represent aspects of the dream, and placing them on top of your dresser or on a windowsill.

⚕ EXERCISE: Seek out a story that touches you. See the Online Resources for some suggestions of where to start. You might try going back to stories you learned as a child, or searching the internet for folktales from your ancestral lineage. Look for themes that attract you. Remember, the goal is not to interpret the stories! Let them inspire and allure you.

10TH ESSENTIAL: BUILDING A CIRCLE OF SUPPORT

"I think that community is the original way of human beings to live. It is really a statement of allowing a human being to become again who we are. I think that for the new culture it is a very important point to have communities around." –Naila, age 21

This book is a paradox. Ultimately, a rite of passage into adulthood requires a community for one to be initiated into. Initiation is simply not possible without it. How can you be an adult, what does that even mean, when no one else around you understands or has a sense of what you've been through?

And yet, after several decades of studying rites of passage in the places I am from and in places very, very different from mine, I have become completely convinced of two things: 1) rites of passage into adulthood are part of healthy communities, and 2) that rites of passage will not happen in most of the communities in the United States unless the effort is led by young people themselves.

If this is true – that initiation requires community, and in these places and in these times the effort must be led by young people – then there is one simple solution: young people must create the community around them in which they will be initiated.

Earlier in the chapter, you explored the importance of learning to be alone. In this section, the task is the opposite. It's about learning to be with others, in an open, honest, and vulnerable way. Specifically, it's about how to call together mentors and peers, two important elements of a healthy community that will allow for a true initiatory experience for you. As you reach the end of this book, you will be invited to consider your role in supporting the next generation, where true intergenerational communities can begin to emerge.

MENTORS

"My grandma has been just an unbelievable mentor. I would not be the same if it weren't for the impact she's had on my life. It's just been monumental on my way of thinking about things and seeing the world."
–Zachary, age 22

When I ask young people about their mentors, the vast majority talk about their primary caregivers. While it's wonderful when young people can learn from their parents or caregivers and confide in them, mentorship through initiation into adulthood needs a different sort of support. It needs the mentorship provided by other adults, whether those adults are blood relatives or chosen kin. When young people are stepping into adulthood, parents and primary caregivers are in the midst of their own rite of passage as well, needing their own support to loosen the strings.

I first met Stan Crow, whom I mentioned in the beginning of the introduction, when I was thirteen years old. Relatively short and rotund, quite bald on top, he must have been about 50 at the time. He was part of my life for decades, as my mentor, supervisor, and more.

Stan passed away suddenly at age 68. The night he died, a spontaneous gathering came together, to celebrate him, share our grief, and to share stories. One by one, each of us shared. Every person echoed the same theme: Stan touched us by trusting us to be more than we thought we could be, and so we became more capable than we had known possible.

We were not the only ones. At Stan's memorial, five hundred people showed up to honor this man who had touched them deeply, many of them through direct, one-on-one mentoring in their youth and young adulthood. This capacity to be present with young people, and offer blessings in the form of listening and encouragement, continued as a theme throughout his memorial.

Stan's death devastated me. With each challenge I faced, I lamented that it would've been Stan that I would have turned to if he were still alive. What would he have done for me? I wondered. The answer was simple. He would've listened, and offered me his blessings. Simple acts, profoundly reassuring results.

Talking about working with young people, Stan frequently said, "if you're talking more than 10% of the time, you're talking too much." His listening had a powerful effect of instilling my faith in myself, in my own wisdom and capabilities.

I use the term mentor because that was the term Stan used. Over decades of working with young people, he began to see that one of the biggest needs was for mentors. He saw this as an essential element of rites of passage. He was very clear: young people cannot initiate themselves, nor each other.

After his death, I felt left behind with riddles to decipher. How was I to make sense of a life lived quietly as an example? There was so much I hadn't yet thought to ask him, and that I didn't understand. Since then, I have come to discover the powerful legacy that Stan left with me: when I think I cannot make it through a challenge, Stan is always there, in my mind and heart, to remind me that I can make it. What's more, I must, because the needs are so urgent. What greater legacy can an elder offer?

You may not have a Stan in your life, but you undoubtedly have someone that you can ask to serve as a mentor. But it's important to be discerning about who you invite into your inner world! There are many folks who wish to be of service, but sometimes they wind up making it more about them than about you. Mentorship relationships are reciprocal, but you shouldn't feel like someone is putting their needs onto you. If you don't really feel like they are listening to you, or what they're saying doesn't resonate or it seems more about them than you, they might not be the mentor who can support you on this journey.

Often someone who shares a similar background or aspects of our identity is what we need in a mentor. Karla, age 19, puts it this way: "I can not have a white person be my mentor because they don't know what a Person of Color is going through. If I have a mentor who looks exactly like me and helps me go to where they are at, that makes a good mentor." Knowing this about herself, and what she needs, allows Karla to seek out adults that can meet her where she's at as she figures out where she wants to go.

Even if we find someone we can relate to based on identities or experience, this won't necessarily make them a good mentor. Since many adults have not had the opportunity to receive mentoring themselves, they may not be very skilled at offering it. You can support those mentoring you by naming clearly what you need. Usually, this has to do with listening, and asking questions. You may want someone to reflect what they are hearing you share, but to be sparing in offering you advice. Dante describes it this way: "A mentor never tells you what to do. Sometimes they tell you things that you really need to hear, but they never tell you how you should act."

In looking for mentorship, look for someone who honors and respects your creativity in the world. You want to find someone that will respect the natural drive for innovation and the creation of new ways of doing things that are part of the gift of the time of life that you're in. Look for someone you also respect, and can trust that if you ask for confidentiality they will honor it.

⚜ EXERCISE: Reflect on someone that you would call a "mentor" in your life so far. What did they provide you with? Consider writing the person a letter and thanking them for specific things they offered. You don't have to send the letter unless you want to. If you haven't had anyone serve in this role, what comes up for you?

⚜ EXERCISE: Identify one or two older people in your life who can listen and be open-minded as well as call you on your stuff, and ask them if they'd be willing to serve as mentors throughout this journey. Don't choose someone because you feel like you "should!" Practice listening to your intuition. Who *feels* right to ask to support you in this way? Choose accordingly. When you make the ask, have a conversation about why you're asking them and what you know of what you need, like asking for them to listen, ask you questions, perhaps give sparing suggestions. If they agree, identify a schedule of how often you'll check in with them (I encourage at least once per month to start).

> Remember, if you need them, it's your responsibility to reach out. I rarely, if ever, check in with my mentees because I want to give them space to learn and grow, and to practice reaching out for help if they need it. This practice—of knowing when you need help, and asking for it—is part of the power of having community-based mentoring relationships.

PEERS

"Whenever anything happens to me that triggers me or that makes me unhappy or not in peace in the situation, my first impulse is to find people." –Naila, age 21

In addition to finding mentor support, an added task is to find or create a circle of peers to support you on this journey. This helps you avoid isolation, reinforces your own capabilities so you don't get dependent on the support of older folks, embeds you in community, and gives you the opportunity to bear witness to the challenges and triumphs of other people's experiences so you don't get too caught up in your own.

For many of us exploring the edges of mainstream culture, it is easy to experience social isolation. The idea that no one understands us or our experience can be strangely seductive. It is important to avoid this trap and keep ourselves squarely in relationship with others in the world around us. While these relationships may include engagement online, it is important that we try our best to cultivate these relationships in direct proximity to people that are actually, physically around us.

For Naila, growing up in an intentional community in Portugal, this sort of support came naturally. When she is struggling, her first impulse is to reach out, and share what's going on for her: "I find someone that is kind of close to me and just speak to them. I don't try to keep thinking straight by myself. I just go to someone and say 'This is my inner state. I know it's bullshit, but please can you just be an opposite for a moment?'"

Naila recognizes that her experience is unique. "I never had this feeling that I had to hide anything that I am. We all carry a certain history about not just being who we are. And yet fear of not being able to show who you are was not confirmed in my life, because I was never told in this place that 'You are completely weird or you are not okay or you are too much.' So there is a place in myself that I can really say, 'I like myself, I like who I am.' This feels like a huge gift."

While you likely have not grown up in the same sort of loving, supportive community as Naila, where people strongly

---

SHIFTING YOUR RELATIONSHIP WITH YOUR PARENTS OR PRIMARY CAREGIVERS

As you step forward on the path to adulthood, one thing you've likely noticed already is that your relationship with your primary caregivers is inevitably impacted. Growing into a new life stage requires changes in the relationships most central to our lives, and this impacts everyone in the system. If you have grown up close with your caregivers, you may find that you're able to talk about the changes relatively comfortably, and navigate them without hardship. Or you may suddenly feel yourself making distance, and this may be supremely uncomfortable, even painful. If your relationship with your immediate family has been more challenging, difficult emotions may be a significant part of how you relate to them, and this process may or may not soothe those feelings.

Wherever you are at, as you embark on this journey, there is an invitation to consider how you do and don't want to include your most immediate family in the process. Especially if your family is not a safe, supportive place for you, it may feel good to keep this separate and turn to the circle of community you are creating for support. On the other hand, this process can be an opportunity to include your immediate family without your relationship as the focus. Surrounded by a circle of mentors and peers, you can invite your family to join and witness you in the presence of others that do offer you safety and support. In the right circumstances and with the right container, this has the potential to be healing and transforming not just for you, but for the whole family system.

welcomed all of who you are and gave you tools and strategies with which to be completely honest, you can begin to cultivate this openness and transparency now. One way to do this is by inviting folks to join you in this process, in which case you truly have companions on the journey.

However, perhaps this isn't something they have the time, space, or desire to engage in right now. In this case, much like you invited mentors in to support, you can invite one or two friends to serve as your witnesses and support. Together with your mentor(s), they can listen to your progress, perhaps on a monthly or seasonal basis. If it feels right and safe for you, you can invite their reflections.

Slowly, over time, this sort of openness and sharing creates the conditions for a deep, ongoing community.

THE JOURNEY AHEAD

Whew! Just packing this backpack of essentials is a lot, isn't it? And we haven't even yet left home! At this point, there is no expectation you have skills in utilizing these tools. You may pack your map before setting out on the trail with only rudimentary knowledge in its use; it is through miles on the trail that the skill is honed. So, too, we have just scratched the surface with what these tools and practices may provide for you. When the going gets tough on this journey, turn back to this chapter and consider which of the Ten Essentials you can pull out of your backpack to support you.

☾

Chapter Two:

NO LONGER A CHILD, NOT YET AN ADULT

"I don't know if I'm an adult or when I will become one. I find the Western idea of adulthood to be somewhat limiting. I am an adult in the sense that I've gone to college, and I'm working to support myself financially. But I feel that there is still so much growth left to happen that it's hard for me to say exactly where I'm at in the process." –Zachary, age 22

"The joke at my job is that because I started there when I was 16 or 17, and I just turned nineteen not too long ago, they were like "Oh, you're 19, you are an 'adult' now, right?" The joke is like, no, I've been an adult since I started working! At a young age I had to be well-rounded and mature. I had to start putting money towards the table at home. I felt like I had so many responsibilities in my household, I didn't really get to enjoy my youth. When I walk into certain spaces now I am not considered a youth, I am considered an adult now. But adult is just a word." –Karla, age 19

In my work with teens and young adults, I ask them to place themselves on an imaginary line. Childhood is at one end, adulthood is at the other. "Where are you on the journey?" I ask. "Place yourself precisely." Usually, they move slowly, unsure of where to place themselves, looking around to their peers for guidance. Try it yourself, no matter how old you are. Take out a piece of paper, and draw a line with childhood at one end, and adulthood on the other. Place yourself on that line.

Why did you place yourself where you did?

I've noticed that where folks place themselves only vaguely corresponds to their actual age. I've seen four 24-year-olds place themselves at four different points across the spectrum, literally from one end of the line to the other.

When I ask folks why they place themselves where they do, their answers also vary widely. Sometimes, they base their placement on how independent they perceive themselves to be, or what they've gone through so far in their lives. Sometimes, it instead seems like a personal inventory of what they don't like about themselves, like a young man who placed himself at the childhood end of the line because he couldn't control his temper.

When I go on to ask these teens and young adults how they'll know when they're adults, I hear a multitude of answers: "When I turn 18," "When I can drive," "When I can legally drink," "When I graduate from college," "When I have sex for the first time." Sometimes I hear "When I buy my first house," or "When I have a child."

Gloria, age 22, illustrates the complexity in understanding what adulthood means. "Even when I had my baby I didn't feel like that made me an adult," she says. "I feel like that made me a mother. Now that my daughter is two, and I have taught her how to speak, and being her mom and guiding her through the world, that is what started making me feel, like 'Oh, I taught my daughter how to sing songs, I read to her, I taught her the alphabet!' I feel like I have a lot of people that rely on me. I don't know if that is what an adult means, but I have to have a certain amount of energy and I have to have a certain amount of perseverance for myself to help my people."

Confusion over when adulthood begins is a culturally specific phenomenon. Many communities have practices for initiating young people into adulthood in ways that help them to know and understand their changing role in the community. However, in dominant Western culture, we rarely have explicit, precise, shared agreements about what it means to be in various life stages like childhood, adolescence, adulthood, and elderhood. This leaves folks muddling around, unclear about their place within their community, often afraid to move forward into the next stage because they're not sure what it will mean for them. We need a collective understanding about the way we grow through various life stages, known as the *human developmental process*.

All elements of the natural world have their own developmental processes. A dandelion seed sprouts little leaves, for example, then grows a stem and bigger leaves. Eventually, it grows a flower bud, which one day blooms, then turns into a fluffy seed head. Soon the seed head scatters, and the plant dies back and decomposes into the earth. We can count on each and every dandelion to do this, if the conditions are right. Humans, too, have a particular developmental process. Understanding this process can help you navigate into adulthood in ways that will set you up for a meaningful and fulfilling—though not necessarily easy—life.

A SIMPLE DEVELOPMENTAL FRAMEWORK: THE FOUR SHIELDS

Developed by Steven Foster and Meredith Little of the School of Lost Borders, the *Four Shields* draws on Indigenous teachings, specifically Cheyenne and Mayan, as well as the teachings Stephen and Meredith received from a number of teachers, and their own experiences in the natural world.

There are many different models similar to the Four Shields, coming from many earth-based cultures around the world. "Medicine wheel" is a term that is frequently used.* These mod-

---

*Medicine wheels are ways of understanding and making sense of the world particular to a given culture. In the next chapter, we'll discuss cultural appropriation, or taking parts of people's cultures other than your own. I thought a lot about including the Four Shields here, given that it's based on Indigenous teachings, shifted and evolved through the understandings and experiences of white settlers, even ones grounded in direct relationship with Indigenous teachers and the more-than-human world. Ultimately, I included the Four Shields for two reasons. One, it is foundational to my own understanding of human development. Two, grappling with complex issues like cultural appropriation is important for those who have benefitted from theft of land, labor, and culture. I believe we can not shrink back from these issues but instead need to name them, explore them, and find our way forward.

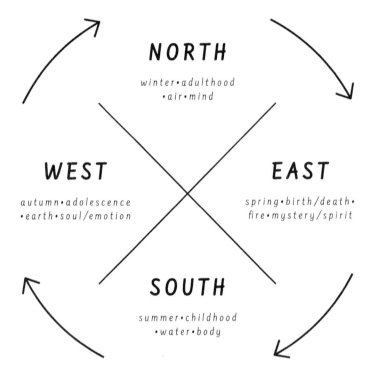

The Four Shields as described by Steven Foster & Meredith Little

els generally share basic structural elements: they are circular (as opposed to linear), they are typically broken up into quadrants, and the quadrants pertain to different elements of life and the natural world, like the directions, the seasons, times of day, and phases of a human life.

While it seems simple, the fact that the Four Shields model and other similar models are circular is important. They remind us that all of life is a cycle, with no beginning and no ending, just like each day fades into the next. It can be hard to wrap our minds around thinking of time and development as circular: in Western cultures many of us have been taught to view time as linear. But in fact this is a minority view of humans throughout time.

Because these models are maps based on the world around us, it makes sense that they are different based on where you are. In the Northern Hemisphere, for example, the south is frequently associated with summer, because the sun's peak is in the middle of the day when the sun is due south in the sky. In the Southern Hemisphere, it's the opposite—the midday sun is in the north.

I like the Four Shields because they provide a very simple roadmap of the changes that occur over a human lifetime, connecting the processes in our lives with the cycles happening in the natural world. The major life stages are each given a place on the wheel. Childhood, in the South, is a time of exploration, adventure, and rapid growth. This time of life is associated with the body, with engagement in the physical and sensual world. Adolescence, in the West, is a time of introspection, exploring shadow and darkness. It is associated with increasing self-reflection and soul exploration. Adulthood, in the North, is a time of responsibility and serving the community. It is frequently associated with the mind, with our capacity for critical thinking. The terrain from the North to the East moves through elderhood, a time of guidance and wisdom as well as a return to innocence. In the East, we have the line between death and birth, associated with spirit, with the unexplainable mysteries.

In this model are many simple but profound truths. They include:

- To live a full and complete life, we must go through each of the phases; if we stop moving we are denying the natural order of things.

- A healthy, whole, and vibrant community requires folks in all four phases. No part is more important than any other.

- Each of these domains exists within us at all times, to greater or lesser extent. While we have one that is dominant in a given time in our life, we can also access the other parts of us—and, in fact, this is required to be whole and healthy.

Because this is a book specifically on the transition between adolescence and adulthood, we are going to take a deep dive into what's happening in these two stages of life. You'll see that in the material I present, there's some contradictory information about where adolescence ends and adulthood starts. As you read, please keep an open mind about where you're at in that process. At the end of the chapter you'll get a chance to reflect on your own developmental journey. But before we get to adolescence and adulthood, there are a few words to say about the end of childhood.

THE DEATH OF CHILDHOOD

Vicki knew what it was like to give things up. At 21, she stopped drinking, and learned what it was like to live life sober. Yet at 28, she felt like she was still unable to give up parts of herself that would allow her to step fully into adulthood. "I'm 28 years old, and I don't even know how to do my taxes!" she exclaimed in frustration, as she described her internal ambivalence over whether or not she wanted to move forward in her life.

As Vicki prepared for a ceremony to step into adulthood, she knew she had to begin with letting go. A fire was lit, for her to burn items of the life she was leaving behind. She cried gently as she first offered an inventory to the ceremonial fire, detailing what she learned each year during her schooling, about what gives her strength and value. She burned the American Express card she carried though rarely used, a symbol of her economic ties to her father that she felt ready to release. While she offered these items to the fire, she held tight to a Winnie-the-Pooh bear, saying, "I am not yet ready to let you go."

Ideally, childhood is a time of exploration. Like a plant growing stronger and healthier in fertile and healthy soil, a child raised in a safe, loving, and secure environment will roam and wander, learning about the world around them all the time. A healthy childhood is a time full of experimentation and play, adventures both big and small. One of the most important developmental tests of childhood is developing a sense of oneself as separate from others—discovering words like "I" and "me." This focus on one's self, and one's own needs, wants, desires, and aversions, is critically important. Yet there comes a point when things need to change.

Cultural activist and author Stephen Jenkinson says that in order to step into adulthood, you must first *kill the child*. Killing the child—this is not a gentle, light-hearted image! A child, one who relies on others to meet their needs, loved and protected and nurtured, will never willingly choose to die. This is why we have so many folks walking around in adult bodies, yet acting like teenagers!

In cultures with strong rites of passage into adulthood, there is enough social pressure to become an adult that one wouldn't consider avoiding an initiation, even if it involves a death of sorts. Who wants to stay at the little kids table when all their peers are moving into a new status?

In the dominant culture today, the problem is the opposite. Who wants to take on additional responsibilities when no one else is? Who wants to think of the greater good when social pressures encourage us to focus on our own personal needs and be cynical about those that devote their lives to the community? To make the transition into adulthood, you need strong inner fortitude, long-term vision (as in, many generations), and to keep cutting the ties that bind you to a faulty way of seeing the world.

For Vicki, the death of childhood never came. She remained attached to her father, and he allowed—even supported—her staying attached. This kept her from being able to fully engage in her adolescence, much less step forward into adulthood.

Never having experienced a Death of Childhood is part of why many young people have a strong attraction to death imagery.

While many in Western culture perceive this as dangerous pathology and mental illness, I understand it as a deep inner knowing that it is time for some part of us to die. The danger is in confusing the *part* of us that needs to die with our entire life. This can lead to risky, self-harming behavior.

Before we get to talking about adulthood, what do you know about your own crossing out of childhood? Did you ever formally leave it behind? Was your childhood a safe haven at all, or were you forced to grow up before you were ready? How did this time come to an end? Has it? Were you able to formally say goodbye to your childhood, grieve its loss, let it die?

As you consider these questions, a lot of emotion may emerge, including sadness, anger, resentment, bitterness, numbness. This is why it's so important you packed the Ten Essentials for this journey! If it's helpful, take some time to thumb back through that section, and see if there's something that can support you in considering your childhood years.

> ⚘EXERCISE: Ask yourself: What is ready to die? What do I need to let go of, to step fully into my life? Find or create a symbolic object that represents something you need to let go.

DOING ADOLESCENCE WELL

"I think a lot of older people don't understand that, just because we're younger, doesn't make us lesser. We will, eventually, be in the same place they are today, and while putting people down as 'Not understanding' and 'Not knowing' is common, it's untrue. Younger people go through stuff too, we all have. It's a part of growing up, actually." –Ben, age 16

"When we're adolescents, we are learning more about ourselves. I think that was part of a time when I started to question who I am." –Nadia, age 30

Cade, 17, remembers when he first became a teenager: "Other parents and adult figures were warning my parents and myself, 'Well, it is about to be survival!'" Cade didn't like how those around him were describing his life stage. "I felt like that whole connotation," he said on a podcast interview a few years later, "that whole idea of the teenage years being a rough time to live through, was a negative outlook. I feel like you can make your own life instead of having to look at it in a negative way."

Wherever he turned, Cade found those messages reinforced. "...A lot of people... were always telling me that my ideas didn't really matter, almost like I was delusional because I was a teenager. Like I didn't understand what the bigger world was. I felt like this was not only a misunderstanding, but did not represent the teenagers well. I felt like I could make my own decisions and contribute."

Many young people have experiences like this. Perhaps you have, too. Some young people withdraw from adults, and seek solace by themselves, with peers, or online. Others lash out in anger and frustration, trying to find a place for themselves. Others "go along to get along," but underneath feel unseen and misunderstood.

Cade decided that he wanted answers. He spent his senior year of high school studying what is happening in the life stage of adolescence, in order to arm himself and other young people with information to help them separate fact from fiction, and advocate for themselves.

Understanding this stage of life is something that can benefit us all, not just Cade. Where did the word "adolescence" come from? Have the stereotypes of young people always been there? And what can we do about this? These are just a few of the questions we'll explore in the coming pages.

ANTIQUATED STORIES ABOUT ADOLESCENCE

Adolescence is a common word these days, but this hasn't always been so. Before the early 1900's, adolescence wasn't considered very important in mainstream United States culture. In early US history, for example, boys as young as ten worked alongside young men in their twenties; the most important criteria defining the work of each was physical size and capability.

This remained true until the turn of the 20th century, when psychologists began to identify adolescence as a particular life stage marked by "sturm und drang," or storm and stress. The common story throughout much of the last century was that adolescence is a life stage innately and universally a time of turmoil. In 1958, Psychologist Anna Freud even wrote, "to be normal during the adolescent period is by itself abnormal."

As people increasingly began to hold this negative perception of adolescence, it quickly became the basis for how many of society's institutions relate to adolescents. This stage of life became a sort of pathology, setting the stage for radical shifts in public policy, primarily in the education and juvenile justice systems.

Over the last hundred years, many researchers found gaps and inadequacies in these models, similar to other social science research at the time. Still, as Cade's story earlier in the chapter points out, these stereotypes of adolescents persist.

CURRENT UNDERSTANDINGS OF ADOLESCENCE

The word "adolescence" is a fairly awkward and scientific word to describe an amazing (though also sometimes awkward) life stage. The word comes from roots meaning "to nourish, ripen, grow up." It is a time of rapid growth and change happening on all sorts of levels: a time of both possibility and risk. There are lots of ways to understand this phase of life. The two that have been most helpful for me are to understand what's happening in our brains and understand what's happening with our souls.

IN THE BRAIN

"Learning about how our brains function has given me a whole new understanding of what it means to rewire my own habitual thought patterns...I've realized how malleable our childhood/adolescent brains are, and how negative thought patterns are rampantly ingrained into our everyday processes." –Kelly, age 25

In recent decades, the field of neuropsychology, which helps explain human feelings, thoughts, and behavior through what's actually observable in our brains, has provided new insights about what is happening during adolescence. Thanks to people like author and Professor of Psychiatry Dr. Daniel Siegel, what might otherwise be very technical research has become accessible to a broad audience (the rest of this section draws heavily on his work).

We've learned that from a biological perspective, adolescence is an essential life stage primarily because of the important development that is happening in the brain at that time, as our minds change in the way we remember, think, reason, focus attention, make decisions, and relate to others. Other changes, such as hormonal shifts, are secondary.

The adolescent brain, which begins at around 12 years old and concludes around 25, has distinct and special qualities. Siegel uses the acronym ESSENCE to remember these special qualities available in the adolescent mind:

Emotional Spark: Brain changes often create an emotional intensity in young people. This emotional intensity brings passion, a sense of meaning, and vitality, and helps young people fight for change and justice. It can also create mood swings and extreme reactivity!

Social Engagement: Teens are much more focused on peer relationships than adults, as areas of the brain that help folks manage distress from social exclusion are developing. The shift from family orientation to peer group orientation can help young people develop a sense of personal identity, while it can also lead youth to isolate from adults.

Novelty: Seeking new experiences that engage us fully and stimulate our senses, emotions, thinking, and bodies in new ways results from shifting brain chemistry. This change helps young people be open to change and seek adventure and new opportunities. It can also lead to dangerous risk-taking with serious consequences for self and others.

Creative Exploration: Adolescent brain development creates new capacities for conceptual thinking and abstract reasoning, which often manifest as questioning of the status quo and thinking "out of the box." These capacities can make adolescence the most creative time in one's life. Experiencing new ways of thinking can also lead to a crisis of identity, lack of direction and purpose, and vulnerability to peer pressure.

The biochemistry of what creates these unique qualities can be boiled down to five major changes happening in the brain. First, during adolescence a massive "remodeling" takes place in the prefrontal cortex, the brain's place of integration where all signals from other parts of the brain, the rest of the body, and the stimulus from the outside world come together. Located right behind the bridge of the nose, this area regulates decision-making, planning, judgment, expression of emotions, impulse control, and allows for conceptual and abstract thought. It's one of the last parts of the brain to fully mature, usually complete by the mid-twenties. While this process is happening, the area is like a construction zone: sometimes functioning in ways simply not possible before, and sometimes entirely offline.

Second, the limbic system (located right above the brainstem, which processes and manages emotion) is also developing and is more active than in childhood or adulthood. Despite the fact that it's not fully mature, it stands in for the underdeveloped frontal lobe to process emotions. Siegel points out that it's as if you take a detour when the main road is closed for construction (the prefrontal cortex) and find yourself on a road that's really not suitable for lots of traffic! This causes more mood swings and impulsive behavior.

Third, during adolescence, levels of the pleasure-seeking neurotransmitter dopamine shift, raising the threshold needed to stimulate feelings of pleasure, as well as possibly creating a baseline lower than during other life stages. Activities that were once exciting for children may no longer be so exciting. In addition to spurring impulsiveness and thrill-seeking behavior, shifting dopamine levels also increase susceptibility to addiction.

Fourth, gray matter in the brain begins to thin as synapses (the links between neurons that transmit and receive information) undergo a process of pruning. Up until this point, lots of neurons and synaptic connections are being produced, which means that we can learn new things very quickly. But during adolescence, we rapidly discard the synapses that we haven't been using. This is why it's good to learn foreign languages, musical instruments, and begin athletic training before adolescence. Vulnerability in the brain's makeup during childhood—caused by any number of things, including genetics, toxic exposure, or adverse childhood experiences—may come to light in adolescence because pruning is pairing down existing, but sometimes insufficient, numbers of neurons and their connections. This is why many mental challenges become apparent during adolescent years.

"If we are to survive on this fragile and magnificent planet, we are going to need all the ingenuity of the rebellious adolescent mind to find solutions to the grave problems that our and previous adult generations have created in this world."

–Dr. Dan Siegel, brain researcher

In the fifth major change happening in the adolescent brain, a thin sheath called myelin covers the membranes among interlinked neurons. Myelination enables the passage of the electrical flow among the remaining neurons, and improves the connectivity between neurons by speeding up and synchronizing communication between cells. Frequently used parts of the brain are strengthened, while parts that are used less frequently weaken and die off. Pruning and myelination help the adolescent brain become more integrated, which allows for increased brain coordination and, as a result, more big-picture thinking. Healthy development during adolescence allows us to continue to grow and evolve throughout adulthood.

What we learn through brain science can help us create a deeper understanding of the unique opportunities of this time of life, both in setting the stage for the rest of an individual's life and for our communities as a whole. Capacities emerge that were simply not possible during childhood; they are also way harder to cultivate in adulthood if they are not nurtured in adolescence. This is a great opportunity for you, if you're lucky enough to still be in the adolescent-brain-developing stage. Our brains develop in the ways we direct them to.

The ESSENCE of Adolescence as described by Dr. Dan Seigel

🌱EXERCISE: Reflect on these questions: Are you still in the midst of your adolescent brain development process? If so, what have been the most difficult parts of that process for you? What gifts do you have to offer to those around you? If you're not in that time any longer, how do you look back on it now?

IN THE SOUL

"My soul is extremely skilled in the art of camouflage. When the lighting is perfect, the season is right, my mood is curious, and there are no other distractions I have caught a glimpse and felt a twinge of a soul worth reckoning. I believe my soul is the counterbalance to my current identity, patiently waiting for enough time, space, and attention to be expressed."
–Gretchen, age 26

Another important way to understand what's happening in adolescence is how we are developing at a soul level, in relation to the larger web of life. We'll talk more about the soul in Chapter Five; for now let's just say that the soul describes the deepest essence of who you are, uniquely. Bill Plotkin, a psychologist and wilderness guide, has spent decades taking people out on the land in ceremony, paying close attention to what was happening for them at a deep soul level, and then writing about what he noticed. Through working with thousands of people, he has noticed repeating patterns and themes. Like other psychologists before him, he noticed there were discrete stages that people passed through over the course of their lifetime, commonly known in psychology as phases of human development. Part of what Plotkin was paying attention to—different than many psychologists—were the phases of soul development he began to observe.

One thing that's important in Plotkin's model is that adolescence is more than one stage. For him, there are two different, identifiable stages of growth between childhood and adulthood. In fact, childhood and adulthood are also two stages, as is elderhood.

As people make the passage out of childhood, their focus shifts from their family and immediate surroundings and into the broader world, particularly to their peer group. Typically beginning around the time of puberty, figuring out how you fit in (or what to do if you don't fit in) often becomes a major focus of energy. I remember my own early adolescence: I lived near a lake and my mom would suggest we go down there and go swimming in the summer, but I didn't want to be seen with her! All I wanted was to hang out with my friends.

This stage is all about developing the social self: who I am in relation to the people around me. There are two important aspects of the social self that need to be allowed to fully develop and mature: security and authenticity. A secure social self means that you know you belong. You are able to trust that the people around you love you, will have your back, and care for you when you need it. An authentic social self means that you are able to express who you are, in alignment with your true nature. Many people are able to develop a secure social self by hiding certain parts of themselves; others express themselves fully but aren't accepted. But to really complete the work of this stage of early adolescence requires a reasonable amount of support to do both.

Plotkin writes that each of the eight stages has its own gift and that the gift of early adolescence is fire and passion, a time in our lives where culture "becomes a fabric for us to refashion." It was in my early adolescence that I learned about ecological disasters. I remember how outraged I was that people would allow the earth to be harmed in that way, and imposing strict rules on my mom about how we would be washing and reusing bags so that they wouldn't go to waste.

One important element of Plotkin's model is that the stages are not necessarily connected with age. In fact, he believes that most folks in Western society never move beyond the Early Adolescent stage, because it is so difficult to be able to be both secure and authentic given the expectations of Western culture. It's a beautiful life stage, early adolescence—but not if 90% of the culture is in the same developmental place!

Those who do cross from early adolescence to late adolescence are able to make the transition because they've developed the grounding both in belonging to their community, and being true to themselves. Having done this, soon they find that it's time to leave the safe harbor they've created for themselves—to leave home and go out into the world in some way (or down into the depths), face challenges and true unknowns, in order to discover an even deeper part of their essence.

What this means is that before you step into adulthood, you construct a socially acceptable, viable identity. But to continue growing toward true adulthood, you must eventually let that identity dissolve, as you undergo, like the caterpillar in a cocoon, a refashioning of the *true self*. This true self allows you to emerge into adulthood with a sense of your soul gift and unique place in the world.

The gift of late adolescence is access to mystery and darkness. This is a stage where individuals can go into the deepest, darkest places, and from these places bring forth incredible treasures like creativity, soulfulness, inspiration, and courage—not just for themselves, but on behalf of the whole community.

⚘ EXERCISE: Part of the work of early adolescence is developing a secure and authentic social self. What is an area of your life where you don't feel secure? What's a part of you that doesn't feel totally authentic?

CHANGING TIMES, CHANGING PERSPECTIVES

"Young people are just as capable as "adults." It is solely perception that determines we are not adults, not age." –Alex, age 17

Our society's understanding of adolescence is changing, but public opinion needs time to catch up with scientific advances. Even with the great research that's been done on brain development, these understandings are just beginning to make inroads into the institutions that matter in the lives of young people. This is why we still think of storm and stress as a defining characteristic of adolescence, even though this perspective has largely been debunked.

There are factors that create more rapid change, however. For example, the percentage of the population that is of adolescent age can strongly shift the way we think about and treat adolescents. In 1776, half the US population was under 16; consequently, young men in their teens were key on the frontlines during the Revolutionary War and young people were often primary breadwinners. To think of teens as needing more time before taking on adult responsibilities was impossible: they were desperately needed by their families and society. Now, with the population more evenly distributed, the situation is different.

Economic changes, largely influenced by technological changes, are another key factor driving rapid shifts in how we societally think about adolescence. High school became commonplace during the Great Depression, for example; previously it had been available only to the wealthy. In the 1930's, with extremely high rates of unemployment, young people were legislated out of work in order to create more jobs for adults. Soon, the majority of teens were enrolled in high school, setting the stage for age-based segregation and the development of a distinct youth culture. For the first time, the state held responsibility for the education and socialization of youth for a large portion of their waking hours.

It wasn't concern about what is happening in adolescent brain development that created the original push for widespread secondary schooling. Rather, the economic necessities of the times created it. We now think of adolescence as a time period of experimentation, education, and preparation—but this is the result of shifts in cultural beliefs over the last several hundred years that have been driven primarily by economic factors.

Economic impacts continue to change the role of young people in the United States. Though this is starting to change now, over the last decade or more, young people stayed in school longer because of fewer professional opportunities. When I graduated from college in 1998, I never considered that it would be difficult to find a job that paid well, and that I wanted; there were plenty of jobs to be had. The same was not true for the folks that graduated college in recent years.

A fourth factor in how we think about adolescence is driven by actual biological changes. Puberty is coming biologically earlier for people who menstruate; there's been a decline of four months per decade since 1850 in the age of menarche (which means the onset of menstruation) in the United States. Scientists believe that sexual maturation is tied to nutrition, so as diets have increased in fats and proteins, menarche is coming earlier and earlier. This in part accounts for a societal shift towards younger and younger folks identifying as adolescents rather than children.

⚘EXERCISE: Think about a couple of different adults in your life, and how they treat you or treated you during your teenage years. Based on what you just read about adolescent development, how aware are/were they of what was happening for you developmentally?

MAKING THE CHANGE: RITES OF PASSAGE

"I became an adult at 19 when I moved out of the house to be on my own and in college. I was given an heirloom, a journal, passed down by my dad, when I left." –Nick, age 25

In the geographic heart of India, there is a sovereign Indigenous village called Mendha Lekha, the home of Gond tribal members. Traditionally, Mendha Lekha had an important local building, built of teak from the surrounding forests, called a Ghotul. For many generations, this building served as a gathering house for young people and the home of education and preparation for their initiation into adulthood.

The villagers in Mendha Lekha depended on the teak forests for their livelihoods and cultural traditions. After Indian Independence, however, the government wanted control of the valuable teak resources. It began a policy of assimilation, requiring village children to attend school in the nearby town. Authorities dismantled the Ghotul gathering house. Soon, village life looked very different. Children began leaving the village, and traditions broke down. Poverty and alcoholism became significant issues.

The elders gathered to find a solution to these problems. Soon, they concluded that without the Ghotul, the center of community life was broken. So they set about building the structure out of teak, a resource they could no longer use freely. It was a key symbol of their cultural life as well as a symbol of what the government was withholding through laws and regulation.

Overnight, men traveled into the forest, harvested teak, and constructed a new Ghotul for the young people. In the morning, the forest wardens set about destroying it, despite the villagers' declaration that they would simply construct another in its place. By nightfall, the Ghotul was gone. That night, the villagers harvested more teak and again rebuilt it. The next day, the forest wardens tore it down again. Both the building and the tearing down were repeated a third time.

Finally, on the fourth night, Mendha Lekha constructed a fourth Ghotul. This night was different—many nearby villages did the same thing at the same time. That final morning, the wardens declared that they couldn't keep tearing down the Ghotul, or the villagers would go through the whole forest. The Ghotul remained, and the young people returned to take part in this ancient cultural tradition.

With this victory, the villagers gained confidence and once again began to pass on their traditions to their young people. They gained the courage and the strength to fight and eventually to gain recognition as a sovereign tribal nation.

I was in awe when I learned about their story. For many years, I had been exploring rites of passage, focusing on how important they can be for individual young people. Hearing the villagers tell the story of their struggle and victory, I began to see that they are important not just for young people themselves, but for whole communities.

WHAT HAPPENS WHEN RITES OF PASSAGE ARE MISSING?

When the elders of Mendha Lekha got together to consider how to reverse the challenges they were facing, why did they prioritize rebuilding the Ghotul? Simple: they knew that the health of their community depended on raising healthy young people.

In Western cultures, we often don't have such an immediate opportunity to reflect on the cause-and-effect relationship; for many of us, our rites of passage have been lost for generations. Yet over the last hundred years, a rich body of scholarship has emerged detailing the consequences that follow when we don't provide clear and culturally-relevant pathways to adulthood for young people.

Research shows that when young people lack access to intentional, meaningful rites of passage, they initiate themselves. Adolescent brains are hardwired for risk and challenge. Young people thirst for testing and initiation; it is an actual, biochemical need. If the culture isn't providing positive outlets for this drive, it is not surprising that teens and young adults experiment with all sorts of other avenues for initiation: alcohol and drug abuse, self-harm, risky driving, and risky sexual experiences, to name a few. These behaviors stand in for what meaningful, culturally-supported rites of passage provide: opportunities to explore and assert your identity and autonomy, to find connection, and to be tested.

Whether because of lack of access to those few initiatory experiences that are common in our culture (like high school graduation ceremonies), or because they perceive that those experiences carry little validity in terms of true testing or meaning, when the adults and elders in their lives fail to create opportunities, young people create their own. The many forms of hazing, whether into fraternities, clubs, or street gangs, are powerful examples of this that have been long documented as stand-ins for culturally sanctioned rites of passage. In the 1950's, a study showed that youth without access to culturally-sanctioned initiatory experiences turned to gangs to meet this need. More recent studies have uncovered similar results. In fact, gang initiation contains many of the key elements of a rite of passage, like the presence of "elders," being assigned a new role, and community recognition.

Another major consequence of inadequate or inconsistent rites of passage is that essential community or cultural values and skills aren't transmitted. Rites of passage are an important training ground to equip young people with the skills and knowledge they need to be adults in our culture. They are a nexus point between the ancestors and future generations, where traditions are shared with young people that will carry them forward to share with the next generation.

At the same time, culture is evolving and malleable, changing in large part based on the physical needs of a group of people. Traditions fade when they no longer make sense, and new, more relevant symbols emerge. Cultural values evolve as well. Strength and courage may be essential in times of war or in places where big game hunting is essential for one's livelihood, for example. Yet generosity and compassion may be the most important values to foster in another community, at a different time. Rites of passage celebrate and reaffirm the wider community's culture, traditions, values, mythology and beliefs within the context of a particular time and place, and the needs of the community at that time. At the end of the day, rites of passage aren't just about what's best for *you*; they're also about the health, vitality, and resiliency of the larger community.

In Mendha Lekha, when young people stopped being prepared for adulthood and instead went to school in the nearby town, they began to be drawn away from the traditional values of the community. Cultural values break down so quickly; traditions that have existed for thousands of years can be largely lost within a single generation.

There's a final consequence of Western culture's rite of passage drought: we are semi-consciously, or unconsciously, prolonging adolescence. In traditional cultures, rites of passage were (and in some cases, still are) markers between childhood and adulthood, and that time was often, though not always, relatively short. In cultures where the time in between childhood and adulthood is longer, there is still usually an intact community context in which roles, transitions, and expectations are clear. But now, with everything from someone having sex for the first time to buying a house perceived as markers into adulthood, this liminal time can be years, even decades.

By its very nature, adolescence is the liminal, threshold time between the life stages of childhood and adulthood. A liminal stage is necessarily a time of intense anxiety and confusion; by definition, you lack any culturally-defined status or role. By prolonging adolescence, we as a society unintentionally stretch out this time of heightened anxiety and intense role confusion.

ADAPTING TO LIFE WITHOUT RITES OF PASSAGE

My partner, Dave, is a wildlife biologist, and he's always reminding me to look at the biological underpinnings of human behavior. When I talk about the consequences that come from not having widespread, meaningful rites of passage, he makes note of how humans are hard-wired to adapt. The ability of young people to meet the need for initiation on their own, when culture doesn't provide it, represents an evolutionary adaptation to a less-than-ideal environment. It points to the resiliency of our species.

By not intentionally initiating young people into shared community values, mainstream culture promotes and reinforces a "do-it-alone" mentality that may be what we unconsciously (and sometimes even consciously) perceive to be the most valuable survival skill. Years ago, I noticed that the most common answer when I asked young people to identify when they reached adulthood was, "When I get my driver's license." It certainly speaks to what we value as a culture—freedom to come and go as we choose.

Unfortunately, this is a maladaptation, an adjustment that makes things work in the short-term but is actually unhealthy in the long term. It stems from collective trauma, the result of human communities enduring colonization, genocide, cultural disruption, and outside oppression rather than slow cultural shifts. Ancestrally-rooted rites of passage have been lost because they were forcibly taken away.

Now, as more and more people from different cultural backgrounds assimilate into Western culture, they largely leave behind their traditional ways of initiating young people. Intentionally or unintentionally, with the promise of a dollar or the threat of a blade, they trade their rites of passage for the institutions and understandings of what young people need to succeed in the Western world. If you're reading this book, it's likely because your ancestors did this at one point or another, whether they chose to or were forced (or a combination of the two).

At the same time, institutions serving and educating young people in the Western world today are large and complex, trying to meet the needs of many diverse stakeholders with different and often competing values. How to prepare young people for their future is a source of great political contention. Are schools and colleges designed to prepare young people to be effective citizens, and if so, who gets to define what this means? Are schools designed to create skilled workers? Are they designed to create responsible adults, many of whom will become parents? Are they warehouses for people we want to keep out of the workforce? There is not a broadly-shared consensus about what is most urgently needed for young people on their path to adulthood. Historian Thomas Hine, in *The Rise and Fall of the American Teenager,* says "The principal reason high schools now enroll nearly all teenagers is that we can't imagine what else they might do." Colleges are increasingly plagued with the same issue, and have the added consequence of saddling young people with more and more debt.

Another path is possible. The life stages of adolescence and young adulthood are fertile, creative times. Hours in front of screens and engaged in mindless tasks don't use these gifts to their fullest! If we reimagine the adolescent stage as being a multi-year rite of passage, from closing the door on childhood to stepping fully into adulthood, we could change the future of humanity for the better.

These complex issues desperately need exploring, at local, national, and international levels. But if you're reading this book, that might not matter much to you at this moment. You're probably looking at a much more pressing issue: figuring out how to move forward into adulthood with the toolkit you've been given. This likely includes questions about how to earn a living, how to find work you enjoy, and perhaps make a difference in the world. Likely, you also have questions about love, romance, possibly long-term partnership. Maybe you struggle with a debilitating mental health challenge or physical impediment. Perhaps you don't feel safe in your own home, or on the streets of your neighborhood.

It would be a great thing if we as a society could get our act together, learn from brain science and the other innovative models, and transform the way we raise young people to really bring forth the unique gifts of each stage. This would set us up well as a species for what's needed! But that's not where we're at. So the goal here instead is to put some tools in your hands, and equip you with some knowledge so you can make the best use of this life you've been given.

MOVING FORWARD INTO ADULTHOOD

"When I think about it, the word adult is just a word. Anybody can be an adult, but it is all about the knowledge that we hold. That is what makes us adults—because "adult" is just another way of saying you are mature now." –Karla, age 19

"Adulthood is responsibility and working to death." –Dawson, age 16

As I sit with folks in their late teens, twenties, and thirties, preparing to begin a rite of passage ceremony, I constantly hear reluctance to step into adulthood. Fear, ambivalence, even outright hostility at the idea are ever-present themes.

Responsibility. Independence. Hard work. These are the words that folks commonly use to describe adulthood. What's fun about that?

The challenges young people face as they grow older, and the options that society is usually telling you that you have before you, are often rooted in false assumptions about what adulthood is. These assumptions, which are tightly woven into the fabric of our culture, profoundly get in the way of one's ability to actually move into adulthood.

One false assumption is that adulthood is a fixed, static time. The commonplace question "What do you want to be when you grow up?" reflects the idea that you will have one career, and that who you are is defined by your work. Yet many, if not most, folks change careers multiple times over the course of their lives, and who we are is far more than our work. While changing, this idea is still represented as the norm in our media and ways of thinking and talking about the world, particularly to young people.

Another common conception is that adulthood is defined by independence. This is a constant thread, most typically related to finances. This seemingly simple idea creates deep pain and misery, which we could correct simply by teaching the difference between freedom and independence. Freedom is the ability to follow the truth of your heart, to live the full, inspired life that is yours alone to live. This is how life is meant to be lived, where each of our unique gifts and passions are nurtured so that they can be fully embodied in the world. Independence is the ability to live without being beholden to others or having others beholden to you. This stands in strong contrast to Indigenous worldviews and ecological realities, which understand that all things are related; nothing exists on its own.

A big part of adulthood is responsibility. Responsibility can feel like a lot of pressure, like something it's better to avoid at all costs. Yet in a community, responsibility doesn't have to be burdensome. It simply means having the *ability* to *respond*. And there are so many things in the world today that require people to be able to respond.

This is a big step, to orient your life towards something bigger than yourself. It stands in contrast to almost every commercial you have watched, the messages you've likely received in school, the values of our consumerist-driven society. It is a hard step to take. But the health and vitality of our communities depends on it. And this step is a necessary one on the path to true adulthood.

☾

Chapter Three:

RESTORING CULTURAL HABITAT: RITES OF PASSAGE FOR JUSTICE AND HEALING

"Rites of passage weave the threads of the past with the threads of the future." –Luis Rodriguez

About ten years ago, I found myself sitting in the flickering light of a small campfire, part of a circle of women from around the world. Native Hawaiian activist Pualani Case had invited us together to share the story of her daughter's initiation.

To the best of her knowledge, Pualani began, it may have been the first traditional Hawaiian coming of age ceremony for a young woman in generations. As the fire lit up her face, Pualani

Case shared the process that she and women in her community reconstructed. Her daughter spoke as well, saying the experience changed her life forever.

Her story inspired another young Indigenous woman to share the traditional coming of age ceremony she had experienced. She spoke of days of ceremony, and shared how much having been initiated into womanhood in her traditional cultural ways meant to her. At the end of her detailed, lively description, the woman ended with, "and any of you here, you're welcome to use this ceremony yourself, if it would help you in your community."

Pualani Case responded, thanking the young woman for her generosity, while simultaneously encouraging everyone present to instead turn to their own cultural traditions in developing rites of passage for their young. She described the impact that turning to her own ancestral traditions had on herself, her daughter, and her community; they felt enlivened reclaiming their own roots.

This experience transformed my understanding of rites of passage, as I realized for the first time that I, too, came from people rich with cultural traditions, even if they were so far back I had no idea what they were. Hearing Pualani Case's reflections, I began to understand how vital the community and cultural context of a rite of passage is to its impact and real transformative power. I realized that rites of passage—the actual, specific ceremonial acts—are non-transferable: *their power comes from the community context in which they're held.*

Many Indigenous peoples have been saying this for years, even decades and centuries. But it was the first time I could actually feel as a white person what this meant for me. I began to reflect more deeply on my own experience with the rite of passage movement as it has shown up in primarily white communities. While my coming of age ceremony was deeply impactful, not all of the teachings I received were helpful in the long-term. In fact, some of them were outright harmful for me and for Indigenous peoples whose cultural elements were included in my coming of age ceremony. This realization sent me on a journey looking for alternatives that would create less harm, and more healing.

CULTURAL HABITAT RESTORATION

The phrase *cultural habitat restoration* describes what I believe is the ultimate aim of restoring rites of passage in community life. This idea first came to me when I was offering a class called "Restoring Youth Rites of Passage Leadership Intensive." For about two weeks, we camped on the edge of a river where a major river restoration project had just taken place. Many communities are making efforts to repair our natural habitats like rivers, streams, and wetlands. Even in places that have been deeply damaged, these efforts can help restore the conditions necessary for life to once again thrive.

We spent our days and nights exploring how to bring forth meaningful rites of passage for youth. Teaching sessions took place along a side channel of the river that had just been reconnected to the main channel to create habitat for young salmon that need slow water and deep pools to mature before their journey to the ocean and adulthood. Heavy machinery had recently resculpted the terrain, and subsequently hundreds of trees and native shrubs were planted along the shore. The land was raw and clearly disturbed by these efforts; trees were caged in chicken-wire to give them time to grow without local deer nibbling them down to nothing.

The landscape mirrored our inquiry into what is necessary to restore healthy rites of passage today. We saw the connection between the young trees in cages, and the many literal and figurative cages in which young people find themselves. Our human communities have also received harm, and need help restoring the cultural conditions necessary for human life to thrive.

What exactly cultural habitat restoration looks and feels like is something I'm still learning, and I imagine I will be for the rest of my life. One thing I do know is that it requires attention to both justice and healing. In many ways, struggles for justice are like the heavy machinery changes I saw along the river. Justice requires significant changes to the physical landscape around us. The work of healing is the more subtle but also essential day-to-day tending that allows the changes to have a positive result for the long term, like planting native trees and shrubs and making sure they have what they need to thrive. What follows is some of what I have learned about what justice and healing looks like in the world of rites of passage today.

UNDERSTANDING POWER AND PRIVILEGE

"Always ask questions; don't take anybody in a position of power for granted. Question why they're there. Use your gut, too, because I think there are some people who do make sense in some ways with their position and I'll trust that. I'll trust what my gut tells me. Most people will make my stomach hurt. Question that and follow that. Always question power. That may sound cliché, but always question power." –Serena, age 25

In order to create healing and just rites of passage, we need to understand how power and privilege work. Understanding power and privilege is part of understanding culture—one of our Ten Essentials from the last chapter. Neither power nor privilege is good or bad, though both of them can be used in healthy or harmful ways. Both are important to understand so they can be used responsibly and for maximum benefit for all. Working with power and privilege is like learning to read the landscape for what changes will allow a salmon to once again travel back up a stream, or reduce the chances of a catastrophic wildfire.

POWER

Martin Luther King, Jr. defined power as "the ability to affect change and achieve purpose." It has to do with our ability to influence and impact our own lives, and the world around us. Understanding power helps us make sense of how things work politically and on larger societal levels. It also helps us understand how things work even in intimate personal relationships, like with friends, family members, and romantic interests. Though it can often be hard to see and even harder to name, power impacts how we relate to each other on the largest and smallest scales. As J. Miakoda Taylor, lead steward of Fierce Allies, says, "Power is at play in every relationship and at just about every moment."

> *"Power has such a bad reputation that many people do not want it, do not believe it can be embodied responsibly. I disagree. If we want to embody it responsibly, we must become intimate with it and its potential entrapings. We must dance with it, fall with it, create with it, destroy with it, witness it, analyze it, question it. Power is alive, do not intend to know it. Intend to develop a deep understanding of its patterns."*
>
> *–J. Miakoda Taylor*

Here are a few things to note about power:

- *There is not just one type of power.* Activist and author Starhawk teaches about three types of power that exist in our relationships with each other and with the world around us: "power-over," meaning domination and control, "power-from-within" meaning personal agency and internal spiritual authority, and "power-with," meaning the power that comes from two or more beings joining together to combine forces.* "Power-over" is largely how we think about and define power in Western societies today. We can also distinguish different forms of power, like economic, political, social and military power as well as different sources of it, like authority, physical strength, endurance, creativity, resilience, and more.

- *Power is not good or bad, it just is.* To say that one person has more power in a given situation is not to place judgment (though it might feel like a judgment), it is to name and be transparent about interpersonal dynamics. Power can be used in healthy, loving ways, and it can be used to manipulate and hurt. The more that we can have open and honest dialogues about how power is operating, and come to shared values around how we want and do not want to use power, the more we can learn to trust one another.

- *Power is a form of energy.* Power works best for the greatest number of people when it flows like water rather than being

---

*As J. Miakoda Taylor pointed out during their review of this chapter, February 25, 2022, Starhawk's "power-with" analysis lacks equity analysis and application. While I agree that equity must be a core aspect of any liberatory power framework, I am using Starhawk's framework here as it serves as an accessible place for people to begin to explore what power is and how it works.

POWER OVER

POWER FROM WITHIN

POWER WITH

Three Types of Power as described by Starhawk

trapped in the hands of a few. The idea that all humans inherently want to consolidate power and hold onto it is one cultural perspective, *not* a universal truth. Pools and reservoirs can be beautiful to look at but without proper circulation they can also stagnate. When power doesn't move, it begins to fester. When we allow our social currencies to flow, they can refresh and revitalize. Imagine having a sports coach that tells you what to do all the time, and seems to wield power over you. Then imagine having a coach that treats you as their equal, providing guidance, support, and challenge along the way. Both of them may have the same amount of power, but one uses it to empower others while the other hoards it. Which coach would inspire your care, commitment, and best effort?

- *Feeling powerful is different than having power.* Whatever type of power we're talking about, however much or little of it may exist, it can be difficult to convince someone that they have power when they don't feel powerful. Yet just because someone doesn't feel like they have power in a given situation, doesn't mean they don't. Power that comes from one's place in the social hierarchy, based on things like race, role, age, gender, economic class, ability, and more, has real-world implications. That's why it's crucial that we each study how and where we have power, what we want to do with it, and invite open dialogue and reflections from others on themes of power. I've observed that I can make far bigger shifts in myself than I can make shifts in anyone else—and one of these shifts is to band together with other folks to work to change oppressive systems of power.

PRIVILEGE

Privilege is a hot-button word these days. People have such a strong reaction to the word that I'm almost inclined to leave it out, but it's really important to understand and be able to talk about it. If you're someone who gets turned off by people talking about privilege, hear me out, because part of stepping into adulthood is understanding, owning, and *using* our privilege.

Privilege is related to power, but it's different. It refers to advantages, including access to dominant forms of power, that are enjoyed by some, but not all. Frequently, it's associated with those advantages held by people in positions of power in a certain arena: like white folks with regards to race, men with regards to gender, owning class people with regards to socioeconomic class, and heterosexual people with regards to sexual orientation. When people experience privilege, they are often unconscious of the privilege they experience, because for them it is the standard and it's all they know. But folks that lack that same privilege can make a detailed list of all the advantages that they go without.

Hearing these detailed lists often leaves folks with privilege feeling guilty, ashamed, frustrated, feeling like it's not their fault that they have the privilege. That's true! Whether we want it or not, growing up in the Western world means being socialized into a highly stratified, hierarchical society. Abolitionist and organizer Kruti Parekh breaks this down in what she calls a "Social (in) Justice Framework."

This model shows how our relative power and privilege in this culture is defined by many criteria: skin color, age, physical ability, gender—just to name a few. And like the chart shows, this system is a prison for all of us, and we're going to need all of us to figure out how to break out of it.

The ranking we hold for all of these different criteria are not based on a natural order of things, nor have they remained fixed over the centuries. They are unique and particular to this specific time and culture. Not all cultures are hierarchical, for example: some have complex social systems based much more upon widespread equality. Even among cultures with more hierarchical power structures, the hierarchies they use may be very different from our own. While it may seem natural to some folks that people with mental health diagnoses or physical disabilities would have less power and privilege, for example, in many cultures these folks have been, and still are, revered for their access to different ways of sensing and relating. These gifts, rarely seen as valuable in dominant culture in the United States, are treasured in another context. So much is gained in our communities, and by society in general, when we nurture, support, and appreciate

SOCIAL (IN)JUSTICE FRAMEWORK

CATEGORY →

← MORE POWER & PRIVILEGE | LESS POWER & PRIVILEGE →

RACE	GENDER	ABILITY	FAMILY/ VILLAGE	CLASS	SPECIES
WHITE	CISGENDER MEN	PERSON WITHOUT A DISABILITY	FUNCTIONAL, LOVING AND SUPPORTIVE	OWNING /RULING	HUMAN
LIGHTER SKINNED				MANAGERIAL /UPPER	
	CISGENDER WOMEN		DISCONNECTED	MIDDLE CLASS	
DARKER SKINNED				WORKING CLASS	
BLACK AND/OR INDIGENOUS	TRANSGENDER/ NONBINARY /INTERSEX	PERSON WITH (VISIBLE OR INVISIBLE) DISABILITIES AND/OR DIVERGENCE	IMMEDIATE LOVED ONES DEAD AND/OR INCARCERATED, UNABLE TO BE PRESENT	POOR AND WORKING POOR	NON HUMAN

Note: This is offered as a starting place for discussion, not as fixed and rigid classifications. Specific circumstances can and do shift.

Other categories to consider: sexual orientation • documentation status • education • religion • culture • indigenous ancestry • national origin • age

Social (In)Justice Framework from the Ecology of Power & Privilege, 2017.

the unique gifts that come with each person's different ways of sensing, thinking, and moving through the world.

As much of a prison as a hierarchical, stratified society can be, understanding what's happening can help us work our way out of it. Looking at the chart, you can consider where you can find people who identify with your challenges, who can relate and teach you how to live with them. The chart also helps to identify folks facing more barriers in a given area than you face. As a cisgender woman, I am keenly aware of how I struggle and am marginalized as a woman in society. For most of my life, however, I have been less aware of how many more barriers are faced by transgender and gender-nonbinary folks. When I see things through this model, I can both stand up for myself and be reminded to use my relative privilege in support of those more marginalized in any given area.

Dante, age 21, puts it this way: "Privilege is pretty simple: Can you live with yourself if you're getting something at the expense of someone else? For me, that puts it all into perspective and helps me make decisions that aren't coming from my privilege or aren't rooted in my need to hoard all of the things I've gotten because of my proximity to white hetero-patriarchal power."

Despite how simply they see it, Dante acknowledges the way the word privilege can be misused: "I feel like I've been steeped in a weird culture that I don't think is actually counter-culture but feels like it is. It uses language like 'privilege' to almost disempower people and not have them understand power in the way we need to understand it. My relationship to the word privilege right now is "eh" because it's been so stolen and used in the worst ways." While it can be a bitter pill to swallow to feel accused of "privilege," the term— like power—is pretty value-neutral. I find this quote from blogger Sindelókë really helpful:

Being told you have privilege, or that you're privileged, isn't an insult. It's a reminder! The key to privilege isn't worrying about having it, or trying to deny it, or apologize for it, or get rid of it. It's just paying attention to it, and knowing what it means for you and the people around you. Having privilege is like having big feet. No one hates you for having big feet! They just want you to be careful where you walk.

❦ EXERCISE: Free-write for 15 minutes: What does power mean to you? When have you experienced power-over, power-with, and power-from-within dynamics in your life? How do you see these dynamics playing out in your school, workplace, or in the media?

❦ EXERCISE: Draw your own social (in)justice chart, and fill it in like a bar graph of your own relative privilege. Note what comes up for you: what physical sensations, feelings, and thoughts arise?

RITES OF PASSAGE IN A DAMAGED LANDSCAPE: THE HAZARDS OF CULTURAL APPROPRIATION

"Throughout my life, people think they can just take my sacred things and do whatever they want with them."– Serena, age 25

As we try to understand damages to the cultural landscape in the world around us, and explore ways to restore health to our cultural habitat, we need to understand the hazards we face. One hazard that's particularly important to talk about in the context of rites of passage is *cultural appropriation*, or taking elements of other people's culture (including traditional knowledge, cultural expressions, or artifacts) without permission or reciprocity.*

Cultures are constantly evolving and always have been, adapting to changing needs and circumstances. When two cultures come into contact, cultural forms are inevitably adopted from one culture to another. This can be a beautiful thing. However, it can also cause deep harm when people lack awareness, care, and respect. Context is really important.

---

*People use the term cultural appropriation differently, often distinguishing between cultural appropriation and misappropriation. In the end I stuck with this simple definition because: 1) It's most consistent with resources available for a general audience, including dictionary and wikipedia definitions; 2) It's most consistent with writings I've seen by Indigenous authors on the topic; and 3) It emphasizes the need to understand cultural appropriation on a continuum of impact.

The damage resulting from cultural appropriation is on a continuum, from not-so-great to deeply harmful, based on factors like: who is doing the appropriating, what culture they are appropriating from, what cultural practice they are appropriating, and how they are engaging in that action. For example, a white teenager wearing a traditional headdress from a Turtle Island Indigenous community to a music festival is a deeply offensive act. It shows a lack of awareness of the history of colonization and genocide of white settlers toward Indigenous peoples on this continent, as well as a lack of awareness, care, or respect for the sacredness of cultural regalia and protocols about who is authorized to wear regalia and when it is appropriate to do so.

Such acts have a long tradition in the West. In his book *Playing Indian*, author Philip Deloria explores how early American settlers exploited Native cultural symbols. During the Boston Tea Party, for example, revolutionaries donned Native headdresses. This persisted with different faces and fashions over the next several hundred years, leading to sports mascots wearing headdresses and other native regalia. Recent years have seen growing awareness in some communities (for example, several sports teams have changed their offensive names and mascots), but the issue persists.

Cultural appropriation is often driven by stereotyping, as exemplified by this story from Serena, a 25 year old takatāpui Māori (takatāpui is basically the Māori term for LGBTQI+ folks) about *haka*, a Māori ceremonial dance form:

"In New Zealand we have this rugby group called the All-Blacks, and they have their own haka. And people all over the world have seen that, and what that's done is they've attached that to Maori and the All-Blacks and everyone else in New Zealand. [People] have called the haka a war dance. And, specifically, the one that [the All-Blacks] were doing before they wrote their own was a war dance. It was one done for battle. But haka is really diverse. We have ones for battle, but we also have ones where we're happy and we're welcoming you. We have ones for lament. It's like feelings: there's a lot of them. We are a diverse people, and we have a range of emotions. Yet because of [the popularity of the All-Blacks] everyone has looked to my people like we are angry and like we're savage, or like the bad-ass Polynesians.

People across the world, like football teams and stuff, started to do haka, *and they think that's okay because they're like, "We're competing against each other! Let's do this! It's like a battle!" And it's like, "No, that's not what* haka *is." People take on* haka, *and they do it badly."*

As Serena's story highlights, people see something in *haka* that they are attracted to but they don't necessarily have the whole story. The needs and longing are real, healthy, and important, but our attempts to get these needs met can often have unintended consequences.

When I was 13 and found myself attracted to the coming of age experience I eventually participated in, I was yearning for something I couldn't find in other areas of my life. I craved spirituality, but in my family there wasn't a clear tradition I could turn to. My schooling provided access to beautiful cultural practices, but they were often taught as artifacts of other cultures not my own. They lacked a coherent worldview and weren't connected to the place I lived. As I grew older, this absence inside of me felt like a deep void. When I encountered elements of Indigenous cultures, whether through people, practices, or learning about Indigenous history, it felt like the void inside me began to fill.

My culture was unable to meet the needs I had for community, culture, and meaning, and so I sought it outside of dominant culture. The needs I felt were real and important. Yet when they intermixed with consumer-oriented Western culture, cultural experiences became something for me to consume. Because of who I was and the resources available to me through my community, I sought meaningful cultural experiences through the means that felt most accessible to me. This led me, throughout my life, to engage in a variety of harmful acts of cultural appropriation, including sacred Indigenous ceremonies led by non-Indigenous people, medicine wheel teachings, sprinkling my vocabulary with Hawaiian language when I was living in Hawaii, and using herbs like sage to "smudge." It's not that each of these things is problematic for me to participate in regardless of the context. For example, learning and using Indigenous words in the area I am in can raise consciousness, shift ways of seeing the world, and create opportunities for connection. But being really honest with myself about my intentions, *and* my impact, has helped me see many of the problems that have stemmed from my actions.

As I increasingly explored how cultural appropriation showed up in my own rite of passage, I discovered that my experience allowed me to avoid the difficult inner work of healing from the trauma and oppression that my ancestors suffered, including the destruction of their traditional rites and ceremonies. I was also allowed to avoid reflecting on the impact of the oppression caused by my ancestors, and the ways those impacts continue today. With my early rite of passage experiences, I gained tools and practices that helped me seek comfort from the stress of my life and find ways to access deeper meaning in my life. Those needs are real and important—I need those tools, and so do you! I was able to access them without being asked to engage in the painful and dirty work of dealing with the perpetual structural inequity that impacts every aspect of our lives. This experience has a name: *spiritual bypass.*

Spiritual bypass is a "tendency to use spiritual ideas and practices to sidestep or avoid facing unresolved emotional issues, psychological wounds, and unfinished developmental tasks." This psychological defense mechanism helps people avoid disturbing aspects of the world and difficult feelings like shame, "transcending" these things by focusing on spiritual concepts like love, unity, and oneness. This ultimately keeps people from addressing underlying issues, blocking their ability to grow.

In discerning whether or not something is cultural appropriation in my own life, I've come to really appreciate activist and author Starhawk's definition: "taking the gifts of the ancestors without a commitment to their descendants." This means making use of elements of a culture but not participating in the day to day struggles for survival, self-determination, and liberation with the people from that culture.

Here are a few of the ways that cultural appropriation creates harm:

- Cultural appropriation can diminish the cultural and spiritual impact of specific traditions. Songs, stories, ceremonies, names, and symbols function within longstanding cultural protocols specific to individuals, families, clans, tribes, and nations. The intricacies of these protocols are difficult for outsiders to understand, and are often impossible to teach or learn outside of a specific cultural context. As Katheryne, age 26, puts it: "I think appropriation is harmful because it gives people the idea that they can adopt and discard cultures whenever they feel like. I feel like it takes power away from a whole culture for the sake of vanity."

- When people are spiritually or culturally hungry, they can project a lot onto people they perceive as having culture and spirituality. Remember the section from Chapter One on shadow, and the psychological term "projection?" Cultural appropriation comes in large part from projection, from looking around and seeing how little meaning there is in much of our consumer-driven culture, and looking for places of meaning—and believing they can only be found "over there, in other people's cultures." This creates a number of issues: the promise of adoration, financial wealth, and power are very alluring, and being projected upon can distort people's view of themselves. These are issues that Indigenous communities need to work out for themselves, and pressure and idolization from wealthy outsiders makes this work more difficult for them. When Native people are put on a pedestal and expected to perform "Being Indian", it can feel exhausting and dehumanizing. Have you ever felt stuck or pigeon-holed into performing a stereotype of your identity? As you can imagine, this makes it harder to build authentic relationships.

- Native peoples the world over have faced land theft and displacement, wholesale efforts at extermination, the outlawing of cultural practices, continued economic and political exploitation, and more. It wasn't until 1978—the year of my birth—that the American Indian Religious Freedom Act made it legal for Indigenous peoples in the United States to practice their cultural and spiritual ways. In many places, this happened even later. It's this context that leads Indigenous activists Brandi Douglas and Steph Viera to write that "cultural

ASSIMILATION

Like so many other themes of the book, you may have really different experiences with cultural appropriation than I do. Perhaps you experience the impact of others taking elements of your culture, but haven't been the one doing the exploiting. For you, bigger issues may relate to the ways you and your family need to take on elements of dominant culture in order to get by.

One way that people do this is through *assimilation*. Assimilation is when someone from a marginalized group takes on, either by choice, coercion, or violent force, elements of the dominant culture in order to "fit in" with dominant culture. A non-Westerner appropriating Western fashion styles like wearing blue jeans is a form of assimilation, as is celebrating Christmas in order to blend in with the neighbors. Like appropriation, assimilation can be seen as operating on a continuum as well.

Tarek, age 32, tried hard to assimilate in middle school outside of Seattle just after 9/11. "I was starting to connect with my Turkish ancestry at the time," he says, remembering. He made his first trip to Turkey to visit relatives with his family.

"But I was confused to have this connected in some way to terrorism by my peers. Suddenly, I was being faced with harsh jokes towards me, I guess from my name and how I looked. I found myself rolling with the jokes, sometimes even telling jokes at my own expense as a means to brush it off, I guess, and feel connected to the people making those jokes. I remember being hurt and not even able to understand it."

For Tarek, his ability to learn about, connect with, and feel pride in his family's cultural background was impacted by social pressure from his white peers, leading to confusion and belittling himself in order to fit in.

Assimilation is a strategy to survive, and at times even thrive, in a consumerist-driven, white-dominant culture. Have you ever chosen to hide part of yourself in order to fit in? Have you ever put someone else in a choice like this? How would things be different in a healthy cultural landscape?

appropriation is violent, extractive, and profit-driven, seeking to maintain systems of colonialism and white supremacy while silencing and maintaining the invisibility of Indigenous people, our cultures and experiences." When Westerners, particularly white Westerners, consume elements of culture which Native people themselves risked persecution to maintain less than a generation ago, it's like pouring salt on already-deep wounds.

- Cultural appropriation fosters cultural and spiritual confusion. A side effect of my early experiences was learning that authentic, land-based spirituality was something that lived outside of my familial, ancestral, and cultural traditions. In my teens and twenties, I increasingly grew comfortable engaging in practices from peoples Indigenous to Turtle Island—until I learned the term cultural appropriation, and discovered the issues associated with it. What followed was years of confusion about what ceremonial, spiritual, and cultural practices I could legitimately engage in, without harming others.

- Cultural appropriation also creates practical confusion about the culture(s) from which the practice originates. For example, the term pow-wow is often used erroneously among non-Native people to refer to a group of people getting together to discuss a topic. In fact, pow-wows are gatherings of North American Indigenous communities to sing, dance, feast, socialize, and celebrate cultural histories.

- Cultural appropriation promotes a sense of misplaced entitlement and perpetuates consumerism. Entitlement is one of the hazards of privilege, where people develop a sense that they have a right to physical and emotional comfort beyond what most of the rest of the world enjoys (and often even a lack of awareness that others don't have access to these comforts). This can and does take many forms, like beliefs that you, your family, your community, your nation, or even your species have a right to land, resources, and practices. Growing up white in Seattle, surrounded by people with economic privilege, I was trained to feel entitled to comforts like rich foods with lots of sugar, fat, and spices, a house that can be any temperature I want, and new clothing each school year. My experiences with cultural appropriation extended this even further, to my right to beliefs, traditions, and ceremonies without requiring me to understand the history or context of exploitation of Native people. If I could buy it, I could have it.

EXERCISE: Reflect on the following questions:

- How have you engaged in cultural appropriation? What did it give to you (both positive and negative)?
- Have you ever seen elements of your culture or identity appropriated by others? How did it affect you?

PRACTICES FOR RESTORING CULTURAL HEALTH: EMERGENCE, RECOVERY, AND MEANINGFUL CULTURAL EXCHANGE

"Due to lack of reciprocity in the US, people can actually get very intense about appropriation of cultures. Because the culture is not being given willingly. There is no ritual for when people say, 'We want to share our culture. We want to give our culture.'

...There's no dialogue between one peoples and another peoples that can hold the complexity of those peoples...But in most of the history of the world, culture has always been shared. That's the other flip side of appropriation, is that people learn from each other and they mimic each other all the time. So part of our DNA as mammals, as humans, is to copy things from each other all the time...

The question is, is there reciprocity in that relationship, yes or no? When there isn't then I think appropriation comes in. But it is so difficult because sometimes we as individuals think that we can solve the appropriation question. Because that reciprocity is not established, every other relationship on the bottom collapses, because there's no way two individuals can make peace for two peoples."–Activist and founder of Ayni Institute Carlos Saavedra

The last decades and even centuries contain more than just stories of cultural theft, exploitation, and genocide. They also carry stories of meaningful cultural emergence, recovery, and exchange. As we strive to rebalance power, these stories offer a glimpse of what culturally restorative practices can look like in our lives, communities, and nations.

Cultural exchange is when people of different cultural backgrounds share one or more aspects of their culture, in ways that are consensual, reciprocal, and rooted in relationships and relatively equal levels of power. An example of cultural exchange is Tribal Canoe Journeys, where Indigenous peoples from Oregon to Alaska travel by canoe each year, formally asking permission to land in each territory along the way, until after days or weeks (depending on how far away they are coming from) they gather in a Host Nation's territory for days of feasting and sharing with each other. Each day of the journey, the gathered tribes and nations participate in "protocol", sharing songs, dances, and gifts from their culture with the other peoples present. This sharing, which can take many hours and even days, is a chance for each community to share unique elements of their culture. Preparing for Tribal Canoe Journeys is an opportunity for Indigenous tribes and nations in the region to preserve, recover, regenerate and transmit their songs, dances, and stories.

Another example is the way that cultural exchange is happening in the realm of Tibetan Buddhism, where Western teachers like Pema Chodron carry and share the traditional teachings with great care and respect while Tibetan monks and lamas including the Dalai Lama have engaged in mutually enriching dialogues with modern psychologists and neuroscientists. Within the world of rites of passage, there have been powerful moments of meaningful cultural exchange over the last decades, while there have also been many instances of cultural appropriation.*

The word *recovery* comes from a root meaning to regain health or consciousness.** *Cultural recovery* is the painstaking work of unearthing healthy traditions in our own cultural and ancestral backgrounds. Many Indigenous people have talked about how settlers would better serve themselves—and violate Native peoples less—if they turned to their own cultural traditions rather than stealing spirituality from Native peoples. This, combined with efforts to shift dominant power structures, allows everyone the possibility of participating in meaningful cultural exchange. I think back to my own coming of age, where I showed up with yearning and emptiness, and nothing to offer from my own cultural background in exchange for what I was offered.

What does this mean for those of us with ancestors from many different lands, places and traditions that our family hasn't been connected with in generations? How do I meaningfully engage with my ancestral lines, and not just appropriate these

---

*The work of restoring cultures is messy and complex. Sharing stories—of both healthy cultural exchange and cultural exploitation and other missteps—can help keep the same mistakes from being made over and over. A big part of the work for guides and practitioners of rites of passage is unpacking, understanding, reckoning with, and addressing the harm embedded in the legacy of rites of passage communities and related communities loosely affiliating under names like nature connection, conscious dance, circle practice, and more (particularly white and/or settler communities). This is a microcosm of larger cultural reckonings with ongoing harm from settler colonialism, chattel slavery, Jim Crow, growing economic inequality, and more.

Throughout this book, I have struggled with how much to include these stories. In the end, I chose to leave most of this out in the interest of pointing you, the reader, in the direction I think we are trying to go. My hope is that in the coming years we will see the opportunity for more of the stories of the mistakes and missteps to be laid out publicly as we do the culture-building work of re-learning ways of being in healthy accountability with one another.

**There is a connection between cultural recovery and 12-step recovery processes. I've experienced a similar process between my attempts to find the healthy traditions in my cultural background and my attempts to find health in my relationship with mind-altering substances. The steps of recognizing that there's a problem too big for me to solve, coming to believe that I can "be restored to sanity" and asking for support from a Higher Power, engaging a "searching and fearless moral inventory"— all inform the cultural recovery process well. This is similar to efforts to link recovery from white supremacy culture to the 12 steps. Search "12 steps racism" for many meaningful examples.

traditions, too? Part of the work of rites of passage is exploring how your own ancestral lineage informs who you are today—whether you have a great relationship with your family or are totally estranged from them, whether you can trace your ancestry back 15 generations or you lack access to any information about your birth parents. In Chapter 6, you'll be asked to explore your lineage and consider your responsibilities to your ancestors, both to reclaim gifts and to work to end cycles of violence.

Finally, restoring cultural health is also served through *emergence* — bringing forth songs, stories, prayers, rituals, ways of being that come forward for the first time out of a particular group of people, coming together in a particular place and at a particular time.

Sometimes, this involves the weaving of multiple cultural elements into something new, in such a way that identifying a single originating culture is difficult. Rastafarianism is an example of a cultural form that emerged when multiple cultural forms came together, as traditional African beliefs mixed with elements of African-centered Christianity to create something entirely new.

Recognizing the emergent nature of culture highlights that culture isn't fixed but can evolve, adapt, and shift—and in fact always has. My mentor Stan loved to say, "We're going to do it like we've been doing it for thousands of years. We're going to make it up as we go along." I take great comfort in this saying, as it reminds me that co-creating—with other people, with the more-than-human world—is part of what humans have been doing on the earth for generations.

In these complex times of global interconnection, climate catastrophe, and all the rest, and especially when we come together with others across differences, new forms are essential. This has led me to focus on the key question: *What will serve in this place, with these people, at this moment?*

WAYS OF ENGAGING ACROSS CULTURES TODAY

Type	Cultural Appropriation/ Misappropriation	Cultural Assimilation
Definition	When people use elements of a marginalized culture without reciprocity, permission, and understanding of context. Harmful impact is on a continuum.	When people from a marginalized culture adopt elements of a dominant culture that has been imposed on them, displacing their native culture and identity.
Examples	Non-Maori sports teams performing haka. White people donning Native headdresses.	Non-Westerners adopting blue jeans. Non-Christians celebrating Christmas in order to blend in with the neighbors.
Possible Motivations	Shadow desire for cultural meaning. Desire for prestige Entitlement, greed	Survival and/or success in dominant culture. A means to gain power in order to subvert or challenge dominant culture.
Possible Risks	Many; See list in this section	Losing access to one's culture. Creating internal dissonance, loss of esteem.

WAYS OF ENGAGING ACROSS CULTURES TODAY, CONTINUED.

Cultural Recovery	Cultural Exchange	Cultural Emergence
When people who have lost access to their ancestral traditions work to regain access and understanding.	When people of different cultural backgrounds share one or more aspects of their culture, in ways that are consensual, reciprocal, and rooted in relationships and mitigation of power differentials.	When people create new cultural elements by weaving multiple cultural elements
Me connecting with the traditions of my Ukrainian ancestors through learning how to make Ukrainian motanky (cloth dolls).	Tribal Canoe Journeys, where Coast Salish tribes and nations come together and share songs, dances, and stories through protocol.	Rastafarianism, weaving traditional African beliefs with elements of African-centered Christianity to create something entirely new.
Recovering practices and ways of being lost due to assimilation	Genuine relationship, understanding and mutual solidarity.	Creating forms relevant for new contexts.
		Allows weaving of dominant culture with marginalized cultures.
Risks becoming a form of cultural exploitation.	Few contexts exist with truly equal levels of power, creating risk of exploitation.	Can quickly become subsumed and commodified.

✲ **EXERCISE**: Reflect on the following questions:

- Consider the difference between *cultural appropriation* and *cultural exchange*. Have you ever had an experience of cultural exchange? What was it like to experience another's culture? What was it like to share your own?
- What do you know about your ancestors? Where do they come from, and if it's different than your home now, what was their path to where you are now? What are some of the struggles they have faced over time?

RITES AND RESPONSIBILITIES

At the beginning of this chapter, I shared this quote from activist and poet Luis Rodriguez: "Rites of passage weave the threads of the past with the threads of the future." Over the last seven or so years since I heard this quote, I've reflected a lot on what this means. I've come to really understand how rites of passage tie together the generations, connecting us with our ancestors as well as our descendants, our elders and mentors as well as our younger siblings.

In this chapter, I've tried to pass on some of the context informing our experiences today. Understanding where we've been and some of the pitfalls we face is very important to understanding how to move forward. Part of being human is making lots of mistakes, and hopefully, learning from them. Too often as people get older, we try to hide away our mistakes and pretend we know what we are doing. This can create brittleness and rigidity in us and in our relationships. Part of being a true adult is being capable of change and being in interdependent relationship with other people.

In American culture, we have a strong emphasis on the idea of "rights," just as I've talked here about your *right* to a rite of passage! People in the United States learn from a young age about the "Bill of Rights," the set of entitlements that are considered a pillar of democracy here. Yet too much of anything can start to be unhealthy and problematic, even rights.

A number of leading Indigenous activists over the years have spoken about the danger of emphasizing "rights" as a way to win their struggles for self-determination and sovereignty. They instead highlight the significance of their "responsibilities" to protect and uphold the health of their culture, their language, and their traditional lands. It's not so much about their rights to a certain piece of earth, they say, but rather that in order to fulfill their cultural responsibilities they must be able to provide for the well-being of a place. This definitely challenges the notions of entitlement I spoke to early in the chapter.

As we engage in rites of passage, and step into healthy adulthood, our personal power and autonomy becomes less about our individual freedom to do whatever we want, and more about our sacred responsibility to fulfill our purpose and bring forth our gifts for our community. This begins with taking responsibility for our lives and our choices, as well as the impacts of choices made by those before us.

This might not feel fair—and indeed it's not! For survivors of childhood trauma, doing the hard work of healing from the violence that others inflicted is not fair. And, it's still part of what is required to become an adult in our world, and to learn how to give and receive love. Many people who don't engage in their own trauma healing ultimately inflict violence and harm on others. A little further on, we'll explore how this phenomenon is the root of much cultural violence today. Meaningfully addressing the collective violence that has been inflicted, and continues to be inflicted, in our society requires that we take a big step into acting like adults and taking responsibility.

This means considering your responsibilities to the place and peoples of the land you call home, and taking action in solidarity with the Indigenous peoples of your community. As you navigate the rest of the material in this book, seeking to be initiated into adulthood, you will be asked to do so with the parallel processes of engaging more and more deeply in understanding the people that you come from, and the peoples of the place in which you live.

A FEW FIRST STEPS FOR SETTLERS TO BEGIN TO TAKE RESPONSIBILITY

People who benefit from colonization can begin to take responsibility for their impacts on Indigenous people by engaging in basic education about where they live. One aspect of this learning includes traditional elements of the culture. This might include exploring things like what tools people traditionally used, what medicinal and food plants were common (and may remain in active use today), learning traditional stories, developing an understanding of the cosmology and spiritual life of the people, or studying a local Indigenous language. In fact, many prominent Indigenous scholars and leaders say that it is not possible to fully know a place without knowing an Indigenous language of that place. Taking the time to learn place names, greetings, and other basic words in the local Indigenous language is a sign of respect and care for the lands, and people of the lands, on which you live, work, and play.

A second element of basic education is to learn the story of colonization of the area. How and when did settlers arrive, and from where? Had disease reached and shaped the community before these settlers arrived? What were the stories of removal from the lands, of massacre, of removal of the children? Did Peoples sign a treaty, and if so, what were the conditions of that signing. Have treaties been honored? These are the wounds of the land and the People; part of opening ourselves up to connecting means understanding as much of the full story as possible, and reckoning with these truths.

A third aspect of this education is to explore issues affecting the daily lives of the Indigenous peoples whose lands you live on. Depending on where you live, those people may have been largely removed and live now in distant reservation communities. They may have assimilated into the region. Learning about the continued struggles of Indigenous people surviving amidst the legacy and ongoing impacts of genocide is an important part of connecting with your place – as is looking for places where you can take action. It is also important to note that just as there is a legacy of genocide and violence that have deeply impacted Indigenous peoples, there is also legacy of foreigners coming in and wanting to help, taking up time, and then disappearing from the community. What serves is slowly and humbly building real relationships over time, based in mutual support, care and respect.

Indigenous peoples have often lived in their homelands for thousands of years; many of their stories share that they have been there since the beginning of time. For any of us that are not Indigenous to a place, understanding that we are newcomers, settlers, and recent, often uninvited guests (even if our ancestors have been on these soils for generations) is important to cultivating strong relationships, both with the place and the peoples of the place. This takes lots of patience and humility; like ancestral research, this is not a journey that fits in well with an instant-gratification culture.

As you can see, the work of creating meaningful, healthy rites of passage is very complex in our world today! This chapter has covered some of the many nuances and complexities, but nowhere close to all of them.

When you feel discouraged, remember to turn toward your intuition. In doing this work, you are standing on the shoulders of generations of ancestors, elders, and teachers who see a different future possible for humans on this earth. Trust their guidance! Through this struggle, true *cultural exchange* exists: times when people from different backgrounds, all of whom have learned and grown and rooted themselves in cultural practices, are aware of the power dynamics at play in their coming together, and bring their gifts to one another to create just what's needed in the moment. Cultivating the trust to listen to what's wanted in a certain moment, to let go of forms and structures and show up with what is alive, can be challenging, humbling, and ultimately transformative. As we bring forth meaningful rites of passage today, we uncover ancestral traditions, as well as create emergent ceremonies relevant to the people that surround us, on the lands where we are, today.

⚕EXERCISE: Reflect on the following questions:

- What Indigenous nation(s) have always lived in the place you call home? Visit Native Lands website or download the app for a searchable map.

- What is the history of colonization in the place that you live? What treaties were signed, and what were the conditions of that signing? How are those treaties being upheld and/or broken today?
- Where are the Indigenous people(s) of the lands on which you live today? What are the main issues they are facing? What Indigenous-led sovereignty movements exist in your community?
- What does what you're learning now compare to what you learned about Indigenous people growing up?

You may have difficulty finding answers to some of these questions; now is a time to begin this research, knowing that it may take some time to find the answers. See the Online Resources for suggestions on how to get started.

⚘**EXERCISE**: Translate this learning into a simple creative expression to bring the learning out of your head and connect with it on a physical and an emotional level.. Draw a map, write a poem, create an offering of items found on the land and gathered with care, or whatever else calls to you.

☾

Chapter Four:

SEX, DRUGS, AND RITES OF PASSAGE

"I received very conflicting messages about love, intimacy, and sexuality. My dad tried to teach me to respect women. But we have never once talked about sexuality. My mom indirectly taught me that it is ok for men to treat women badly. Music also taught me to treat women like objects. I don't think that I have ever had a positive influence on views of love and sexuality." –Tim, age 29

Several years ago, as I was packing for a move, I read through all of my old journals. Since I kept a journal faithfully starting when I was 10 years old, it took me several days to read through them.

It was an intensely uncomfortable exercise, as I discovered that page after page, year after year, I had written almost exclusively about one thing: boys. On and on I went: whom I liked, whether I thought they liked me, what I wanted to happen and how I felt when it did or didn't. After I read them, I packed the journals away in storage. I dreaded ever having to see them again, but I was somehow unable to let them go.

Fast-forward three years. A wildfire swept through my community, and most of my journals burned up. While there were other things that I felt sad to lose, I felt total relief that those embarrassing pages had been wiped off the earth. I would never have to read them again.

When we are ready for transition, the forces of life move in wild, magical ways.

Years before the fire, my partner and I had decided to explore an open relationship, where we could explore intimacy and sexuality with other people—a challenging choice in the community where we were living. By the time the fire swept through my community, I was consumed by a dramatic, intense, and exhausting love triangle. While the evidence of my hyperfocus on boys (and eventually men) in the form of the journal pages was gone, I still saw how I was expending so much energy on that one part of my life, at the expense of others.

Meanwhile, that same summer, I gave up drinking. After years of wondering if I had a problem, I finally admitted that I did. Getting sober was a powerful initiatory experience for me, far more difficult than fasting alone in nature or any other ordeal I had experienced to date. I experienced a complete reworking of my identity, a rewiring of my brain, and important shifts in my social roles and sense of community.

Growing up with rites of passage and related practices woven into my life, I felt like I had all the tools I needed to navigate through any transition that life could throw my way. Yet now I was navigating something that felt far different.

Looking back, I can see clearly that my experience with rites of passage had laid a solid foundation for these new life challenges. Having had these experiences didn't mean that life felt easy or happy all the time, or even that I always made good choices. But the experience did help me trust the process of change when I found it happening. Changes keep coming, no matter what, for our whole lives! This is why we need tools to face change head-on, and navigate its turbulent waters.

How we relate to sex and drugs can be critical in our development toward true adulthood. For many young people, explorations with one or both of them are primary aspects of our initiatory journey toward adulthood. Even when we develop in healthy ways in other areas of our life, we can simultaneously set in place unhealthy patterns that take years to unravel. That's why it's important to take some time to understand some of the messages we receive about sexuality and mind-altering substances, and identify ways to explore this terrain that are fun, exciting, and safe for you now, and healthy for you in the long run. This chapter won't provide answers to all the questions you may be holding, but it will provide a framework to help you make choices to care for yourself and others physically, emotionally, and spiritually. It will help you identify gaps in your knowledge and find tools to address them.

⚘EXERCISE: A tricky thing with this book is how to provide information and make important aspects of initiation accessible in a culture that generally doesn't provide this, at least not in healthy ways, while at the same time helping readers understand the limitations of a book to guide your journey. Some of the places where the limitations are clearest are in this chapter. As you move forward through this chapter, please schedule a time to discuss what you're reading with the mentor you identified in Chapter One, or another caring adult. This is also an area where many adults are also still doing our own work, so it may be that this is a place where you want to seek out mentors skilled and experienced in working in this terrain specifically. You can check out some places in the Online Resources.

FROM "JUST SAY NO" TO RECLAIMING THE SACRED

I am not the only person for whom sex and drugs are important themes on the path to adulthood. As you may know from your own life, experimentation is part of many young peoples' transitions into adulthood—and not only young humans! Juvenile dolphins, for example, have been documented getting high on puffer fish.

Two of the most powerful doorways of initiation are sexuality and ingesting mind-altering substances, allowing us to access our deep yearnings in immediate and direct ways. Perhaps this is why these themes fill the arts, from today's popular songs to Shakespeare's plays to the poetry of 7th century mystics to ancient rock art.

Yet as you may also know from personal experience, these doorways are not without peril. They are in fact quite dangerous. Their power can be seductive, at times driving away rational thought and wise-decision making. Their consequences can be serious, altering the course of one's life trajectory: unwanted pregnancy, sexually transmitted infections, long-lasting trauma, heartbreak, bad trips, overdoses, addiction—these are just some of the challenges that can ensue.

You may be among the many young people today navigating the realms of love, sexuality, drugs, and/or alcohol without adequate support, mentorship, and guidance. Rather than being prepared to work with powerful plant medicines or the healing forces of human sexuality, and being held in strong containers with clear boundaries for such exploration, young people are mostly told simply to wait, abstain, or left to go at it on their own. Laws and societal messages about safety, ethics, and legality are confusing, contradictory, and often arbitrary.

I believe this breaks trust between young people and adults. That's what happened for me. Because I wasn't sure what information I could trust, my peers and popular culture became primary sources of information. I made my own choices. Some of these choices were great, some left me spinning in circles, and some meant I spent many years dealing with long-term consequences of fleeting, ill-informed decisions.

As I reflect back, the main thing that was missing for me was any mention of the sacred in discussions about sex or drugs. In the dominant culture, we continue to hold a split between the sacred world and the profane world, and sexuality and drugs long ago became divorced from the realms of spirit. But the forces of both are intensely healing domains, when their power is understood and channeled in healthy ways. This chapter explores love and sexuality, and substances which alter our consciousness, as gifts bestowed on the human species, part of the reservoir of wisdom handed down to us from our ancestors.

LOVE AND SEX

"The erotic is a measure between the beginnings of our sense of self and the chaos of our strongest feelings. It is an internal sense of satisfaction to which, once we have experienced it, we know we can aspire. For having experienced the fullness of this depth of feeling and recognizing its power, in honor and self respect we can require no less of ourselves."
–Black American feminist and author Audre Lorde

Not everyone is as focused on love, romance, intimacy, and sexuality as I have been over the course of my life. Where my unique personality characteristics, chemical make-up, and set of life experiences encouraged me in that direction, other people respond differently. Some find their interests take them in other directions, others would like to explore love and/or sexuality but feel utterly inept, and some lucky ones manage to attain some level of balance naturally.

Regardless of what your wounds, challenges, and interests are in this area, we all have the right to explore *eros* in our lives, on our own timing, and the responsibility to do so wisely. Eros is the Greek god of love and sexuality (the word *erotic* is derived from his name). The Greeks distinguished different types of love—like the love between friends, the love between parents and children, and the love between lovers. *Eros* is the word for the latter; it includes sexuality but is not limited to it. *Eros* can be described as both the creative life force, and the experience of sensual pleasure. While it may be an unusual word to bring into the conversation about sex in some circles (and perhaps you've never heard it), in other circles it is a commonly-used word.

Whatever we call it, the forces drawing us towards *eros* are strong, and have an important place to play in our lives and in our culture. After all, humans are hardwired for connection. Love, intimacy, and sexuality—these are ways that we connect and bond with others of our species, express ourselves, establish kinship ties, and experience joy and pleasure.

MIND ALTERING SUBSTANCES

"[P]lants and fungi with the power to radically alter consciousness have long and widely been used as tools for healing the mind, for facilitating rites of passage, and for serving as a medium for communicating with supernatural realms, or spirit worlds." –white American Author Michael Pollan

Consciousness-shifting plant medicines are an important part of cultures across the globe, seen as sacred gifts from the earth that allow humans to pray, gain wisdom, address depression and anxiety, expand their ways of thinking, and connect. For many cultures, proper use of these plants is part of the Original Instructions handed down to them from the spirit world.

Indigenous ceremonial practices (including those with plant medicines) were outlawed and persecuted under colonization, in many places well into recent decades. In the United States, for example, this didn't change until the 1978 Indian Religious Freedom Act. In Canada, such practices were outlawed until even more recently. Despite attempts to destroy access to traditional cultural practices, many Indigenous cultures have retained or reclaimed traditional plant medicine ceremonies. Recent decades have seen increasing attention among Westerners to both ceremonial use of plant medicines, such as ayahuasca, as well as recreational use of substances held by many as sacred, such as peyote and psilocybin mushrooms.

Problems come when these sacred substances and practices come in contact with Western consumer culture. Questions arise: Does the use of sacred plants outside of well-held traditional cultural practices dishonor the plants, and change their medicine? Does the use of synthetic substances further separate us from our true nature? Certainly, in places around the world, the pressures of production for mind-altering plants leads to overharvesting, environmental destruction, and even violence.

Even when plant medicines are held in ceremony, there are still issues around how the use of such plants by Westerners intermixes with cultural exploitation and consumerism. How does the exchange of money and commodification of sacred plant-based ceremonies distort the medicine, put pressure on traditional practitioners, and give rise to folks profiting off another's culture?

Research has grown in recent years around the impacts of psilocybin and other hallucinogenic substances to promote mental health and well-being. This research points to the importance of how, where, and with what intention one engages with plant medicines, reinforcing the importance of a shift away from recreation-oriented approach toward one more deeply rooted in spiritual discovery and wellbeing.

One thing is clear: consciousness-shifting substances are part of human cultures. Humans have literally evolved alongside plants that can serve to deepen our connection to the sacred. The question is: how do we engage in responsible ways that honor this healing power?

MAP OF EXPLORATION

So, how do you explore these realms in ways that are healthy for you and healthy for your community? Through my teaching and research, I've come to believe that there are at least four domains to consider: consent, pleasure, safety, and connection. Each of these domains require some baseline level of experience, skill, and understanding when exploring the realms of sexuality or substances. And each domain is a universe that you could spend a whole lifetime exploring! Collectively, they comprise a map that you can keep traveling around, going deeper and deeper, allowing for new possibilities for satisfaction, transformation, healing, and growth.

As you explore these domains, a lot may come up for you. Many of us have had very difficult, painful, or even traumatic experiences with sexuality and/or substances. Learning about all the things you weren't taught earlier may bring up anger or grief. Or you might build excitement, and want to go out and try things! Whatever comes up for you, this is a great opportunity to revisit the practices of tracking your sensations, emotions, and thoughts, and resourcing to help you stay grounded in your body, described in Chapter Two.

CONSENT

For Vicki, age 29, early experiences with sex and drugs were wrapped together. The week after she graduated from high school, she and her friends rented a house on the New Jersey shore. "We just got drunk," she says, beginning to describe the experience. "Everyone that I knew would do this. That is the rite of passage that I went through after graduating high school."

At the time, she told herself it was fun, "but I ended up breaking my shoulder, getting a concussion, and being raped all in the same night." She woke up one morning after a blackout, and found that she felt like she'd had sex, but she had no memory of it. Her friends confirmed it, and told her there were pictures taken. "Thank God it was the time when disposable cameras were a thing," she says in reflection, "and people didn't have smartphones. Because if it was a time that smartphones and social media play the role that they do now, I have no idea what would have happened to me. I think it would have been 10,000 times worse."

After it happened, Vicki acted like it was consensual, and tried to pretend it was no big deal. But as she's gotten older, her perspective on what happened has changed. "I would never call him a *rapist*, but that is what he did," she says. "I think that the word rape is so harsh that no one wants to use it. It's such an extreme accusation. But on paper and legally I was raped and therefore he is a rapist. But in my mind, this person that I know and that I have known since kindergarten, can't be a rapist."

While there are many things to say about Vicki's story, one really important thread is about *consent*. Vicki's level of intoxication (she was so drunk that she had blacked out) left her unable to consent to sex. If Vicki and her peers had received adequate education in what consent is all about, they might have made different choices, both during the incident and after—choices that could have left Vicki feeling a deeper sense of health and

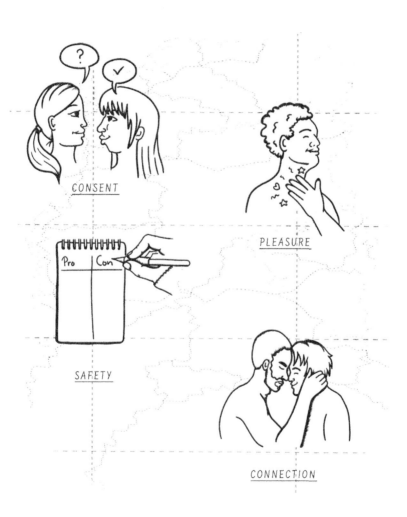

Map of Exploration

sovereignty in her body, and prevented the young man who raped her from being a perpetrator of sexual assault.

Consent is a word increasingly used in classrooms and popular culture, most commonly in reference to sexual encounters. It's been a legal concept for hundreds of years, and a deeply studied and practiced subject in sex-positive and anti-rape circles for decades. Recently, it's become more of a household concept, especially in the aftermath of the #MeToo movement, the social media phenomenon in which thousands, if not millions of people, mostly women and trans/nonbinary folks, have spoken up to say that that they experienced sexual violation. Many public figures, mostly men, have faced public humiliation, loss of their careers, and sometimes legal charges. Questions of consent are finally being addressed (though threatened by a growing backlash).

Understanding consent ensures that you don't violate your own or another's boundaries. Even as notions of consent become more commonplace, we still live in a world where things frequently happen to us without our permission. Sometimes, this is as extreme, or even more violent, than what happened to Vicki. But most of the time it's far subtler, like the person behind you in line touching your shoulder or asking a really personal question. Sometimes it has less to do with someone personally violating space, and has more to do with systems that violate, like the expectation that while in school we'll sit quietly at our desks even when we can't concentrate and our bodies need to move. Whatever the form, most of us regularly receive messages to deny what's happening in our bodies and in our hearts, and submit to the needs and desires of others.

For many of us, this started early on. Part of the natural process of human development includes learning about personal space: where I end and where you begin. The way a child learns about personal space is through a combination of experimenting with asserting their needs and boundaries, and experiencing others doing the same. Ideally, we come to develop a strong awareness of what we want and need for ourselves, while at the same time gaining awareness of the verbal and nonverbal cues that others use to signal what they want and need, as well.

However, in dominant culture, we are frequently taught to override the wants and needs our bodies and emotions are signaling, and to collude with others to do the same. Because so many of us receive this conditioning, we often come to believe that this is normal. This leads to pervasive boundary violations of those around us, in subtle or not-so-subtle ways. By the time folks are in their twenties, they are typically very good at denying messages from their own bodies, and ignoring the nonverbal (and sometimes verbal) cues that others send as well.

As consent becomes a more widely discussed topic, communities are grappling with how to integrate new generational perspectives that are shifting cultural tides, while at the same time preserving meaningful cultural values that have served the communities for generations. "I agree that consent is everything," Nadia, age 27 wrote to me after reading an essay I wrote on consent. "[We] rarely were taught to have choice," she continued, offering a nuanced perspective from her experiences growing up in Madagascar, "and setting boundaries is something really debatable because in my culture for example, choosing boundaries can be a sign of selfishness, which can go against one of our societal values: 'Fihavanana' or the concept of kinship which is a form of solidarity and mutual support."

As a young woman from Madagascar who has been educated abroad, Nadia is grappling with how to honor consent, and honor tradition, and integrate these two perspectives. When I spoke to her three years later, she reflected on her early experiences. "I used to be someone who hardly said no. For me that was a sign of disrespect, and also I was longing for acceptance. I would just say yes because I wanted to be accepted. But inside me it was not right. That's not what I need right now. That's not how I should feel. That's not what I should do."

In her early twenties, Nadia traveled to Boulder, Colorado several times to take part in Surfing the Creative, a movement-based rite of passage developed by Melissa Michaels and the Golden Bridge community (whom I mentioned earlier from my own studies). "During Surfing the Creative, we were given choices. I learned to see in each situation, I would feel ok to say 'yes,' ok to say 'maybe,' and ok to say 'no.' I'm still learning right now. I learned that when you are exposed to different cultures, to different ways of doing things, there's some similarities with other people's way of doing things, but sometimes there are differences."

Nadia's story can remind us that in finding our own ways with consent, we are still in relationship with those around us. So much of what we grapple with around consent is social and cultural. How I exercise my sovereignty impacts others. Yes, I absolutely can, should, and will say no when something doesn't work for me. And, when I have the opportunity to say no in ways that build trust and intimacy with someone, I try to do so.

What about when boundaries are crossed, and consent violations occur? This happens all the time in violent, extreme ways across the globe. It also happens in smaller ways, every day, in the lives of many of us. I look back on friendships, working relationships, and sexual relationships I've had, and I can count dozens of times my no's have been ignored or I haven't felt safe to speak, and dozens of times I haven't tracked carefully enough no's that others have tried or wanted to express. This is where accountability comes in, something we'll talk about toward the end of this book.

Consent violations are often related to power. Like we talked about in the last chapter, there are always power dynamics in any relationship, whether or not they are understood or acknowledged. Power dynamics develop from a range of places, like social locations, roles, verbal skills, charisma and strength of personality, and more. Those with more power typically feel more comfortable encroaching upon the physical, emotional, mental, and spiritual space of those with less power, and those with less power typically feel more comfortable overriding their own needs and desires in order to please others.

For example, those that are socialized as female are typically trained to say yes in attempts to please others, even when something doesn't feel good to them. The peer pressure that can lead to substance use is another example of how one individual (or the power of the group) can cause someone to do something that doesn't feel right to them.

Paying close attention to how we ask for and give consent helps us each become simultaneously empowered and humble.

The root of the word consent literally means "to feel together." This definition speaks to the empathy and partnership required to really know that consent exists in any given situation, paying close attention to the subtle forces playing out for everyone involved.

There is so much power in the spoken word, and so much power in asking permission, even if it's just to put a loving hand on a friend's back while they cry. I've noticed how helpful it is, for example, when someone asks if it's okay before offering words of advice or feedback to me. I can actually feel my body relax and become more open to receive what they have to say when I feel I've had the opportunity to choose. In a world where so many of us have things happen to us (even small, innocent things) that aren't what we actually want, changing the culture to one where we ask can be empowering, even healing.

Engaging deeply in the practice of asking for consent means being open to the possibility that consent will be withheld. To actually ask for consent is vulnerable—it means you might have to drastically alter your plans, and it means you might be sad and disappointed. It's hard to be rejected. Yet supporting others to maintain their boundaries—even when those boundaries are with you!—helps to develop trust and deepen connection in the long run. Besides, engaging with someone who has any level of ambivalence about what's going on is very unsatisfying.

It's a practice to ask for consent, and it's also a practice to encourage others to ask *you* for consent. "Hey, would you mind asking before you touch me?" you might say to someone you work with. "Mostly I don't mind, but sometimes I do, and I appreciate the opportunity to choose." Short and to the point, asking for what you need with those around you can both help you assert your own boundaries, and encourage folks you know to be more conscious in the rest of their lives and relationships, as well.

Many traditions extend the practice beyond the human world, and toward the more-than-human-world, asking permission before entering a place, picking up a rock, or harvesting a plant. This lesson really hit home for me a few years ago, when I was part of a beach cleanup in Hawai'i, at a place called Kamilo Bay. Because of swirling ocean currents, this beautiful stretch of shoreline receives tons of plastic refuse annually from as far away as Japan and the Pacific Northwest of the United States, earning it the sad nickname Trash Beach. Every few months, a local group hosts a beach cleanup. Before folks approach the Bay to remove the garbage, a traditional Hawaiian practitioner offers an *oli* to the place, a chant to ask permission to enter the area. And then the group waits for a sign: perhaps a breeze, or a bird flying over, some sort of indication that the place wants them to be there. It is a powerful and humbling exercise as a Western-socialized person, where permission is dictated by laws, land ownership, permits, and the like, to ask the earth and the beings of a place for permission. It is also great training in the subtleties of consent.

Ultimately, consent is far more than asking before kissing or touching someone. It's a whole way of orienting to the world, a political stance that believes in respecting the sovereignty and dignity in our own being, and in others. It has to do with developing the ability to listen to what is a true "yes," and what is not, and learning how to hear the answer from your own body and heart, from other humans, and from other beings in the world.

Being able to honor our own boundaries, and the boundaries of others, is an important part of being a true adult. While all so-called adults don't necessarily have this skill in our world today because it's so often poorly taught, part of taking responsibility for ourselves, our communities, and current ecological realities means grounding our relations in consent.

> ⚘ EXERCISE: Find someone who you trust to do this exercise with you. Please note that either of you can pause or stop the activity at any time.
>
> Start by standing about 10 feet apart. Put your hands out in front of you, and use hand gestures to signal "come closer," "stop," or "back up," to your partner. As they move, notice what it feels like inside your body, what sensations arise. Pay attention to your breath, and practice maintaining slow, steady, deep breaths. Gesture for them to stop whenever you have the impulse, and then gesture for them to continue to come towards you however close feels

right. You can gesture for them to back up at any point. Notice what happens in your body based on another's approach and proximity.

Now it's your partner's turn to give you cues as you move toward them. Notice what happens in your body as you follow their instructions. How much or little attention are you able to pay toward your sensations while following their lead?

You can experiment with a few variations: doing this activity without hand gestures, with voice instructions, moving toward each other at the same time, engaging more or less eye contact. Keep practicing, noticing the sensations in your body.

Take a few minutes to debrief together. What did you each notice about the physical sensations you were experiencing? Were there differences between your comfort zones? What were your internal cues of what "yes" and "no" felt like for each of you? Were there moments when you overrode those cues, and what did that feel like? This is a very intimate activity! For best results, do this with someone with whom there is not strong desire or attraction (at least at first). This makes it easier to notice subtleties and develop a baseline map for your body's cues without intense charge.

☥ EXERCISE: Over the next few days, pay close attention to your interactions with others, and what you witness in your day-to-day life and in the media. Make note of any instances when you observe or experience folks acting toward another without first gaining permission, or examples of folks taking the time to gain consent before getting in their space (emotional or physical).

❡**EXERCISE**: Practice operating from the perspective that all beings have choice and agency—everything you come into contact with, from your friend, to your friend's dog, to the salad greens on your dinner plate.

To begin, go out into nature and seek out a plant that you find interesting. Approach the plant with curiosity. Introduce yourself and share why you chose them. Ask for permission to approach and touch. Then wait for a response, and act according to the response you sense.

Experiment with this. Ask a number of different trees, plants, or rocks if you can touch them, sit next to them, pick them. Track what you notice inside and outside of your body, and look for patterns. What does "yes" feel like? What does "no" feel like? When you are done, express gratitude to the being you've approached, for sharing this moment with you.

Often, I experience a lightening in my chest and upper body when something is a "yes." I feel a constriction, heaviness, and downward pressure when something feels like a "no." Other people experience other bodily cues. Some folks look to cues in nature, like a breeze picking up or a call of a bird.

When you practice, move very slowly. Notice the distractions that make it more difficult to observe consent when words are taken away. If you've never done this before, it might seem really silly or awkward at first, or impossibly difficult. It's actually a very common practice and any of us can do it with time and practice. Most cultures around the globe understand that all beings have their own sovereignty and dignity and that it is possible to communicate with them. There is a very different feeling when you engage with non-human nature in this way. It's a powerful exercise about what consent actually *feels* like.

A word of *caution*—please DON'T start going around experimenting with nonverbal consent with other humans, unless you have established an agreement with them to do so.

PLEASURE

Gretchen began working with Planned Parenthood and advocating for sexual health and education when she was 14. Throughout her teens, she sought out information, peer groups, and opportunities to help foster a culture of empowerment regarding sexuality. Now 26, she observes that "sexual well-being" is a theme that has persisted since these teen experiences. She says, "I have created and told a confident story about my practice and expression of sexuality and relationship with myself and other people."

This past year, Gretchen uncovered a new layer of herself as a sexual being. In particular, she recently noticed that her understanding of pleasure is evolving: "Not long ago I would have said that pleasure is most accurately used in a sexual context," she says. "I would now say that in addition to intimate, romantic, and sexual situations, I experience similar feelings of pleasure in activities like dance, running, rock climbing, eating certain foods, music, and other immersive situations.

"I also see a pattern in my past stories of "doing things" that I thought, or that even my culture told me, were pleasurable. However, many of my feelings were not specifically pleasure but more feelings of unfamiliarity, exploration, and curiosity. The more I labeled the array of these new feelings as pleasure the more that I lost the understanding of what pleasure actually felt like. Not being able to recognize pleasure led me to performing, acting, or even mislabeling other feelings to imposter feelings of pleasure internally and externally.

Recently, I am realizing that by understanding and articulating my needs and desires, I can create situations that allow me to just be in states of pleasure. Without the effort of so much experimenting, I am able to pay more attention to the unique feeling of pleasure. What distinguishes it from other feelings? What is pleasure of the mind, body, heart, spirit and soul? What is embodied pleasure? What is holistic pleasure? What is mutual pleasure? If I can exist comfortably with my needs met and my desires honored, I allow myself to be able to be pleasured!

It almost makes me feel shy to expose that I am realizing all of this as a 26 year old! Shouldn't I have learned this as a teenager? It makes me curious to explore how other people in my life relate to pleasure! Do other people have an inauthentic, or partial understanding of pleasure? How is our culture influencing us to lose, or to repress pleasure? So many questions are alive for me right now!"

As Gretchen's story of her sexual unfolding highlights, one of the great gifts of sexuality is that it provides opportunities to experience pleasure. This is true of what intoxicating substances can do for us, as well. Pleasure comes from being deeply engaged in an experience often rooted in our bodies. Touch, taste, smell, sight, hearing—our senses are the portals of pleasure that our human bodies contain. Certain chemicals our body produces like dopamine and oxytocin (not to be confused with the highly addictive drug oxycontin) heighten our experience of pleasure. These chemicals can be released by our bodies naturally, or can be ingested.

It is both a gift and a challenge to be a human in a physical body. Our bodies are vulnerable, and can experience pain and limitations. They are also able to experience sensual pleasure in ways that can be hard to see as anything but a gift from God, or the gods, or whatever mysterious force may exist for you in the spirit realms!

But over the past several thousand years in the Western world, sensual pleasure has often not been seen as a gift from beyond but rather a sign of our fundamental immorality as humans, a force to be overcome. The separation of the body from the mind, where the body is seen as the house of carnal desire that needs to be overcome by the intellect, still deeply impacts our lives today. For example, most of us do not receive an education in what pleasure actually feels like as children. Because pleasure is seen as being connected to sex, drugs, and other taboo acts, it's not something that many parents talk about with their children, or that is talked about in school. While children naturally explore and follow the pleasure they experience in their bodies, they are rarely offered the context and vocabulary to understand and share what brings them pleasure and what doesn't. Children's budding sexuality is definitely taboo. So we grow up and enter into adolescence and young adulthood—a time of experimentation with our peers—without adequate context, understanding, language, or mentorship.

We typically fear that which we don't understand. And when we feel fear, we often react with attempts to control or suppress. Since we don't understand pleasure as a culture, we try to control or suppress it. We drive our innate human birthright to experience sensual pleasure into the shadows.

These are the underlying conditions that have created a world that simultaneously encourages excess in eating, drinking, sexuality, and other sensual experiences, and then shames us about these experiences. A consequence of this strange hypocrisy is an inner conflict which often causes us to dissociate, cutting off part of ourselves from our physical experience. When we disconnect our hearts and/or minds from our bodies, we then lose access to our actual bodily cues about what we're experiencing.

The root of the word *pleasure* is closely related to the Latin word *placare*, which means, "to soothe, or quiet." The word came to us all the way from our far-distant linguistic ancestors the Indo-Europeans. Based on these early roots of the word, it seems they knew that pleasure is good for us! It is actually physiological; it can be defined, studied, and even measured, as a biological response that promotes health. Some cultures never forgot this.

Author and long-time intimacy educator Betty Martin points out that pleasure serves to regulate our nervous system. She describes how, when something feels pleasant, if you bring your attention to it, the pleasantness grows as you recruit more brain cells to attend to that experience. This engages your parasympathetic nervous system (the part of your nervous system that leads to relaxation). Consequently, things in your body actually begin to shift as you "follow your pleasure." The rate and depth of your breathing, your blood chemistry, your blood pressure, your muscle tone—all these change. Once these changes kick in, you become increasingly receptive to what's happening. As Martin says, you're able to follow the pleasure where it leads.

When she describes this phenomenon, Martin is quick to point out that you cannot *push* pleasure. When you do something because you think you should enjoy it, it actually builds patterns in the opposite direction. Pushing through engages a part of your brain that turns off your ability to relax and settle into the pleasure. Martin says she thinks of it like this: "Imagine a goddess in the forest, holding a lantern. A pleasure goddess. Your job is to go toward her, not tell her she's in the wrong place in the forest."

As you can see, there is a whole science behind pleasure. Just as pleasure releases chemicals in our bodies, the chemicals in our bodies impact our ability to experience pleasure.

One of the most helpful distinctions for me has been exploring the difference between satisfying a craving and experiencing pleasure. When I'm experiencing pleasure, I'm deeply rooted in my physical body and all parts of me are aligned. When I'm satisfying a craving, by contrast, I'm generally disconnecting from my body on some level, and some part of me (physical, emotional, mental, spiritual) is not aligned with what I'm doing.

Food is an easy place to observe this. When I'm satisfying a craving like, I'll admit it, my addiction to jelly beans, I'll eat most of a bag, and really quickly, sometimes almost a handful at a time, and wind up feeling ill at the end of it. But when I allow eating to be about real pleasure, I move much more slowly and consciously. I take the time to savor the flavor and texture of the food on my tongue. I eat only as much as I can truly enjoy. When I stay rooted in my body, I feel satisfied, not sick.

The difference partially has to do with what I'm going for: am I going for a full engagement of my whole being, or am I going for a quick fix of dopamine to be released in my brain? Going for the quick fix is more about satisfying a craving than about

Following the Pleasure Goddess as described by Dr. Betty Martin

SEX, DRUGS, AND THE BRAIN

The adolescent brain is uniquely wired for novelty, adventure-seeking, and seeking connection with peers. High-intensity experiences like sex and drugs provide this ready stimulation. What exactly is happening?

The secret is in our brain, where neurotransmitters fire impulses to other nerve cells, creating brain connections which then lead to thoughts, feelings, and actions. Different neurotransmitters are made from different amino acids, and they lead to different emotional and physical states. For example, dopamine causes pleasure, motivation, euphoria, and alertness. It's commonly released when we fall in love, have sex, and use stimulants like coffee.

Dopamine is great, and it's totally healthy and natural to seek out ways to support its release. But because of the changes happening in the brain like *myelination* and pruning, high-stimulus behaviors can become wired in, making it more difficult to release adequate dopamine through lower-intensity experiences. This is why many young people who use pornography find that they become unable to experience arousal in flesh-and-blood contexts. In addition to hard-wiring habits, many substances deplete our natural ability to release certain neurotransmitters, which leads to physical addiction.

Since adolescent years are a time of a lowered baseline of dopamine, it's a natural time to seek out easy options to gain a high. But there are lots of ways to stimulate dopamine release! Exercise, listening to music, and proper nutrition all support the release of dopamine at lower levels, in more sustainable ways.

Another important neurotransmitter is serotonin. Where dopamine leads to a "high," serotonin creates feelings of relaxation and well-being. Low levels of serotonin can lead to depression, anxiety, and more. Things that support serotonin release are emotional connection, physical touch, and foods rich in tryptophan, like turkey.

Many pharmaceuticals are also taken to adjust our serotonin levels. High rates of depression, stress, and anxiety among young people have fueled a greedy industry, which has led to an alarming rate of pharmaceutical use. Like illicit drugs and alcohol, pharmaceutical use also wires itself into the brains of children, adolescents, and young adults.

experiencing pleasure. It's what leads to, and then results from, patterns of addiction.

Jelly beans are not the only place where cravings can get in the way of our experience of pleasure. One place where this is a big issue is with pornography. As highly interactive porn has become widely accessible, this has affected the ability of many, particularly boys and young men, to experience genuine pleasure. According to social psychologist Philip Zimbardo, the average boy watches 50 porn clips a week. He points out that our brains and bodies don't understand the difference between making love and watching porn. What they do understand is the biochemical impact of being able to access highly arousing images at any time, that we can change at the click of a button as soon as we grow bored. Zimbardo's conclusion is that "boys' brains are being rewired in a totally new way for change, novelty, excitement, and constant arousal,"* impacting their ability to be aroused and engaged with others in person.

Pleasure is our birthright as humans. It is one of the gifts of having bodies, and is a beautiful thing to move towards and follow. Exploring pleasure has led me to a simple formula for tracking my experience of pleasure:

Sensory Engagement + Speed that allows me to stay present in the moment, and present with other(s) + Alignment between the desires of mind/heart/body = Pleasure

✿ EXERCISE: Choose an activity which you know yourself to enjoy, that engages your senses. Maybe it is preparing a nice meal, or going for a walk outside, snuggling with a friend or family member, or exploring a neighborhood farmer's market. Whatever it is, take some time to, as Betty Martin says, "follow the pleasure." Open up your senses and practice breathing in the experience. Afterwards,

---

*It is unclear how Zimbardo defines boy, but I am assuming male-identified, assigned male at birth. There are other researchers in the field that have challenged Zimbardo's conclusions, but Zimbardo has held fast to his findings; more details and links are available in the comments of the video cited in the endnotes.

spend a few moments in reflection. What did you learn about what brings you pleasure?

✿ EXERCISE: Every day for a week, do something simply because it brings you real pleasure, and take the time to fully relish in the experience. Try different activities each day. Maybe you pick yourself a bouquet of flowers, or listen to a song that you really love, or take a long hot shower.

✿ EXERCISE: Journal on these questions: What is truly pleasing to you? What did you learn about pleasure when you were growing up? How often do you take the time to create pleasurable experiences? What more challenging feelings (like guilt, fear, sadness) come up for you when you think about pleasure, and why? How might you bring more pleasure into your life on a daily basis?

SAFETY

Tim's parents divorced when he was two, mostly due to his mom's alcoholism and drug addiction. He and his brother were raised by his father, a very strict authoritarian. As Tim grew older, he began to experiment with drugs and alcohol, and began to struggle with his own issues of addiction. As he navigated the always-complex time of adolescence, Tim was dealing with really intense stuff, like smoking crack with his mom. He would hide his stash not for fear of being caught by her, but for fear that she would steal it.

Trying to escape his abusive and confusing family dynamics and his own patterns of addiction, and out of a strong sense of duty, Tim joined the Marines when he was 18. But he couldn't escape the hold that drugs and alcohol had on his life, and the models of masculinity he found in the military made it worse. "In the Marines," he says, "drinking was expected and encouraged." Over the course of his service, Tim's alcohol abuse grew worse. When he was two months away from the end of active service, he found himself in jail, dishonorably discharged from the Marines as the result of three DUI's. "It was really hard on me," he says. "I envisioned myself a career Marine. I was going to stay in for 20 years. My alcoholism drove me to the point of dishonoring my service and not being fit for duty. I felt a lot of shame about that for a long time. I still do actually. I think that part of my amends to the Marine Corps is living an honorable life and regardless of whether I am actively enlisted or discharged, still honoring my oath."

Now 29, with several years of recovery under his belt, Tim is deeply reflective about his upbringing and history. "I can't say for sure how exactly it affects me," he says. "But I have a strong feeling that it subconsciously does. Even today, having a relationship with my mom is really strained because of the way that I feel about all those things. And it probably made me aggressive in a lot of circumstances that didn't really require violence, but that was the way that I knew how to handle things and protect myself and the people around me. It probably made me a lot more fearful than if I hadn't been exposed to those situations. Probably made me a lot more selfish."

Maybe your home life growing up was as challenging as Tim's, or perhaps far less intense. Regardless, as we grow into adulthood, each of us have to make choices about how we will and won't explore the worlds of substances, trying to grow up without damaging ourselves or others.

As we've talked about, both sexuality and substances can be healthy, even healing, when used in the right ways, by the right people, at the right time. They are powerful forces, with the capacity to forever change the course of our lives. This can be beautiful, as when sexual touch is offered in a way that it can be deeply received and bring long-term healing to a wounded part of another, or when a plant can be used to alter one's chemistry and bringing healing when nothing else has worked. But these strong powers can also bring trauma and destruction.

How do you find your own path, one that feels true and authentic to you, while keeping yourself and others safe from physical, emotional, and spiritual damage?

Safety is another word that comes to us from an Indo-European root, this one meaning "whole, well-kept." Keeping this definition in mind can be a secret (and sacred) touchstone for you to cut through all the confusing information, and decide what's best for you at any moment. You can ask yourself: "Do I feel reasonably certain that this activity will support my wholeness as a human being?"

Of course, first you have to figure out if you even have the information you need to answer the question! When I took people into the wilderness to climb mountains with Outward Bound, I learned a lot about risk management. One of the things that I learned is there's no such thing as perfectly "safe." Rather than trying to completely eliminate risk, I would ask myself: *Are the consequences of an incident either small or unlikely enough to make the likely rewards worth the risk?* My task as a mountaineering instructor was to weigh the hazards of an activity against the outcomes I was seeking, and then make an educated choice. With the health and well-being of others in my hands, I would make tricky decisions by imagining myself on the stand in a courtroom, explaining to a jury why I made the choices I made. If I felt like even in the worst-case scenario, I could stand behind my decision, I would continue on. If I couldn't, I'd find an alternate activity. Sometimes, the circumstances would change mid-way through an activity, and cause me to reassess.

There are a few things that have to be in place in order to make a risk management assessment. One, you have to have enough information to have an accurate understanding of the hazards and your ability to manage them. Two, you have to have some experience that can lead you to decide if the gains are worth the risk. Three, you have to prepare.

I'm going to speak frankly here: these tasks are super tough as a young person. There's so much contradictory information that you have to choose what to believe. This can often lead us to seek evidence for what we want to believe, a phenomenon known as *confirmation bias*. I'm sorry to say it, but as a young person you often don't have the life experience to fully and accurately decide if the risks are worth it. And, as a young person you have less experience knowing how much you can trust your own judgment—especially given that altered states of consciousness, including the chemicals released when we are attracted to someone, impact our judgment.

This all puts you in a tricky position, having to make decisions that you're not totally equipped to make yet. A trusted adult or mature peer can help you weigh the consequences of your choices and decide what's best for you.

As you consider your choices, remember that hazards aren't just singular events. Your choices are forming patterns in your brain. There are subtle, ongoing ways your life is shaped by your choices, as happened with me and my drinking. Substances alter your brain chemistry in ways that can make you less able to find both excitement and a sense of peace and relaxation without them. Like we've talked about earlier, in my childhood brain I developed new connections and pathways constantly. But with *pruning* (where the unused synapses begin to thin), and *myelination* (where ones that are used are made stronger and more efficient), my adolescent and young adult substance use literally wired itself in my brain, becoming a habit. Social connection and coping with my emotional world became tied to substance use. Over years and further pruning, this evolved into patterns of addiction.

Like we can learn from our own bodies about pleasure, we can learn from our own bodies about risk, as well. This is a big part of what we choose to consent to, and what we don't—a powerful place to listen to our inner "yes" and "no."

A few questions to ask yourself with any activity:

- Do I feel reasonably confident that I have a full understanding of the risks associated with this activity?

- Do I have the ability to manage the risks sufficiently and/or deal with the consequences? What is my safety net (like a designated driver, or a friend who knows where I am and what I'm doing)?

- Based on previous experiences, how confident am I right now that I have good judgment? Is this the right time, place, and experience to test my judgment?

As you move forward and consider the choices you'll make with substances and with sexuality, you can work on developing

RISK MANAGEMENT INVENTORY

Some Potential Hazards of sex and/or use of mind-altering substances
- Disease
- Addiction / brain patterning
- Bodily harm of self and/or others
- Pregnancy
- Poor decision-making while intoxicated
- Heartbreak
- Loss of trust
- Betrayal of self or others

Some Benefits:
- Sensual pleasure
- Learning new things about the world, excitement and adventure
- Experiencing connection with others, and with the world
- Stress management / relaxation / supporting parasympathetic nervous system

Ways to Mitigate the Risks, and Maximize the Benefits:
- Use physical protection, and educate yourself about physical protection
- Having frank conversations, and don't engage in any activities with people with whom you haven't taken the time to build trust
- Build a community with a shared sense of values and norms, that can hold you and others accountable
- Don't make decisions in the moment; decide beforehand what your limits and boundaries are and stick with them
- Remove yourself from situations if you find that you are not able to consistently maintain set boundaries
- Avoid "mixing medicines"*
- Share everything with a trusted, nonjudgmental mentor

---

*Mixing medicines can refer to the specific interaction between two chemical compounds, or between various spiritual practices. Just as Western medicine warns people to be careful when they take multiple drugs at the same time, because they can have potentially harmful effects when they interact, so too mixing substances, sexuality, and/or various spiritual practices together can create dangerous, unintended consequences. Even just bringing together two ceremonial practices can have unintended effects.

As I gain more skills, it's my responsibility to both address the ways I impacted others, and to care better and better for myself. As you travel around the map of exploration, coming to new levels of understanding and experience around consent, pleasure, safety, and connection, you may find that you, too, need to go back and revisit some of your earlier choices. Here are a couple examples of what this looks like.

UNDERSTANDING VIRGINITY

"My second rite of passage was my first sexual contact with a man. This was really magical because for me it was of course exciting, a next step in life that I did not at all want to just do it somehow, somewhere. So, I invited thirty people. We had snacks and drinks and we danced and we made 'love declarations' to each other. It was a celebration of contact and love. My parents were there. It was also simply a joyful community happening. From that space, we went to a room and we came back and people were still there. It felt like yes from community and back into a community. It felt like somehow an adequate step and felt right. It is how I wanted it. A lot of my friends had an afternoon of celebrating that we are alive and that we love." –Naila, age 21

As you read the above quote from Naila, perhaps you feel a little envious. Or maybe it weirds you out a little, or makes you sad. For myself, hearing her story, I was really struck by the difference between her experience, and my own first time having sex. I wondered what would have been different for me over the next twenty years, if my experience had been more like hers.

Hearing Naila's story made me reflect a lot on the notion of virginity. Benjamin von Mendlesohn, one of the leaders at the Tamera community in Portugal, talks about what a strange phrase "losing virginity" is, and how it places the emphasis on something being lost, given up, through experiencing a sexual encounter with another. Though things have changed quite a lot in many communities over the past centuries, there is still lots of baggage bound up culturally in the notion of virginity. For example, the idea persists that women maintaining sexual "purity" makes them more attractive than having had many sexual partners, and for men there remains the stereotype that they are somehow lacking if they remain virgins beyond a certain age (as per usual, gender liminal folks are left out of the equation altogether).

Whatever your story around virginity is—whether you've had sex or not, whether your first time was fantastic or whether it was assault—our life experiences continue to unfold, and can bring us new insights and healing. The powerful initiatory experiences of sexuality remain available even if we didn't have the opportunity to engage in ways that were conscious and healthy at the outset.

SOBRIETY AS INITIATION

"Culturally, I was initiated in "young adulthood" with drugs and alcohol. However, this was a negative initiation that set my life down a pretty dreary path for a few years. It wasn't until I went to treatment and got sober that my life changed directions for the better. I think this was a positive initiation that allowed me to really connect and step into my authentic self. It was a challenge to be with myself and figure out who I am and who I want to be. With substances there was always a cloud over that person and idea, something preventing me from truly authentically relating to others and myself. I think that is one of the greatest gifts of sobriety and treatment." –Vicki, age 33

Almost invariably, people I meet who have become sober describe it as either one of the most powerful transformative experiences of their lives, or more commonly as the single-most important rite of passage they have gone through.

In each of their cases (as in mine), they reached a point where the life they were living no longer worked. They had to accept a radical letting go of their old lives, leaving behind friends, family, well-developed coping strategies, and leap into a complete unknown. What they found was a powerful process of recovery designed to support their initiatory journey, complete with fellow journeyers, mentors, and elders, and clear steps for how to move forward. There is much to learn from the recovery community about what spiritually-rooted, multi-generational initiation process can look like!

This chapter does not condemn sexual exploration, nor exploration with consciousness-shifting substances. Still, as we've already discussed, in a culture such as ours you are taking risks opening up these doorways for yourself, especially while your brain is still continuing to develop. Part of the work that we need to do in stepping from adolescence into adulthood has to do with addressing our addictions. Addictions, which can take a range of forms from biochemical dependence on substances to subtle habits that we have wired into our developing brains, keep us from exercising our full agency and choice in the world.

As you step forward on your path, a critical step is bringing consciousness to your choices. Allowing yourself to clean up your addictive tendencies (mild, moderate, or severe) and doing what you can to prevent yourself from developing new addictions, is critical—and might wind up being one of the most satisfying, powerful parts of your initiatory journey.

THE PATH FORWARD

"The power to be intimate however you want: it's like the difference between living your life by a rulebook and creating your own thing from the mud. It's so much better." —Dante, age 21

What would it be like to grow up in a culture where sexuality and plant medicines were both seen as sacred healing arts, and where young people grew up learning about them step-by-step ways when they were physically, emotionally, and spiritually prepared?

That's certainly a different world than the one that I grew up in, and likely it's different from the one you're growing up in. Just as our cultures had their rites of passage destroyed or commodified, or willfully gave them up in the process of seeking a better life, so too our relationship with sexuality and substances became distorted and destroyed, and these powerful creative energies festered in the shadow for generations.

In the Online Resources you can find a host of resources to help you be part of the healing. But please remember! Go slowly, at a pace that allows you to be deeply rooted in your body. These are lifelong journeys, and there's no need to get ahead of yourself.

☾

The biggest challenge that I face as a young person today are the questions I have yet to find the answers to. Where do I belong? What does it mean to be Asian American? How can I balance a life of passion with one of purpose? What, truly, can I offer the world that is unique and meaningful? What does it look like to be unique in a world where everything feels like it's been done before, perhaps better than I could ever hope to do it?

—Lauren, age 26

PART II:
CULTIVATING IDENTITY, BELONGING, AND PURPOSE

Chapter Five:

WHO AM I?

"There are details about your identity that you alone will have to discover, and that's what you have come to initiation to find out...a person who lives in denial of who he really is must have a hard time living, because he would have to invent meaning and purpose from the ground up. No one can tell us who we are or how we must live. That knowledge can be found only within." –Malidoma Somé, Dagara Author and Teacher

As I sat against the rock face awaiting my turn, I felt calm and curious. Three days of fasting alone had left me comfortable with time moving slowly, and I was in no rush. As if in a dream, a dark figure emerged from a gap in the boulders, beckoning me toward it. I followed silently. We wound our way through the rocks into a natural amphitheater. Others waited for me there, staring blankly forward. I jutted out my chin fearlessly and strode up to them. Impassively, they watched my approach. I stopped and stood facing them. "What is your name?" one figure seemed to ask. "My name is Darcy Jane Ottey," I said confidently.

As the words tumbled out of my mouth, I immediately regretted them. My birth name couldn't possibly be the *right* answer. I felt like I'd just failed the test.

What followed was excruciating. More questions seemed to follow, invitations for me to express myself. With each inquiry, I felt clumsy, awkward, and wrong. Meanwhile, the mysterious beings looked on, without a trace of warmth. Soon, I found myself slinking back to my solo spot in the desert, trying to reassure myself that it was okay. I spent the last 24 hours of my time alone replaying the scene, feeling foolish.

This experience was a chance to express *who I am*. Name is certainly part of who we are, a key identifier. Other questions were further opportunities to express my deepest self: my essence.

For most of my life, I've been someone who gets things right. I'm a great test-taker, good at learning the right answer and parroting it back. There in the amphitheater, face to face with only mirrors of myself, I lost track of who I was and got totally caught up in trying to be who I thought I should be.

Feeling like there's a "right" answer and a "wrong" answer is part of my personal challenge in understanding who I am, and authentically being that person. Each of us has our own wounds, challenges, and coping strategies that make it difficult to identify and express who we are. While we live in a very individual-oriented culture, where we are taught to center our lives around what we will need, feel, and think, we aren't typically given tools to truly make sense of who we are.

By developing a relatively holistic understanding of ourselves, we can step into adulthood with a clear sense of who we are, prepared to navigate successes, disappointments, losses, and transitions with an enduring sense of our individual gifts, talents, missions, and personal purpose. That's what this chapter is about: exploring answers to the BIG question, "Who are you?"

THE BODY

"I have really grown to love my body, to the point where I have written it letters of gratitude for giving me life. My body is a canvas that holds stories and memories in its scars and muscles." –Katheryne, age 26

As humans on this earth, we are, first and foremost, our bodies. We are the fibers and tissue that connect us into solid form. We are the synapses that fire through our brains, the behaviors that we instinctually and repeatedly exhibit and therefore become habits. So much of who we think we are comes from the patterns lodged in our bodies: the ways we know to seek pleasure or avoid pain, the traumas we carry around that lead us to confusing reactions.

Our bodies are capable of radical change and transformation. From the moment we are born, we physically evolve, gaining new skills and receiving new limitations. Because our bodies are constantly changing, they teach us that we are not fixed beings. We must constantly adjust how we see ourselves and see the world. This also means that the reflection we're getting back from the world about who we are is constantly changing.

When asked about what life experiences have made her who she is, Dani starts with two simple words: "My hair." When she was 10, Dani began to lose her hair in clumps. She went to the doctor, who diagnosed her with alopecia, brought on by stress. She remembers saying, "I'm 10! I can't be stressed out!" But the truth was, Dani was very stressed. She had suffered significant and ongoing abuse for years, and as far as she can tell, her hair loss was the result of this trauma.

Dani and her mom spent several years looking for cures and treatments for her hair loss, until at age 15 she wound up in the hospital on death's doorstep after an allergic reaction to a medication. "I had a rash over my entire body that acted as a third degree burn, so no one could touch me. I was in so much pain. My liver and spleen were enlarged, twice the size they should have been. While that was happening, all of the hair everywhere on my body fell out."

When she recovered from the allergic reaction, Dani returned home. Soon she had to return to school, which she dreaded because she wasn't sure how to face people without hair. So she got herself a wig. She says, "That was a rite of passage. I had 15% of the hair left on my head, and at that point I chose to shave it, because otherwise it would be uncomfortable. Total hair loss set me on a completely different life journey than I had been on."

That life journey was very painful at first. "I hibernated in my room for almost a whole year," she says, describing the deep depression that overtook her. "I gained 50 pounds. I barely looked in the mirror, and every time I did, I did not know that person, I did not recognize them, and it looked like a monster to me. I was ashamed of myself."

After a year of isolation, Dani began to venture out into the world, but she was a changed person. She disconnected from the friends that had supported her through her hair loss, and began to surround herself with people who did a lot of drugs. "People that would not look me in the eye, or care about my hair, they only were together to kind of congregate around that one substance," is how she describes her social world looking back. "I felt comfortable around them because they didn't care about me." She became addicted to cocaine. Her mother tried to get her to treatment, but she refused to go, choosing instead to live with her father—the man who had abused her as a child.

Now 25, Dani looks back on her hair loss and says, "My hair is really what shaped me." This formative experience has helped her understand the impact of how she looks and relates to her body as a key part of her identity. She says, "Sometimes, when I think of myself, and then look in the mirror, I do not see the person I think I look like."

Dani's story highlights so many powerful things about how deeply our physical body impacts who we are. One is the way that our feeling of attractiveness impacts our identity. Physical appearance is extremely important in dominant culture. Someone who is considered quite beautiful by Western standards is treated differently, for example, than someone who might be considered ordinary-looking. Both of these folks experience day-to-day living differently from someone who has a physical disfigurement where other people avoid their gaze or stare. Dani's experience walking through the world allows her to intimately experience the way that her physical appearance impacts others, and impacts her own sense of herself. In fact, she describes herself as having two different identities: "I am a Gemini, the twins, and that relates to my relationship with hair. I feel like two different people a lot of the time. I am bald, and I also wear my hair." She grapples for the words to describe the different parts of herself: "Without my hair, I'm around people who I feel really comfortable with. I'm a relaxed and honest person who speaks from the heart and is allowed to be themselves, and kind of play and wonder and feel free. But with my hair on, I'm constricted. I don't go swimming with my hair on, I don't go out in the hot noon sun. But I feel sexier, more alluring, more mysterious, and a side of me comes out that asks a lot of questions and lives a little more on the edge, almost, a little dangerously. My voice maybe even is different when I wear my hair."

Many of us may not experience the dramatic change in our physical appearance that Dani experienced at a young age, nor one that allows us to shape-shift as we walk through the world on a daily basis. Yet for each of us, our sense of who we are is deeply impacted by our bodies. How our bodies look to the outside world, and how they look and feel to us, tremendously impacts our sense of self, our behaviors, the choices available to us, and the choices we make.

If we listen to them, our bodies tell us precious information about how the outside world is shaping us. Dani's story highlights the impact that the trauma she endured had on her body, how it shaped her as she grew toward adulthood. Both her hair loss, and her subsequent descent into cocaine addiction, were connected with suffering abuse and the related un-discharged trauma she carried in her body. This external manifestation of her inward suffering was a powerful survival mechanism that helped her get the help and support she needed.

While Dani's story is unique to her, all of us have brain patterning that impacts our health, well-being, and choices, so much so that we can come to associate our identity with this patterning. "I'm an anxious person," we decide, unaware of the roots of our anxiety and the ways it has become a habit, not an intrinsic characteristic. Tracking what is happening in our physical bodies, and the relationship between our bodies, feelings, and thoughts, is key in encouraging *healthy* patterning and preventing *unhealthy* patterning from setting in. Then, we can make choices to move this energy through physical exercise, safe emotional release, creative expression, and more, so that it doesn't remain stuck in our bodies and continue to impact our health. As we talked about already, the adolescent brain is in the perfect developmental position to establish and reinforce both healthy patterns like regular movement and stress release, and unhealthy patterns like addiction and self-harm. And even if, like me, your brain has long-since finished its adolescence re-wiring, you can consciously build new healthy neural pathways, and leave unhealthy ones behind. In this way, and over time, we can come to be free of characteristics we previously thought were just "who we are."

Of course, it's really important in all this to make your own conscious choices about what healthy and unhealthy mean. We've been conditioned by a society that says that only bodies with a certain percentage of fat on them are healthy, or that there's something bad or wrong with us if we have differences from the norm in how our bodies sense and move. We receive so many messages from society about what our bodies are supposed to look and feel like, it can be challenging to figure out what is really true for you - who you are.

For Dani, consciously embracing her baldness is part of being healthy today: "I'm always trying and pushing myself to be in a little more uncomfortable situation to get used to it because it's been thirteen years, and I'm still talking about how I lost my hair! I'm still trying to get it back. I'm okay with it not coming back, but I still want it. I'm glad it was mine to experience this because it really is a part of who I am. I don't know who I would be without it. It is a part of me and it's also a part of a process I'm still working on."

> ⚘ EXERCISE: Think back to when your body changed at puberty. How did people around you begin to treat you differently? How did this in turn affect how you saw yourself, and how you behaved?

❦ **EXERCISE**: Look at yourself in the mirror (ideally you would do this with a full-length mirror, and without clothes on). Spend time examining your body close in, as well as standing back. Notice how you feel as you look at different parts of yourself, and the different thoughts and judgments that come up. As you do this, consider where those feelings, thoughts, and judgments come from. Whose voices do you hear as you look at your body? Shake out any voices that aren't your own!

As you do this very vulnerable exercise, you may notice tender, even painful, memories and emotions rising to the surface. This is a time to practice self-compassion and lots of self-love.

❦ **EXERCISE**: Put on one of your favorite songs. Begin to move your body slowly, paying close attention to the physical sensations inside your body. Do what I learned from my embodiment teacher and Golden Bridge founder Melissa Michaels, called a "body part dance." Beginning with your feet, move up your body allowing all of your "parts," hips, shoulders, hands, to follow the rhythm of the music or natural impulses arising from within. Notice where you feel stuck, what parts move easily. What parts feel collapsed, potent, alive? Ask your body: what do you have to teach me? Listen carefully for any sensations, feelings, thoughts, or images that emerge.

❦ **EXERCISE**: Write a love poem to your body, or create another artistic expression dedicated to your own beauty. Take time to offer appreciation for specific aspects of your physicality: how you look and feel; what you can do; your scars, wounds, and limitations; and anything else that your body offers to you.

THE SELF

"I think it has always been hard for me to express and share my deeper emotions with others. When I do share, it feels very unnatural, totally out of my comfort zone and foreign to me. After those moments of vulnerability, I feel a lot of uncertainty, and even shame, insecurity and loneliness. I have often found it easier to connect with strangers. A part of this I think is because there are no preconceived judgments, no boxes and no titles attached to their conception of me." –Cara, age 22

A huge part of who we are as humans is our sense of self. Thousands of books have been written on this subject; it's a lot of what the field of psychology is devoted to studying. Psychologists distinguish the Self from the self. The Self is the biggest conception of who we are—basically what this chapter is about in its entirety. Though many of us often confuse the two, the self is a much smaller part of who we are. It's the part of us that we're usually talking about when we use the word "I" or "me," often called the *ego*. It's the part we know about ourselves, even if we might not understand where it comes from or why it is.

Ego is often kind of a dirty word, but it's a hugely important part of us. It helps us know ourselves and be able to communicate about our needs, wants, gifts, challenges, and more. It helps us to set boundaries and limitations as well as connect and be intimate. Problems come when we get confused that this is *the only* part of who we are, and we use our egos to enact unconscious parts of ourselves in ways that are hurtful to ourselves or others.

A really useful exercise for getting to know the self is the Johari window, developed by Joseph Luft and Harry Ingham in 1955:

The *open area* is the part of ourselves that we share with others, and that we know about ourselves. This includes many of our experiences, opinions, feelings, behavior, skills, or problems. It's our public persona. Our *blank* area* is the part of ourselves that others see, but that we are not aware of. Our *hidden area* is the part of ourselves that we are aware of, but don't want to let

---

*The authors originally called this the "blind" area, and I have changed this to reflect a less ableist perspective.

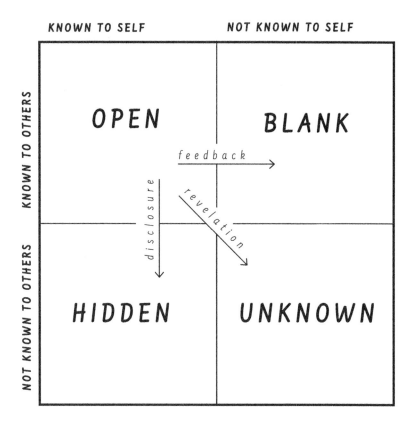

Johari Window Chart

others know about. The *unknown area* includes information that we don't know about ourselves, and others don't know about us either. A large portion of this area is usually common to children or young people, folks who are still in the process of self-discovery and figuring out how to share themselves with others.

What's cool about this model is that what is true about us doesn't remain in a fixed column over time, but might shift and change, through the processes indicated by the arrows in the chart.

OPEN: KNOWN TO SELF, KNOWN TO OTHERS

BLANK: UNKNOWN TO SELF, KNOWN TO OTHERS

HIDDEN: KNOWN TO SELF, UNKNOWN TO OTHERS

UNKNOWN: UNKNOWN TO SELF, UNKNOWN TO OTHERS

Johari Window Illustration

EXERCISE: It's your turn to take stock of your "self," and take a look at the similarities and differences between how you see yourself and how others see you.

1. Draw your own blank Johari Window.

2. Identify a minimum of 6 traits that you possess, from the List of Traits on the next page.

3. Ask at least 2 other people to pick out a minimum of 4 and a maximum of 10 traits from the list that they believe you possess.

4. Things that are on *your* list and *someone else's* list go in the "open" box of the Johari Window.

5. Things that are on *your* list and *no one else's* list go in the "hidden" box of the Johari Window.

6. Things that are on *someone else's* list and not on *your* list go in the "blank" box of the Johari Window.

7. A few things that are on none of the lists are "unknown."

LIST OF TRAITS

able	distant	kind	simple
accepting	dispassionate	knowledgeable	smug
adaptable	dramatic	modest	spiritual
aggressive	dull	moody	sensible
analytical	extroverted	needy	sentimental
angry	fair	negative	shy
anxious	friendly	nervous	silly
arrogant	fearless	observant	smart
assertive	fearful	organized	sneaky
awkward	flexible	patient	spontaneous
bold	goofy	powerful	sympathetic
brave	giving	proud	strong
calm	happy	quiet	tense
caring	harsh	reflective	thoughtful
charismatic	helpful	relaxed	timid
cheerful	humorous	religious	trustworthy
chaotic	hostile	responsive	unaware
childish	idealistic	sarcastic	unethical
clever	imaginative	searching	unhappy
clumsy	impatient	self-conscious	unhelpful
cold	indifferent	needy	unimaginative
complex	incompetent	panicky	unreliable
confident	inflexible	passionate	vulgar
confrontational	independent	passive	warm
considerate	ingenious	perceptive	weak
compassionate	insecure	playful	whimsical
courageous	insensitive	predictable	wild
creative	intolerant	proud	wise
critical	intense	sad	withdrawn
cynical	intelligent	selfish	witty
daring	introverted	self-centered	
dependable	irresponsible	self-conscious	
dignified	judgmental	shy	

❦ **EXERCISE**: Reflect on the following questions:

What qualities currently in the "hidden" box might you want to share with others? What qualities currently in the "blank" box might you feel ready to claim? What qualities in the "unknown" box do you feel ready to explore?

SOUL

"My soul loves colors and landscapes and wilderness. My soul sees the radical interconnectedness cosmic balance of things that there's no escaping life or death and paradox, and is ready to live in the contradictions, confusion, mystery, challenge, difficulty, questions, and the deep, deep longing and desire to be who I can be and give back/pay forward this incredible gift of being alive. My soul loves this land, Olympic mountains, Salish sea, misty days and rainbows." –Cameron, age 29

Several days into a very intense gathering that had left me emotionally drained, I took my seat in the council, waiting for things to begin. An older Hawaiian woman named Puanani Burgess took the seat next to me, a gentle, open expression on her face. Self-conscious of my tear-stained cheeks, I introduced myself. She asked me what I did for work. As I answered, I spoke with a catch in my throat, close to tears even in the midst of this simple conversation.

"You know what you are? You're like a salmon swimming upstream," she said. "Do you know how salmon swim upstream?" I responded I wasn't sure. She informed me that when salmon swim upstream, they turn their bellies into the current and take the full force of the stream right on their most vulnerable spot.

"That is like you," she said. "You're like a salmon swimming upstream, taking the full force of the river right on your tender belly." By the time she finished speaking, I was bawling. When I gathered myself together, I asked her what she did. "That is what I do," she replied. "I see people's gifts and reflect their gifts back to them." This brief five-minute encounter changed how I've seen myself ever since. Burgess' words, rich in metaphor from nature, spoke to me deeply.

Salmon are the lifeblood of the ecosystem I call home. Their spawned-out carcasses provide nutrients to feed the rivers and the large carnivores that prowl the banks of the rivers which in turn feed the forests. The life of a salmon is not easy. Soon after they hatch in a creek or riverbed, they leave their nest for food, making their way downstream. With no elders to guide them, they follow their instincts and the ancestral messages encoded in their DNA on their journey toward the ocean, undergoing bodily changes to prepare them for the open sea. Salmon grow and mature during their time in the ocean, sometimes migrating great distances. When they are fully mature, they make their way back to the place of their birth, swimming back upstream to reproduce and then to die.

Burgess gave me words to understand many things about myself. Her image of a salmon swimming upstream connected with my commitment to living life from a place of deep vulnerability. It gave me poetic language from nature to understand why it is so important for me to explore my role as a white-skinned person in the Western world today, committed to exposing the underbelly of being white in a society built on the backbone of colonialism, genocide, and slavery.

What this wise woman saw and reflected back was an image of my soul. *Soul* typically refers to a deep part of ourselves, a part that many spiritual traditions believe existed before our bodies did and continues after death. The word has its origins in "coming from the sea" or "coming from a lake," places of transition between the living and dead among ancient European tribes.

While our self and our body are always changing, *soul* is not. Still, images of soul continue to reveal themselves over time, getting richer and richer as we go. Years after my encounter with Puanani Burgess, I learned that salmon turn their bellies into the current because it loosens their egg sacs so that they can deposit their eggs. I take guidance, comfort, and direction from this story of salmon. It describes a stance of living from a place of vulnerability, and knowing that one's gifts come forward directly due to this vulnerability.

The image helps me stay focused even in times of difficulty, which is one thing exploring the mysteries of one's soul can offer.

Yet where uncovering the self can lend itself to an inventory like the Johari Window, the soul is very different. It remains on the edge of our senses, revealed not in checklists but in landscape, poetry, dreams, art, myth.

I've come to think of soul as something to be tended, much like a fire. If we don't tend our fire, soon it goes out. Its warmth and light diminish, and the world goes cold and dark. *Tend* comes from the same Latin root as attend, attention, and intention, and means "to stretch." When we tend our souls, we stretch ourselves into new places. We stretch our capacity for love, for hope, for faith. We stretch our capacity to be fully human, fully ourselves, and to live from this place.

Our souls cannot keep up with the modern world. Bruised by the constant jostling chaos, our inner callings retreat, waiting for still, quiet moments where we look up, take a breath, and notice what's around us. Slow down. As Hannah, age 25, says, "My soul strives for genuine human connection and community with nature."

"The soul is like a wild animal— tough, resilient, savvy, self-sufficient and yet exceedingly shy. If we want to see a wild animal, the last thing we should do is to go crashing through the woods, shouting for the creature to come out. But if we are willing to walk quietly into the woods and sit silently for an hour or two at the base of a tree, the creature we are waiting for may well emerge, and out of the corner of an eye we will catch a glimpse of the precious wildness we seek."

–Quaker Author and Activist Parker J. Palmer

In this day and age, to steadfastly follow the yearnings of your soul is a revolutionary act. It can be challenging to spend the evening writing poetry rather than go to a big party, or wander the shoreline combing for treasures instead of binge-watching the latest season of your favorite show, especially when you're exhausted and stressed. There is constant societal pressure to do more, faster and faster, until people burn out and seek relief from mindless, numbing consumption. This is not what we were designed for! This constant information streaming in is a form of violence against our very natures. Thomas Berry says, "In losing our sense of soul, we have trivialized our existence." It's time we listen to the quiet whispers of our souls, and give them more space to be heard. Only here are we able to hear clearly what we are called to do.

This is not necessarily light-hearted, happy work. Tending a fire, we must be careful both to keep it blazing, and to keep it from raging out of control. Fire has a life of its own, and as much as we depend on it for heat and light, as every child learns sooner or later, it can and does burn us. Psychologist Thomas Moore says it beautifully:

"The aim of soul work, therefore, is not adjustment to accepted norms or to an image of the statistically healthy individual. Rather, the goal is a rich elaborated life, connected to society and nature, woven into the culture of family, nation, and globe. The idea is not to be superficially adjusted, but to be profoundly connected in the heart to ancestors and to living brothers and sisters [and siblings] in all the many communities that claim our hearts."

This work is always difficult, yet in a culture that provides little context or doorway for encounters with soul, it can be profoundly dangerous indeed. Still, uncovering and embodying our unique place—our soul—allows us to be the human that only we are capable of being.

> ⚘ EXERCISE: Reflect on what you know already about your own soul. What images from nature, poetry, art, music have been particularly important to you over time? Free write, create a collage out of magazine images, draw pictures, or find other ways to gather and express parts of the world that have important meaning for you. Don't worry about it looking good or making sense. Let these expressions collect over a period of days or weeks. Once you are finished, take a step back and reflect on what you've created (or perhaps even share with a friend or mentor). What do you notice? What patterns begin to emerge?

✤ EXERCISE: Write your soul a letter. Tell your soul that you would like to form a relationship, and that you want to listen to their voice. Consider what you might need to give up, in order to hear that quiet voice speak to you.

✤ EXERCISE: Spend an hour a day alone and technology-free for a week. Explore what you're drawn to, without these distractions. I know this is a huge commitment! If you're drawn to this exercise but it feels inaccessible, think about starting smaller and moving toward an hour as a goal.

SOCIAL ROLES

Who we are is not ours alone to define. A huge factor in who we are, and how we see ourselves, relates to the social roles we play in the lives of others and the broader community. Like our bodies grow and change, the roles we play shift as well. Some of these roles have to do with the relationships we have with others (like daughter), and some of them have to do with our function within a community (like being a teacher or a student). All of these are part of our identities, part of who we understand ourselves to be.

Understanding that these roles are fluid and ever-shifting helps us navigate the inevitable changes in life. When my friend's only brother died unexpectedly in a car accident, suddenly she stopped being an older sister, and instead became her parent's only living child. Losing a job, relationship, or community role inevitably requires a shift in identity. This identity shift can be difficult and painful, sometimes equally as painful as the loss of a person or responsibility that we cared about. Our social roles help us to understand who we are. Without them it can feel like we've lost a part of ourselves, and suddenly that we are not enough.

Many people run from losses of social identities for years, even decades. They quickly replace one career with another, or one mate with another, avoiding having to confront the deeper questions of "Who am I?" that come with the loss of a social role.

Identity loss often feels like falling through a trapdoor in the floor. Suddenly a ground that may have felt solid for years and years gives way, and you find yourself falling and don't know where or sometimes even if you'll land! Yet as scary and painful as these losses can be, they help us know ourselves more deeply. Buddhist teacher Pema Chodron says, "Only to the extent that we expose ourselves over and over to annihilation can that which is indestructible be found in us." And she should know; a painful, devastating divorce left her completely unmoored, but ultimately opened the door for her to become one of the most influential Buddhist teachers in the West.

Some of the roles we find ourselves in may not be roles that we want. They may feel foisted upon us by our parents, peers, adults, or society at large. Sometimes, the labels that come with the roles have come to mean some unpleasant things. For example, many folks I work with in their twenties do not want to be considered adults. Adulthood for them has come to mean a life filled with drudgery, mind-numbing work at a job they don't like, and just the next step toward getting old.

It's important to pull back society's understanding of social roles, and consider what might be deeper and more significant behind it. Adulthood can also mean one who is fully prepared to bring forth their unique gifts in service to their community, in the way that only they can. This is an honorable and important social role.

> ⚘ EXERCISE: Reflect on the roles you occupy in your social world. Which of these roles are satisfying? Which of these roles do you feel stuck in? What roles do you want to move into, but aren't sure how? These may include:
>
> - Roles in family (child, parent, sibling, etc.)
> - Roles with your community (friend, partner, mentor, mentee, volunteer, etc.)
> - Professional roles (student, worker, etc.)

SOCIAL LOCATIONS

"I identify as a queer woman of color. Depending on the situation, each identity has the power to isolate or empower. I'm constantly wondering which part of my identity will stand out to others on any given day."–Katheryne, age 26

"I feel like there's this expectancy to always know what I'm doing because I'm a straight white male, I've got the easiest path, so why wouldn't I have it all figured out?" –Zachary, age 23

History and culture have given meaning to other key parts of our identity, including skin color, gender, socio-economic status, sexual orientation, immigration status, and a host of other factors. These elements of our identity are sometimes referred to as *social locations*. Trying to make sense of how these elements do and don't define us can be contentious and confusing.

In the last fifty years, overt discrimination by race, gender, and other factors has generally become less and less socially acceptable. What emerged to take its place was the ideal of a level playing field, where everyone stood the same chance regardless of their background. The thought was that if differences were ignored, they would go away. This ideal impacts our social norms, and the way young people have been raised for decades. Folks with more privilege in certain arenas were taught that they are not supposed to notice differences, and they were certainly not supposed to talk about them.

Despite decades of trying, awareness has grown that ignoring differences doesn't work to level the playing field. The disproportionate impacts of COVID on Black and Brown communities, the 2020 uprisings sparked in the aftermath of George Floyd's murder by a police officer, and the troubling trend of increasingly mainstream white nationalist ideology throughout the US and Western Europe have rapidly increased public consciousness about the fact that like it or not, our social locations do impact us in many serious ways.

One simple way to describe these impacts is known as the *Four I's of Oppression*:

- *Ideological oppression* describes the impacts of belief systems that value one group of people over another.

- *Institutional oppression* refers to the ways that an institution (like society as a whole, a workplace, or a school) is structured to benefit some people over others.

- *Interpersonal oppression* refers to the ways in which one person from a dominant group puts down or dismisses someone from a less-privileged group.

- Finally, *internalized oppression* refers to the ways that an individual from a less-privileged group comes to believe that they are less valuable. *Internalized privilege* is the flip side of internalized oppression, and refers to the way an individual from a more privileged group comes to believe that they are entitled to certain benefits.

Study after study backs up the persistent impact of these types of oppression. Of course, people who experience oppression every day don't need studies to prove these types of oppression exist; evidence is there for every Black person who feels fear when they are pulled over by police, every young trans person affected by laws undermining LGBTQIA+ rights, every Indigenous person struggling to protect land and water while seeing nearby white communities remain unaffected, and countless other examples.

Yet even with all of the evidence, and even with awareness growing, change comes painfully slowly. Because it's woven deeply into our worldviews, social structures, interactions with others, and ways of thinking and feeling, oppression can be very difficult to root out. As humans, we are hardwired to observe patterns, to make meaning out of them, and to build systems that reinforce them.

The ways that we see each other includes noticing differences like skin color, accent, and gender. These characteristics come with a whole set of stereotypes that become deeply ingrained over the course of our lives, regardless of what we consciously believe. This is known as *unconscious* or *implicit bias*; you've likely heard of this.

Here's the truth: we're going to notice differences no matter what. Our brains are designed for this. And differences have a deep impact on our lives, so it's important that we do notice them. In order to move toward equity, justice, and unity, one of our tasks at this stage is to make conscious and acknowledge our social identities, and healthily incorporate them into our sense of who we are in the world. Our social identities can then become empowering, giving clues to our unique social responsibilities at this particular moment in our cultural history. This is in contrast to saying there are innate differences, like men are smarter and that's why they perform better on tests. That route has produced some truly awful results. It's saying instead that there are huge differences in how men, women, and gender non-binary people are raised and treated, and therefore they face different challenges and opportunities, which in turn gives them different perspectives and roles in addressing issues related to building healthy culture, with equity and justice.

Coming to recognize the ways that oppression shows up in ourselves, between each other, in social structures, and in our worldviews is critical, and it takes time. It is also a necessary prerequisite to a world where our social locations do not inform our identities in the same problematic ways they do now.

The first step in doing this is unpacking the impacts of our various social locations on who we are.

GENDER

"Maybe men don't name or speak of that as much, but there's a lot of pressure to live up to all kinds of ideas of being 'man enough' for this or that. There's part of me that's fascinated by gender and how I'm living into that, and there's definitely a part of me that sort of hid from the question for a while." –Cameron, age 29

"I am queer. I am trans. I am non-binary. I am pansexual. I am liminal. I am constantly coming out of the boxes I've been socialized into. I wouldn't want to live any other way. Queerness is non-linear. Queerness

is liberation. Queerness is home....reverence and respect for ALL the queer stories and experiences." —Clement, age 36

"Being a woman is the most important social identity that I have. I am quite proud to be a woman and everything that we have gone through, or past generations have gone through and have made us who we are today. I can kind of feel my ancestors, my female ancestors. And my mom tells stories and it feels quite powerful because as a woman I feel as though we have gone through more than men have and are just coming out the other side." —Kathleen, age 19

Gender has a powerful influence on how we see ourselves and how others see us. For many of us, gender conditioning begins in utero, when parents are informed of sex organs. Studies have found that from birth, babies are treated differently based on their genitalia.* Those perceived as girls are held more frequently, given more nurturing and care, while those perceived as boys receive less affection from the very beginning of their lives. Different social conditioning by gender continues throughout our development, impacting us in both conscious and unconscious ways.

The way that gender has been understood in recent centuries in Western culture is not the only option. Before contact with European cultures, many Indigenous cultures held different roles and responsibilities for certain genders (and often still do today), none of which were valued or respected more or less than each other. This has included roles for folks living beyond the gender binary, who often held (and hold) venerated positions connected with tending to the spiritual needs of the community.

Gender equality, sexual and reproductive freedom, and acceptance of homosexuality and gender non-conformity ended in Western culture during the times of the European Witch Trials. There had been increasing challenges to these rights for some time, but this time of terror (often referred to as "the Burning Times", and manufactured by the elite in order to consolidate wealth and drive the shift toward capitalism), took healthy gender

---

*It's important to note from the outset that the biological basis of sex is much more limited than dominant culture discloses. The scientific bases for sex (things like size/type of genitalia, X vs Y chromosomes, and hormone levels) vary far more within the human population than most of us learn in sex ed class.

expression and sexuality out of the hands of individuals themselves and put the authority in the hands of the Church and state.

As you probably know, understandings of gender are shifting rapidly. Driven in large part by young people rejecting mainstream ideas about gender, this is a time where we can make different personal and cultural choices about how to relate to gender, informed by history and tradition but not bound by it. Already in 2016, 81% of Generation Z believe that gender doesn't define a person as much as it used to. This is a time of reclaiming what was taken, lost, and stolen beginning with the Burning Times. How and where this will lead is anybody's guess: perhaps toward more gender diversity, a dissolving of gender, aggressive backlash oriented around gender binary and hierarchy, or some sort of mixture of all three.

What this means for you is likely deeply impacted by how you relate to your own gender as well as where you live and who you're surrounded by. Exploring this terrain is an important part of stepping into adulthood in a conscious, intentional way. Even as our notions about gender change, it offers a powerful lens through which to explore ourselves.

Gender has often been used to stereotype people. Historically, it's been a powerful organizing system for culture, which has often forced people to live in boxes that don't fit them—and then ranked the boxes as superior or inferior to one another. Men have been expected to be masculine, which is associated with being strong and stoic. Women have been expected to be feminine, often associated with being emotional and caring. Nonbinary and gender non-conforming folks have been left out of the equation altogether. How we relate to these boxes is essential work of stepping into adulthood. For some, this means busting out of the boxes entirely. For others, it means finding a way to make them big enough to hold our whole selves.

As we explore new, emerging forms of gender, can we carry forward what is helpful while leaving behind what's hurtful? For example, many people are served by exploring the archetypal energies associated with gender. Remember archetypes from the

A STORY OF GENDER

As a child, Clement moved fluidly between genders, totally at home and comfortable in their body. "So much of my childhood was about being a gender shapeshifter without shame," they wrote recently, reflecting on their early experiences. "I could pass as a boy if I wanted to and I felt power in that. Or I could be a girl if that felt better in the moment. I wasn't a tom boy. I was a boy. I was a girl. And because of that I was living "a third way" of gender. My body felt right before puberty because secondary sex characteristics hadn't arrived yet."

This all began to change when they hit puberty: "Puberty built a huge dam across my authentic flow of gender. I became "a woman" in the eyes of society and no longer had the gift of shapeshifting." Suddenly, Clement found that they had to try to fit in society's boxes—boxes which did not fit them.

When they were in college, Clement came out as a lesbian. It was a hard transition. Clement's family didn't really understand, but after lots of hard conversations, ultimately their family loved and accepted them. An identity as a lesbian worked for Clement, and became core to how they saw themselves and how they were seen by others. Still, there was something missing. Something felt inauthentic. "I found solace in my coming out as a gay woman," they reflect, "especially as a butch gay woman. It satiated me for some time, until my wise child self decided it was time to embrace my true gender."

When I met them, Clement was deep in this self-exploration. As they prepared to take part in a solo ceremony that I was guiding, it became clearer and clearer that part of the ceremony for them was letting go of their gender. "What I am uncovering is someone who is fighting for identity," they wrote at the time. "I have an intense subconscious disconnect with identifying as female. Could I have been fighting this deeper battle within myself while I was busy developing pride and strength identifying as a gay woman?"

That was a number of years ago now. Since then, Clem's identity has shifted from being female, to being "genderless," to being "genderful," and now to being a "queer guide who walks the way

A STORY OF GENDER, CONTINUED

of the third." They have shifted from using she pronouns, to they pronouns, to also using he pronouns as a way of expressing and being seen in their changing, and liminal, understanding of gender. This ever-changing nature of gender, for Clement, is essential to their understanding of who they are: "I am gender variant and fluid in all ways," they posted on Instagram in the summer of 2019. "I am a guardian of others AND for myself. I know where I belong."

A few years ago, Clement embarked upon a major rite of passage in their search for authentic gender identity and expression: gender affirmation surgery, otherwise known as top surgery. "This is a spiritually rooted gender identity initiation for me, and I am so grateful to be held so lovingly by my community." they wrote to their community on Instagram days in the weeks leading up to the surgery. "After 26-ish years with breasts, I am finally ready and have done the necessary work to release them back. No hatred, just love. And the timing is perfect. I'm shedding my skin and emerging again, and again, and again." Reflecting on this continuing, unfolding journey in their life, Clement concludes: "So much of my adult journey with gender is really allowing myself to reconvene with my child self to become whole in my shapeshifting gender."

---

discussion about myth and story in Chapter Two? Archetypes are symbols or motifs that show up in culture that we can explore and draw upon in our lives. There are gifts available to each of us in the masculine, feminine, and liminal (meaning threshold, in-between, often associated with gender fluidity and gender beyond the binary) parts of ourselves. Some qualities we can associate with liminality might be fluidity, adaptability, and being able to hold complexity. Femininity might be associated with nurturing, intuition, and receptivity. Masculinity might be associated with dynamism, being assertive, and being protective. These energies move through people of all genders. While we may strongly identify with one category and exhibit those qualities most readily, it is also true that each of us has the capacity to explore and embody any or all of these.

The Gender Unicorn, Trans Student Educational Resources. The Gender Unicorn is licensed under Creative Commons Licensing; no permission necessary.

Additionally, these energies can be seen as having *immature* and *mature* ways of showing up. For example, mature masculinity can be associated with protective, decisive energy. When I advocate powerfully for myself, for example, I may be channeling mature masculine energy. On the other hand, immature masculinity may look like bullying or using force to exert my will. This is an important area of exploration for us as we step into adulthood. How do we lay down immature and toxic ways of relating to these energies (which is what we typically see in the media and many of the adults around us) and find our way toward maturity? One way is by bringing consciousness and awareness to the terrain.

As you explore these archetypes, please consider the ways they are and are not connected with gender, and take what serves and leave the rest. The important thing is to honor your own wholeness and complexity, while also making space for others.

✾EXERCISE: Place a dot on each line of the gender unicorn graphic, according to your own sense of who you are. Gender *identity* refers to the gender you understand yourself to be internally, regardless of how you present yourself to the world or how other people see you. Gender *expression* describes how you present yourself to the world, and are typically seen by others. Sex *assigned at birth* describes the way that people understood and referred to you when you were born. *Sexually attracted to* refers to your sexual orientation. *Emotionally attracted to* refers to your romantic/emotional orientation, which may or may not match your sexual orientation.

✾EXERCISE: Reflect on the following questions:

- What do you think about the idea of archetypal energies associated with gender?
- What is helpful and what is unhelpful about this way of seeing things?
- How do you relate to this from your own experience?
- How do mature and *immature* forms of these archetypes show up in you, and what have you seen in others that you care about?
- How might you cultivate maturity, especially in the realms where you most strongly identify?

✾EXERCISE: Looking back at all your work in these last two exercises, consider where you have shame and/or judgment of yourself. Where might you need support to cultivate self-love in these domains? Where might you need support to be your best self?

RACE

"I definitely identify as Black, which sucks at times, in different situations. It might be nice to be white, for like a week! Oh man, I would walk in so many corner stores! It would be so good." –Jess, age 20

"I feel like my work as a white person is figuring out how to show up for people of color, whether that's supporting local Black businesses or showing up at a protest against violence towards Asian Americans, and listening, showing my support financially or however I can. A big part of our work is listening, and just kind of being there, and learning. When feelings of guilt and shame come up, I feel icky. I feel dumb, like there's this stuff going on that I was just unaware of. I'll be honest, sometimes I kind of run from it, because it's work and can be overwhelming and scary, and I'm bound to feel bad at times. When I find myself in a more holistic and ready-to-digest things mindset, I try to go at those feelings and emotions, and ask myself questions." –Zachary, age 27

"With my dad, I would see Mexican culture. I would see how it is so important to love your skin when you are Brown and how, at least when I was with my dad, being brown was something that was super uplifted and loved. You know, I had so many beautiful names that made me confident in my own skin." –Gloria, age 22

"I am Maori but I am also European and that is very clear. I identify primarily as Wahine Maori, or Maori woman, but that's kind of shifting as I embrace my gender fluidity more. I identify primarily as that but I am also very aware, and I should be aware, that I am also white presenting, so I need to take that into account. That can be hard sometimes in spaces because, especially in spaces with other Pacific peoples, I would like to be included sometimes and I would like to be read easily. The best I can do is just wait until somebody asks me or until I have the opportunity to present that. That's difficult, but I also know that being the way I am and looking the way that I am affords a lot of privilege." –Serena, age 25

Like gender, our race has a powerful influence on how we see ourselves and how others see us, whether we are conscious of it or not. For most people of color, this is obvious. For many white people, trained to avoid seeing their skin color and that of others so they won't appear "racist," acknowledging race feels divisive and problematic. This is changing a lot, especially among younger folks, but it's still part of the dominant conditioning white people receive.

For hundreds of years, scientists attempted to justify a system of hierarchy that placed white-skinned people at the top through manipulating studies of biological differences. The most famous studies related to brain size. These studies have been universally disproven. Biologically, there is more genetic difference within a so-called race than between races. As Ta Nahesi Coates says in his open letter to his son, published as the book *Between the World and Me*, "Race is the child of racism, not the father."

As it became no longer socially acceptable to overtly discriminate on the basis of race, the culture shifted towards "color blindness." The idea was that if we just didn't notice race, racism would go away. Yet as #SayHerName, Black Lives Matter, and other movements have pointed out, justice isn't color-blind. Even though it is 100% clear that race has no biological basis in reality, it is equally true that race is a powerful social force, impacting each of our lives in different ways and to different degrees around the globe. For example, as I write this weeks after Russia first waged war on Ukraine and as millions of refugees flee for their lives, reports are emerging of the different treatment Ukrainian refugees are receiving compared to Black and Brown refugees. At the Polish border, White people from Ukraine are met with warm welcomes and open arms while Black people from Sudan are beaten and refused entry.

Finding our way into healthier futures requires each of us to understand our own racial identity, how it impacts our experiences and understandings of the world, and the responsibilities that come with that set of experiences. This is part of growing into mature adulthood. As Interdisciplinary Studies professor Ramon Parish puts it, "I could not express and embody what was trying to come through my soul without acknowledging that I am a Black human being alive at this time in the world." Developing maturity when it comes to race means unpacking dynamics of internalized privilege and internalized oppression, and cultivating the resilience needed to support liberation, justice, and healing for all. This work looks different depending on our racial identity.

❖ **EXERCISE**: Reflect on the following questions:

- How has race impacted your sense of self or the way you see your place in the world?
- What gifts and benefits come along with being the race you are?
- What challenges or limitations come along with being the race you are?
- As you move into adulthood, what might be some unique responsibilities you have as a person of your race? How do you want to relate to this?

CLASS

"When I was in high school, my dad got a convertible Mercedes Benz. He'd drop me off at school and pick me up every once in a while. I was so embarrassed at the idea of being seen as this rich white kid. The reality is that there's a guilt and shame that's been woven in, that's probably just a background reality for me. I've also been curious about the sort of shadow of privilege, the impoverishment side of privilege or affluence: the kind of personal distance in my family…and the lack of connection to culture, conscious ancestral culture and heritage. In the culture I'm from, people have an identity based on certain kinds of intelligence and social positioning, privilege, resources, where you go on vacation, stuff like that." –Cameron, age 29

One thing that I noticed in high school was the lack of resources and the lack of jobs, which in my community meant that the parents were our rock because they were sacrificing a lot to work hard and support their families. If my friends and I traveled, it was to local places and the majority of us would not pay the fares because we could not afford to. We got citations for it, but we were just trying to get to the beach. A lot of young people never went out of their communities even though LA is big. That is one of the things I noticed, is that a lot of young people never went to the Beach, or other parts of the city unless you are from that area. Thinking about going on a hike, visiting museums or having healthy activities outside of school was not something I experienced as a young person. We are all so segregated. But really like there is nothing to do. When the summer came, there was nothing to do. We could walk to the library but the only libraries in South Central are so under-resourced that there are not a lot of books *and you would have to make a request to get a book from downtown which is the Central Library. The fact that there is nothing to do, unless you are getting in trouble and then finding a resource speaks volumes about LA County's priorities for youth.* –Gloria, age 22

Like gender and race, our socioeconomic class status has a powerful influence on how we see ourselves, how others see us, and how we relate to the world. The influences of class are often ignored, downplayed, or rendered invisible in dominant society, yet they impact us on a daily basis. In making sense of who you are, looking at your class background and how that's shaped and influenced you is an important piece of the puzzle. Understanding this can help you step into adulthood, both taking responsibility for building a world that works for all, while also understanding some of the impacts of your upbringing so you can make conscious choices for how to navigate adult responsibilities.

First, a definition: class is a social system that divides people based on jobs, wealth, resources, education, influence, and power. Like the other social locations we have explored, socioeconomic class divides people up into boxes and categories that impact us in all sorts of ways. Poor and working class people, for example, may be limited in their access to secure housing and educational opportunities. Yet within poor and working-class communities, there may be greater access to intergenerational community and social cohesion.

Class deeply impacts the daily realities people experience, as well as the cultural context of some of our beliefs and values. For example, as someone who was raised largely middle class it has been eye-opening for me to reflect on how deeply conditioned I am towards the value of independence—that my accomplishments are my own, they are measured in certain ways, and that the fruits of my labor belong to me. Given that part of adulthood is about surviving economically, understanding at least a bit about the impacts of our class backgrounds and orientations can help us make more conscious choices around values, priorities, and behaviors.

As with race and gender, life is more complicated than the boxes we are offered. Class status can and often does change over a lifetime, through education, employment loss or gain, relationships, and more. If you have grown up with caregivers that have had significant class shifts over time and/or have different class backgrounds themselves, this will likely impact the ways that you interact with the world. Also, larger cultural shifts (like successful organizing efforts by the working class) have led to changes in broad patterns.

☙ EXERCISE: Take a look at the Breakdown of Class Characteristics on Resource Generation's website.

As best as you can, identify your own class background. Is it the same of different than what you thought?

☙ EXERCISE: Reflect on the Following Questions:

- How has class impacted your sense of self or the way you see your place in the world?
- What gifts and benefits come along with your class background?
- What challenges or limitations come along with your class background?
- As you move into adulthood, what might be some unique responsibilities you have as a person with your class background? How do you want to relate to this?

OTHER ELEMENTS OF SOCIAL LOCATION

"My mom is undocumented. Some folks are like, 'immigrants are bad, bad immigrants, bad hombre' quoting Donald Trump. It's impacting me like, 'Wow, you really don't know what immigrants actually go through, have you ever thought about it from their shoes?' That's how it's impacting me. Sometimes it's frustrating. I can tell you from personal experience that's not how it is, we're not here to live off the welfare system, we're not here to be rapists, murderers, all those things he says. It gets me really fired up." –Kay, age 17

There are dozens of other elements of social location that can impact our identities, like sexual orientation, age, physical ability, mental health status, learning challenges, and immigration status. These are just a few of the identities that we assume, or are required to assume, by the world around us. Each of them, whether we benefit from the advantages they may bring or experience additional challenges, impacts how others see us, and how we see ourselves. They help shape us into who we are, bringing unique gifts and challenges for us to walk with for our lives. As we saw on the Social (In)Justice Framework, we can even think about "species" as an element of social location—just think about what being a human offers us around access to power and privilege as compared to animals or plants.

INTERSECTIONALITY

"Another factor that has shaped me is that I have a Black brother, my older brother. Even being aware of the social injustice that is being done and some of the things that he can never relate to me, or some of the things that I can never relate to him, because he is a man and I am a woman and he is Black and I am Salvadorian, there are things that we cannot relate to. But there are things that we can ally and be involved in other movements about social justice and bringing awareness around social justice as well." –Karla, age 19

In addition to the ways each of these social locations affect our identity individually, they also have a compounding effect. This is often referred to as *intersectionality*.

Originally, the term was coined by civil rights advocate and legal scholar Kimberlé Crenshaw to describe the unique challenges that African-American women endure in the workplace, and the ways that anti-discrimination laws consistently benefit white women and Black men (who experience oppression based on race or gender but not both) at the expense of Black women (who experience oppression along both lines). Over time, intersectionality has been more widely adopted to describe the intersections of multiple identities, which have compounding and unique effects.* For example, as a young, Black, gender nonconforming person, Jess faces marginalization based on their gender, age, sexual orientation, and race. All of these factors intersect to give them an experience different from that of a heterosexual Black cisgender women, for example, or a white nonbinary person, or a Black gay cigender male. Similarly, the compounding effect of being a heterosexual white male brings with it an intersection of privileged identities that provide key advantages for Zachary.

Understanding both the ways we experience privilege, and ways we experience marginalization, is critical. When I focus on the ways I have privilege, I can strategically use that privilege to benefit those who are more marginalized, in ways that ultimately also benefit me. For example, efforts for rights of transgender and nonbinary people helps to dismantle the gender-based hierarchy that oppresses cisgender women, as well. At the same time, when I don't speak up about the ways that I am marginalized, I'm allowing those parts of me to be further marginalized and rendered invisible. When I diminish the impact of sexism on my life, I distance myself from the struggles of other women and give tacit permission for unjust treatment. This comes out sideways in behaviors like competing with other women, self-harm, and more.

The balancing act of making space for all the various intersecting social locations we each carry, and understanding how they impact us individually and collectively, is complex. Yet the more that we practice this on our own and with others carrying similar and different experiences than our own, the more that we are able to tease apart who we are from what society puts on us, and join together to make a world that works for all of us.

⚘EXERCISE: Go back to the Social (in)Justice Framework you drew during Chapter Three. See if

---

*Even as the definition of intersectionality extends beyond Crenshaw's original definition in important ways, it's important to remember that, as Crenshaw says, "intersectionality is not primarily about identity, it's about how structures make certain identities the consequence of, and the vehicle for, vulnerability." Understanding these structures can help us to become more sensitive to the ways marginalization in multiple components of one's identity increases the challenge exponentially.

the way you filled it in still feels accurate to you. Are there any additional social locations you'd like to add? How do you relate to this similarly, and differently, from when you worked on it before?

☙ EXERCISE: Using an image from nature (like a garden, landscape, or river), draw a picture of your multiple intersecting social location identities. Consider: what do these identities enable you to do, that others perhaps could not?

CULTURAL IDENTITY

There's a story my spouse, Dave, tells about his grandmother. One day, when he was in his late teens, he told his grandmother that he did not consider himself to be Jewish. In the years since his *bar mitzvah*, he had moved from his mom's house in Cleveland to his more secular father's in the California Bay area. He no longer believed Jewish religious stories or practiced Jewish traditions, except while back home visiting his mom and grandma. When his grandmother heard his pronouncement, she looked him straight in the eye and said, "You'll always be a Jew."

Fast-forward ten years. Dave was again visiting his grandmother, on the heels of an experience that had awakened in him a sense of connection with his lineage and ancestry. He informed his grandmother that he now understood what she meant, that he had come to realize that despite not practicing Jewish cultural or religious traditions, he will still always be a Jew. Again, she looked him straight in the eye. But this time she said, "You're no Jew."

While Dave laughs about the story, it raises a lot of serious questions about cultural belonging. Who gets to define one's cultural identity? Could Dave decide for himself if he's Jewish or not? Did his grandmother get to decide?

And what does it all matter anyway?

Dave rejecting his cultural identity had to have been devastating for his grandmother. A second-generation American whose family fled persecution in Eastern Europe, she grew up in a Jewish neighborhood in New York City, taught from the beginning that family was more important than anything else. She grew up facing anti-Semitism in her neighborhood, fed brutal stories of Jewish persecution along with traditional Jewish foods, understanding exactly how incredible it was that her family had survived after thousands of years of persecution. Now here was her grandson, who thought he could flippantly throw away that lineage just because he wasn't really that into it.

Meanwhile, for Dave, feeling bound to archaic cultural values and traditions was confusing. The traditions seemed irrelevant to his life as a white California teen, spending his free time adventuring in the mountains and hills.

Perhaps in the second encounter, Dave's grandmother felt frustrated: what, her grandson thought he could just pick and choose elements of his ancestry, with no responsibility to the whole? And what must Dave have felt, being told "You're no Jew?" Imagine the implications of being told by your grandmother that you no longer belong to your ancestral people. Then where do you belong?

Maybe you have your own version of this story. Perhaps you've grown up adopted or in a multi-racial family where you don't look like your caregivers or siblings, so you've constantly had to answer questions about how you're all related. Maybe your family's background is different from the dominant culture, perhaps because you come from Indigenous ancestry, or you're the child of immigrants or an immigrant yourself.

Questions of cultural identity have real, practical, sometimes even legal implications. Many Indigenous peoples have rights guaranteed under treaties (and all do under international law), yet colonizing governments have often set the terms for tribal membership without regards to traditional kinship systems. For example, blood quantum (how much of your blood ancestry comes from a particular culture) is frequently a standard under law, even in cultures where membership is traditionally measured through the matrilineal line, and proportion is irrelevant. This has led many Indigenous folks to assert their sovereignty in determining who is part of their community and who is not.

Affirming and transmitting cultural identity has been the crux of initiation into adulthood for countless cultures, and remains relevant today. I like the way these questions are held within the work of the National Rites of Passage Institute, a program specifically devoted to initiation for African-American young people:

Question: Who am I?

Criterion: What values, history, traditions, and cultural precepts do I recognize, respect, and practice?

Question: Am I really who I think I am?

Criterion: To what extent do I have to understand, internalize, employ, and reflect the cultural authenticity of my people?

Question: Am I all I ought to be?

Criterion: To what extent do I possess and consciously apply the enduring cultural standards and meanings which measure the "being" and "becoming" of Black people in terms of our cultural substance and concrete conditions?

For those of us that haven't grown up with a strong sense of cultural belonging, figuring out where we fit in can be very difficult. Micaela, age 25, puts it this way, "I don't feel a strong sense of cultural identity and perhaps that has the largest impact on me. I've always wanted to feel a sense of belonging, in so many aspects of my life, and not having a distinct culture is a part of that. I didn't grow up with cultural traditions or stories. I wish I had."

This quote from Micaela highlights a fairly common experience among people who grow up fitting into the dominant culture: a lack of awareness of the cultural traditions and stories we have grown up with, which typically revolve around consumerism and the accumulation of resources. Generally, positive cultural identity grows from a deeper sense of shared meaning and values than can be found in consumption-oriented culture. If you are like Micaela, the next chapter is designed to aid you in discovering a positive cultural identity. If, on the other hand, you have grown up with a strong, positive sense of cultural identity, the chapter can hopefully provide some additional tools for healing.

WE ARE OUR NICHE

"I feel like my purpose is to speak for those who feel they have no voice. I am an advocate for youth who are waiting for someone to believe in them when they are struggling to believe in themselves." –Katheryne, age 26

"I know my purpose on this earth is to affect the most positive change I can. The gift I have been given for this is my empathetic heart."–Moriah, age 22

The Zulu word *ubuntu* is often translated as "I am because we are." When I learned this years ago, I immediately compared it to the words of Rene Descartes, the so-called father of Western philosophy: "I think therefore I am." The contrast between these two worldviews, summed up in five simple words each, was striking to me.

In the Cartesian worldview, the one typically taught and supported in Western culture, I am my thoughts. My body, soul, emotions, relationships with other people: these do not define me. I am bound and defined only by the limitations of my intellectual and cognitive world.

On a global scale, this orientation is held by a small minority of cultures. Eastern cultures, and Indigenous cultures the world over, generally see the Self as something far broader. Typically, identity is formed through relationships. Who I am is defined by my relationships with those around me, and the qualities, skills, and characteristics I possess, not as stand-alone qualities, but in relation to my community.

That's why when Queer Nature co-founder Pınar Ateş Sinopolous-Lloyd, community organizer Kruti Parekh, and I designed a course weaving social justice and nature connection called *The Ecology of Power and Privilege*, we rooted the course in the ecological concept of *niche*. Niche is a term used in biology, to describe the role or position of an organism within the ecosystem. Different species may inhabit the same niche within different ecosystems. For example, wolves in the mountains of Alaska and sharks in the Pacific Ocean are both apex carnivores in their respective habitats.

There are so many aspects of who we are that we surveyed in this chapter, including our physical bodies; our qualities and characteristics; the roles we inhabit in our families and communities; aspects of our social location like race, class, gender, and more; and our cultural identities. All of them, in the unique mix of us, make up our identities. And this unique mix doesn't exist in a vacuum, but makes sense and exists only in relationship with other beings. Who I am isn't fixed; it evolves and shifts as the system of relationships around me shifts and evolves over time. Figuring out our niche lets us know we have a place, and can give us a sense of what it is that we have to contribute.*

In an intact cultural context, initiation into adulthood would be a time of educating you about the roles you would be playing in the community, roles often prescribed by social position (gender, who your family is, etc). This would also be informed by unique gifts and aptitudes, likely having been observed by family and elders over many years. In Western culture, these social norms are stripped away in favor of individualism, leaving us without shared agreements about who each of us are to be within the broader community. We have to find our own way, yet what options are available to us is deeply informed by the social world.

This leaves us in an awkward position. Social creatures that humans are, perhaps nothing is more significant to well-being than our relationships, and the roles we play in the lives of others. In fact, according to psychologist Dan Siegel, "studies show that the more individualized and isolated our sense of self is, the less happy and less healthy we'll be." As you come to the end of this chapter, take a look around you, at your friends, family, community. Take stock of everything about you: your history, life experiences, where you're from, your gifts, interests, and limitations, your yearnings and passions, your social roles. You inhabit a special place in your community, and without what you have to give, the lives of those around you will be just a little poorer. What is your *niche*, right now, today?

---

*This is similar to how Bill Plotkin talks about our soul as a place. In his most recent book *The Journey of Soul Initiation: A Field Guide for Visionaries, Evolutionaries, and Revolutionaries*, Plotkin uses the phrase "unique ecological niche" to describe "the distinctive role a being plays in sustaining and enhancing life on our planet." (United States: New World Library, 2021). I believe truly finding our unique individual place in the world today requires an understanding that this place is socially situated, in ways deeply influenced by our relative power and privilege.

⚚ **EXERCISE**: A couple of chapters from now, you're going to be asked to create a "statement of intent," to help you concisely articulate who you are, and the transition you are marking in your life. You can begin this process by reviewing your work in this chapter. Go back through the exercises, particularly the ones where you did some writing. Underline words that stick out to you (somewhere between around 5 and 25 words total) as aspects of who you are. These could be parts of you that feel particularly important, curious, mysterious, or edgy. Make a list of all of these words to come back to later.

☾

Chapter Six:

WHO ARE MY PEOPLE AND WHERE DO I COME FROM?

"I am always wondering 'Where did I come from? What about me?' I need to embrace my African origin and my other origins." –Nadia, age 30

The first morning of the Global Passageways conference, I arose early with the other participants and organizers, arriving at Ahalanui Warm Ponds shortly before dawn. There, volcanically-fed hot springs mixed with cool waves coming in from the ocean, creating a still, warm, Olympic-sized natural pool. One by one, members of our group silently submerged themselves. All was still and calm as we drifted in the warm water. Soon, the contingent of Kānaka Maoli (Indigenous Hawaiians) hosts gathered on the rocky berm, waves crashing at their feet. The rest of us followed as they began a traditional *oli* as the sun broke the horizon.

Even with the beauty of that moment, all was not magically idyllic during our week together. The energy of the gathering mirrored the explosive energy of the island, alive with active volcanic forces and constantly weathered by the power of wind and waves. Race, culture, gender, age, background—all were sources of struggle in bringing together more than one hundred people used to taking strong leadership roles in their respective communities. Cultural conflict erupted, to the point where some participants deemed the conference a failure.

The experience was not a failure for me. On the contrary, it was transformative; one of the two most significant and transformative events in my life, with the other being my rite of passage at age 13.

At Global Passageways, I got my first schooling in the complexity of weaving community across diverse lines: Gwich'n, Lakota, Shuar, Diné, Cherokee, African-American, Chicano, Latinx and European-American: these were just some of the cultures represented, all coming together on Hawai'i. We crossed the lifespan, from late teens to elder years, and were professionally diverse, including authors, youth workers, political organizers, nature-based rite of passage guides, and community leaders. All of us shared a common passion for bringing forth healthy young people and healthy communities in a complex, changing world, and a belief that mainstream structures are failing young people. I had the opportunity to meet people whom I had long admired, people whose books I had read in college and whose work was legendary in my world. I was in awe of the ceremonies, the protocols, the teachings. I felt overwhelmed and humbled. I watched, listened, made mistakes, and learned big lessons.

One thing I noticed was that many of the Indigenous people and other People of Color at this gathering were deeply connected with their ancestry. This seemed different than many of the white folks present, and it was definitely different from my experience. As the Kānaka Maoli hosts welcomed us and introduced us to their culture through traditional chants and dances, sharing the lineage of these traditions, I reflected on the lack of songs and stories passed down through the generations in my family.

I listened as Elder Paul Hill, Jr. described his work. Over his career, three generations of young Black men and women had been initiated into their African heritage. It made me reflect on the lack of a clear cultural context within my own work and for the young people whom I guide. I began to realize how essential it is that we each have a sense of ancestral and cultural inheritance.

Before this moment, I had never really considered myself as having a culture, even though as a social scientist I knew I did. Midway through the conference, the question, "Who are my People?" began to ring urgently inside me, demanding an answer.

At this point in human history, we are a migrating global community. Cultures intermix, colonization and imperialism reach tendrils around the whole planet, climate chaos and war drive massive waves of migration, families cross continents, traditions get lost and forgotten.

Meanwhile, we all still deeply need to belong. Who are our People? How do we make sense of where and whom we come from? How do we come to deeply belong to place, when we have no homeland? And how do we do this honestly, when many of our homes are built on stolen land? Is it even possible? These are some of the questions that this chapter will explore.

WHO ARE MY PEOPLE? A QUESTION FOR OUR TIMES

I guess when I think of my People I think of my family and my friends, I think of my extended family. In our family it's not always blood-related. It's the people who have been around in my life for a while, friends that I've been close with, people who have been in my life long enough to the point where I feel that they know how I am and I feel at home with them. –Zachary, age 22

While the question may feel outdated, irrelevant, or even divisive to many in the Western world today, most human beings on this planet know who their people are. "Who are my people?" is asking a question about kinship. Who belongs to me, and to whom do

I belong? Who are the people that I stick by, through thick and thin, and who do I know will be there for me no matter what?

It turns out that the answers to these questions are extremely important, essential to developing a sense of belonging, which in turn is a critical part of mature adulthood. As social animals, hard-wired for connection, we need to belong just like we need food and water. Social isolation literally kills people: studies have shown that it is as dangerous for your health as smoking.

For millennia, rites of passage provided the training ground for folks like you and me to understand where we come from, and our place in community and the natural world. Yet this basic information is part of what we've largely lost with their disappearance. Concerns about violent religious extremism plague political conversations across the globe, but rarely do we recognize that having a place to belong is one of the basic needs driving folks towards extremism.

I began to ask this question of young people I came into contact with. After some warm-up questions, I'd just put it out there: Who are your people?

Think to yourself: What would your answer be?

When I ask, the question is typically met with a pause. People either look confused or begin to stumble for words. Very common answers include "my friends, my family." Another common response is people impacted by the same disadvantages, challenges, or traumas that they have experienced. Sometimes, I hear the reply, "All people are my people."

While heartfelt and genuine, many responses I hear trouble me. Though they may be adequate for children and adolescents, "my friends and my family" is not enough for folks as they move into adulthood. In today's large, interconnected world, we must understand ourselves as part of something larger.

We look out for our People. If we don't feel a sense of connection, of kinship, with others we come into contact with regularly—coworkers, neighbors, fellow students—then we won't look out for one another, or make choices that benefit a broader world. And in a highly mobile society, many of us either live painfully far away from our families of origin, or replace them. For many of us, our families are sources of violence, rejection, and trauma, not refuges of safety and security. This can create an unstable, psychologically vulnerable existence.

But the solution isn't just to jump to the universal, "all people are my people." While this may be true to some extent, it's very difficult to hold the needs of all of humanity in our minds, and to truly live from this place all the time. Holding this sort of broad picture is a lifetime of work, especially for those of us who grew up with Western society's individualism. Remember the term introduced earlier, *spiritual bypass*, used to describe when folks avoid psychologically uncomfortable terrain by going around rather than through it? This is a good example. If I don't know who my people are, whom I belong to and who belongs to me (or don't like those people or what they represent) the question likely brings with it lots of confusion and pain, consciously or unconsciously. Instead of feeling this pain, I avoid it by responding "Everyone!" This type of avoidance strategy may work for a time, but it eventually catches up with us.

Folks that respond that their people are those impacted by the same disadvantages, challenges, or traumas that they have experienced are getting closer to the right-sized frame for early adulthood. Among these groups, we can often get the understanding, belonging, and support we need. As Dante, age 23, describes it, "I feel like an identity that I can hold with pride is queer and that for me is a unifying thing. It almost tells me something about the culture of where somebody's from. I know that we share similar understandings and maybe goals. It feels good to meet somebody that I don't know and I can know that about them and feel that."

As we gain perspective, experience, and healing, our gifts can be readily applied amongst folks that carry similar challenges. I think of how, when I stopped drinking, speaking with other recovering alcoholics was essential to my healing and process of becoming sober.

Yet our disadvantages and struggles are only part of who we are. In answering the question, "Who are my people?" young people I've asked rarely respond by indicating those that have the same advantages and privileges as them. When we cut ourselves off from relating with those with our advantages, we miss an opportunity to use our gifts.

As you continue reading, please take a pause from time to time, and make note of what you're experiencing in your body, and what feelings are coming up for you. Do you notice yourself holding tension in your body? Scrunched shoulders maybe, or a tightened jaw? If so, maybe take a moment to take a deep breath and consciously release the area where you're holding tension. Maybe even get up and stretch. What emotions do you notice arising? What areas of the text bring sadness, anger, resentment, boredom, relief? What questions arise? As best as you can, please note what comes up for you without jumping to analysis or judgment.

THE INNERMOST RING: FAMILY

"I come from a family of loud women. There is so much love between us, and we express it through booming laughter and celebration. And yet, while we encourage our minds and spirits to grow, we endeavor to make our bodies shrink. My grandmother, mother and older sister suffer from eating disorders and too-often debilitating anxiety. I often find the seeds of their conditions planted in my own body. When my sister was at her sickest, I, too, lost weight. Skipped meals and double workouts became normal. I was proud when people remarked on my thinness, and it fueled my misconceptions. The rings I wore, gifted to me by my grandparents, no longer settled on my fingers, instead sliding off should I even wave my hand." –Meggie, age 27

For many people, family is undeniably a huge part of the answer to the question "Who are my People?" This family can be the family of origin, or "chosen family." For better or worse, family of origin, the people who raised us and were raised with us, have a deep and foundational impact on so much of who we are, including the ways we express and experience love and affection, our emotional reactions and expressions, and the ways we understand and engage with the world. We are not bound by our early childhood experiences, but we are certainly deeply impacted by them. No matter how far away from them we choose to live!

For some of us, our families can be powerful sources of support and inspiration. Gloria, age 22, speaks about her mother's migration to the US from Guatemala. She says, "I have tried to ask my mom, 'How was it when you had to migrate from your country?

When you had to experience many atrocities? And how did you overcome the emotions that this journey created for you?'" That her mother went through this experience in search of a better life for her and her family is a source of strength for Gloria. " To come to a different country," she reflects, "many people wouldn't be able to do that. Which makes my mom a sacred warrior and special."

> "You chose to be born within a particular family because that made your purpose easier to fulfill."
>
> –Dagara Author and Teacher Malidoma Somé

For many of us, our families of origin are sites of deep pain, not at all places of belonging. The trauma and social conditioning that our caregivers or siblings received can easily be transmitted to us, and cycles of suffering are perpetuated. For many people, the healthy choice is to seriously limit, and sometimes completely cease, being in relationship with people that have harmed us, especially if those people are not presently capable of taking accountability for their actions and changing their behavior, and the family system isn't capable of providing safety and accountability either.

For many, embracing "chosen family" to provide the belonging we need can be a huge step toward taking adult responsibility for our lives. Serena puts it this way: "Practice gentle love in every safe space that you can. Practice chosen family. Find people who love you for who you are and stay with them. If you have to live with your [family of origin] do the best you can, but always go back to your chosen family because they will keep you afloat. That's done a lot for me and it's important to maintain those connections. Love doesn't have to be difficult and it doesn't have to be filled with arguments."

Part of growing into adulthood is making peace with what we didn't receive in childhood, but should have. Making peace with it does not mean condoning what happened to us, but to working to accept it. It also means making conscious choices. As someone who experienced love and acceptance as a child, but also experienced emotional neglect during key formative years, this has meant finding my way toward acceptance of who my family members are. When I was younger, I used to get in these cycles of really wanting my father to be different. It wasn't until I was about thirty that I was able to accept that he wasn't going to provide me with love in the way I wanted it, and that was okay. I could count on him for other things. Coming to this acceptance was a huge milestone for me on the path toward an adult relationship with my dad. Accepting him also gave me the freedom to accept myself, and to move forward in my life in ways that felt good for me.

> ⚕ EXERCISE: In your journal, reflect on how your family of origin has shaped and impacted your values, beliefs, and behaviors.

> ⚕ EXERCISE: Map your pod, your circle of people you can turn to for support when you need it. This exercise comes from the Bay Area Transformative Justice Collective, and is reprinted under a Creative Commons Attribution 4.0 International License.

> This resource tool helps people identify their support systems. According to Pod Map co-creator Mia Mingus, *"...people who experience violence, harm and abuse turn to their intimate networks before they turn to external state or social services. Most people don't call the police or seek counseling or even call anonymous hotlines. If they tell anyone at all, they turn to a trusted friend, family member, neighbor or coworker."* This tool can help you map your support systems to weather whatever challenges come your way, while building strong interdependent networks of relationship.

POD MAPPING EXERCISE
Adapted from the Bay Area Transformative Justice Collective

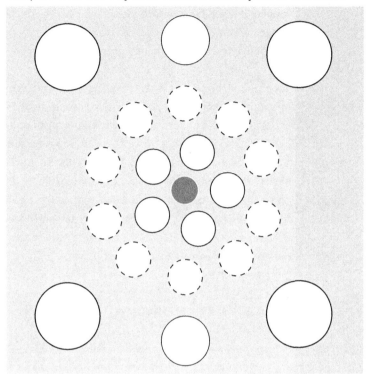

1. Draw a larger version of the pod map above in your journal.

2. Write your name in the middle grey circle.

3. The surrounding bold-outlined circles are your pod. Write the names of the people who are in your pod - actual individuals, instead of things such as "my church group" or "my neighbors."

4. The dotted lines surrounding your pod are people who are "movable." They are people that could be moved in to your pod, but need a little more work. For example, you might need to build more relationship or trust with them.

5. The larger circles at the edge of the page are for networks, communities or groups that could be resources for you. It could be your local domestic violence direct service organization, your cohort in school, your youth group, or a transformative justice group.

Your pod(s) may shift over time, as your needs or relationships shift or as people's geographic location shifts. Take time to actively grow the number of people in your pod and support others in doing so too. Growing one's pod is not easy. In pod work, successes are measured by the quality of relationships with one another. It takes time to build things like trust, respect, vulnerability, accountability, care and love. BATJC sees building pods as a concrete way to prepare and build resources for transformative justice in our communities.

THE IMPORTANCE OF ANCESTRY

"My relationship with my ancestors has really just begun. I have always wondered if communicating with my ancestors came in the form of listening to my gut. I don't always listen to my gut and I wonder if that makes ancestors feel neglected or sad. I am trying to listen more."
–Katheryne, age 26

"I want very much to have a vibrant relationship with my ancestors, yet I feel disconnected. There is a lot of shame, and a lot of anger and grief." –Lauren, age 26

The first time I remember really thinking about or caring about ancestors, in any visceral and not purely intellectual manner, was the opening of a unique nature-based ceremony I had been invited to join. Twelve of us were to go out alone into the desert, in the Funeral Mountains of Death Valley: two men and two women from three different continents. For four days and four nights, we were to be alone, in search of a common vision.

As our white American guides shared the opening they envisioned, which included calling in our ancestors, Scotch and Spesh, dark-skinned South Africans of Xhosa descent, spoke up. "Calling in our ancestors needs to be done a certain way," they said. "It's not something that can be done any old way. Otherwise, they'll be offended. They need money, alcohol, and tobacco. If we call them in, we need to feed them with things they'll like." So a bottle of whiskey was rounded up, along with some coins and some snuff (powdered tobacco that one inhales).

All necessities procured, we began calling in our ancestors in the Xhosa way. Scotch and Spesh kneeled. Scotch poured whiskey and we all laid out change as snuff was sprinkled. Scotch spoke a few mumbled words in Xhosa. We all clapped to punctuate his words. It continued like this for about five minutes, and soon everyone was naming their ancestors, and clapping. The ancestors appeased and called in, we continued on into the next phases of the ritual.

This experience intrigued me. I appreciated the introduction and experience of the Xhosa way of calling in ancestors, and was grateful to Spesh and Scotch for sharing. As I watched the two of them kneel by the makeshift altar, I realized how little I knew of my ancestry. I had never witnessed such overt ancestor honoring before this, had no personal practice of honoring my ancestors, and didn't really even know their names. Certainly, I had no idea how to call in *my* ancestors in the way they wanted to be honored.

As I look back, I'm struck by the absurdity: how could I not have connected with ancestry in the many spiritual and religious ceremonies in which I had been a part? But I hadn't. Somehow, in my life, spirituality had become divorced from lineage—from my kin, the people who came before, whose blood flows through my veins.

This isn't all that surprising. While DNA tests are popular and genealogy is a billion-dollar hobby industry, connecting spiritually with our ancestors remains on the fringes of dominant culture. Commercials for DNA tests pepper our screens, but stories of surprising test results are presented as sources of entertainment, the momentary fulfillment of idle curiosity—not important information with spiritual, cultural, and political impacts.

Before we get any further, let's take a minute to make sure we're on the same page about who we mean when we use the term "ancestors." When I speak of ancestors, I'm talking about those beings who have come before, and are no longer in physical form, those whom we are connected to by blood (i.e. we share DNA), kinship tie (like marriage or adoption), path (like spiritual practice or profession), or collective impact (significant social identity markers we share with them).* This includes both human ancestors (like my great-grandmother Edith Hartshorne Waggoner) and more-than-human ancestors (like our one-celled ancestral kin). In the Western world, many of us are not even taught how to learn about our ancestors, much less how to develop relationships with them or honor them. Before the ceremony with Spesh and Scotch, my only notion of ancestor honoring was the Mexican tradition of *El Dia de Los Muertos,* which didn't have connection to my family traditions or cultural background.

In addition to feeling that such practices are odd, awkward, or archaic, there can also be reluctance to engage in ancestral practices because it brings up (often unconscious) pain and grief. There is so much suffering in our ancestral lines, and many of our ancestors caused suffering for others. Connecting with our ancestors, building relationships with them, requires confronting these difficult truths.

For those of us that are adopted, connecting with our ancestors becomes trickier business still: do we follow the lines of our adopted parents, or try to access information about blood ancestors? The latter can be more difficult to find, as well as sometimes highly emotionally charged.

Given all these barriers, why is ancestry important? Does it really matter where your DNA comes from? I believe what many

---

*An example of this more inclusive perspective of ancestors can be found in the phrase "ancestors and trancestors," which is sometimes used in communities of which I am a part to acknowledge ancestors both of blood and also particular ways of being in the world: in this case, human and other-than-human beings that transcend the gender binary. Gratitude to Shlomo Pesach (who received the phrase from their mentor Pavini Moray) for helping to root transcestry in my heart, vocabulary, and ancestral remembering, and who says "trancestors for me are also movement ancestors, trans historical figures who shaped the future and made space for gender expansive possibilities in my life" like Marsha P. Johnson, Sylvia Rivera, and Leslie Feinberg.

Our Ancestors are at Our Backs

Indigenous leaders, cultural visionaries, and spiritual teachers from a variety of traditions teach: that in order to find our way forward, we need to develop a relationship with our ancestors. By doing so, we can heal the wounds of our past, transform the systems of the present, and forge our collective future.

Our lineage comprises the actual flesh-and-blood of who we are, as well as the carriers of ways of being and engaging in the world that we have inherited. Our ancestors are a source of the strength, courage, wisdom, and tenacity it takes to survive in a complex, changing world. Regardless of who we are, if we are alive today, we are the result of an unbroken line of survivors that stretch back to our earliest human beginnings. The ingenuity, determination, and sacrifice of our ancestors are literally the only reasons we exist. We must learn how to listen to them. Given what they made possible for us, is it not right that we remember and honor them? If we learn to remember our ancestors, our descendants may remember us. If we don't remember our ancestors, and don't pass along the teachings of how to remember them, then surely our descendants—if there are any on this deeply imperiled planet—will leave us neglected, as well.

RECOVERING CONNECTION WITH THE ANCESTORS

"I feel like I am really disconnected with my heritage because I really don't know much about El Salvador. All I really know is that typical food and celebrations, but that is it. I don't know anything about my heritage or my ancestors. My ancestors: who are they? I don't know because I have not had the time and space to connect with my heritage and with my culture. The only thing that I do know is that our ancestors have been able to bring us to where we are now and they are the reason that I am here today and the reason that we are all here and the reason that we are all doing the work that we are doing." –Karla, age 19

"My Dad says that my ancestors were curanderos, which in short represents people that grew their own medicine, were aligned with pacha mama(mother-earth), their people, and used their medicine to heal, support, and transform their people mentally, spiritually, and, physically. Who were like the doctors at the time. In the times my dad describes,

Western medicine wasn't being used by folks in rural areas like his and he remembers many curanderos. People came to talk to them to feel better, similar to what we in the US see as therapists, mentors, and mentees. My mother shared stories of her parents and grandparents being a part of farm workers. My grandparents were also professional tailor folks. I connect with many sides of my ancestors and familia. I too love to be in community, in movement work, and perhaps I am not a curandera now, but I feel like in my own way I am able to heal people." –Gloria, age 22

When I returned home after the ceremony in Death Valley, I began to ask my mom and my grandmother more questions, poured over old photos, and joined an online genealogy site. I painstakingly started to put together a family tree. Inspired by the old ancestral prayers and songs of Indigenous friends and colleagues, reciting back the names of their lineage for many, many generations, I began to learn the female lineage that I was birthed from for seven generations.

Still, I struggled to feel any real sense of kinship with this line. My mother knew few stories. My grandmother was aging and her stories were confusing. All the family history, it seemed, was lost. Nowhere was a sense of who these people actually were, what they cared about—much less any sense of tradition being passed down.

When my grandmother passed away the following fall, a new gateway emerged for me to connect with my ancestors. Suddenly, she was on the other side. She was my ancestor. But I had known her! I had a real, flesh-and-blood relationship that I remembered and could refer to. This connected me in a new way with all my ancestors. Having an ongoing relationship with my grandma (for example, leaving butterscotch candy out for her on holidays, going for walks and talking with her, or just remembering and sharing stories about her) has taught me about how to develop a connection with the many ancestors that I've never met in person.

Traveling to the lands of my ancestors was another significant step in claiming my ancestral lineage. The first place I traveled was to Ukraine, the land of my matrilineal grandfather's family. Coming to Ukraine, I imagined I would find people with access to things that my family had lost on the great ships that traveled across the Atlantic. Instead, I found that in addition to sharing common cultural roots, we shared a common disconnect from and longing for those roots. I learned that when Soviet forces invaded Ukraine, they sought to destroy the culture. Throughout Eastern Europe, families survived through intentionally forgetting their history. They didn't want to know where they came from, because it might get them killed. My ancestors chose to flee, losing their traditions as they assimilated into whiteness in the United States. While the ancestors of the Ukrainians that I met may have stayed when my family left, they too lost their traditions as they willfully tried to survive under Soviet occupation. Realizing that we shared this loss of cultural identity, and that we shared a longing for it, bolstered my connection to these people from my great-grandparents' homeland.

For those of us who didn't grow up with a connection to our ancestors, the barriers to developing this experience can often feel insurmountable. I teach a course where all the students are asked to teach a skill or tradition from their ancestral lineage. For many of them, it is the hardest assignment for the course, provoking a lot of anxiety and sometimes a feeling of inadequacy. Often, long conversations with parents and grandparents ensue, as students struggle to find something to share from their lineage that feels meaningful and authentic.

For those of us disconnected from our roots, this is often a reality. But that doesn't mean you shouldn't try. My students often report that while challenging, this activity is one of the most meaningful of the course. Part of the learning comes when they realize they are not alone in the struggle. Part of it comes from the conversations they have with family, and things they learn through their research. And part of it comes from a sense of connection from learning about the traditions of others, and sharing their own. It is an experience of meaningful cultural exchange; for some the first such experience they have had in their lives.

There are many factors impacting our ability to recover connection with our ancestors. An important one to note is *privilege*. Lineage record-keeping, whether through Indigenous oral traditions or written European nobility records, is a type of privilege that some people have access to while others don't. During chattel slavery, for example, families were separated, records destroyed, and names changed in an intentional effort to disconnect people with their sense of where and who they were from. The poorer the family a person comes from, the more likely that records weren't kept, or were lost or destroyed. This means that many, if not most, of us have large holes in our ancestral narratives. This can bring up frustration, grief, shame and rage at what's been lost or taken from us. But remember, when we are talking about ancestry we are speaking not just about blood ancestors, but also ancestors of kinship tie, path, and collective impact.

There are many ways to recover ancestral connection, though some will be more or less accessible depending on our own unique situations. We can get to know our ancestors through historical research. We can go to the lands of our ancestors, and speak with the more-than-human world and the peoples that live there.* We can learn folk tales, crafts, dances, music, and traditions of our peoples. We can begin to look at our own characteristics and traits, consider where they came from, and talk to our relatives about these traits. We can connect to our ancestors through prayer, developing relationships with those on the other side by feeding them a small plate at meals, creating an altar in our home, or other ways of bringing them into our daily lives. All of these—and more—are valid and important ways to engage (see the breakout box for more ideas).

When connecting with our ancestors, like our families of origin, it's important to exercise clear boundaries and discernment about who, what, when, and how to engage. As we've explored throughout this book, there is so much trauma and wounding in each of our lineage stories. Inviting connection with our ancestors can bring forth these wounds in ways not good for us, or that we are not ready to hold skillfully. Consider going back and reading

---

*Similar to notions of "eco-tourism," ancestral travel has spurred a tourist industry in rural economies, devoted to packaging and commodifying local cultures in service of wealthy descendants wishing to connect with their roots. This type of tourism can be, and often is, extractive and exploitative. While travel of this sort can provide a powerful opportunity to connect with lands where your ancestors' bones are buried, please do so with care, in gratitude for the fossil fuels and other resources that make such travel possible, and in reciprocal relationship with local people as much as possible.

Essential #7: Resourcing: Working with Stress, Trauma, and Difficult Emotions in Chapter One.

As you invite connections with your ancestors, be very clear about your capacity, naming both for yourself and for your ancestors your intentions and what sort of contact you're open and available for. You might do this verbally, or you might share it silently to yourself or write it in your journal. Don't invite in energies you aren't totally sure you're ready to hold, and if you feel uncomfortable very clearly and firmly state your limits. See the Online Resources for more information around ancestral healing and boundary-setting; these resources offer more specific tools for working with ancestry than what we are covering here.

Through my explorations, I have come to understand that at its simplest, my people are those that have come from a common sense of rootlessness, a hunger for home, land, and culture—and are working to find ways to feed this hunger without stealing from others. My people are those that are racially privileged, but culturally impoverished. And my people are also those of all cultural backgrounds that stretch themselves to cross differences, in hopes of building a healthy and just world where all beings can thrive.

Starting out learning the story of my people, I knew very little: the names of both of my grandfathers and one of my grandmothers. That was it. Over the next few years, I came to learn many names, and how to piece together facts about their lives into stories and insights in their lives. As I have gotten better at research, occasionally whole stories have fallen into my lap.

I still don't know the ancient rites of passage of my ancestors. I don't speak their languages, nor remember their ancient stories. So much has been lost. But with each new story I gain access to, my connection to my ancestral inheritance grows stronger. And my will to claim my birthright becomes increasingly fierce.

Mary Hartshorne. Jeremiah Jesson. Emma Lamborn. Samuel Hartshorne. Clara Jesson. Katarzyna Kuzniak. These are no longer just names for me. They are gateways to an unseen, living world, a lineage that reaches back to a time before there were humans, to the one-celled beings that were the beginnings of what we call "Life." All these beings are part of me, flowing through my bloodstream. I feel them with me, encouraging me on, supporting me, giving me clues as I am ready for them. And I realize, deep in my bones, I am never alone.

> **WAYS TO CONNECT WITH YOUR ANCESTORS**
>
> 1. Make foods from your people.
> 2. Learn and practice handcrafts/trades of your ancestors.
> 3. Study an ancestral language.
> 4. Learn folk stories from an ancestral lineage.
> 5. Learn a song or listen to music from your ancestral lands.
> 6. Connect with people who live in the lands your people come from.
> 7. Travel to the lands of your ancestors.
> 8. If your family has photos and archives, spend time looking through them.
> 9. Write the story of your family. Treat it like a myth—don't get too detailed!
> 10. Invite your ancestors to come to you in your dreams, and share with you their stories.
> 11. Look at our own characteristics and traits, consider where they came from, and talk to your relatives about these traits.
> 12. Develop relationships with those on the other side by speaking with them, feeding them a small plate at meals, and/or creating an ancestral altar with artifacts and photos

⚘ **EXERCISE**: In a corner of your room or a spot outside, create a space to connect with your ancestors—whatever that word means to you. Clear this space of any clutter, and add objects and photos that remind you of them. You might add flowers or food as an offering; perhaps a candle or some water. Ask that only those ancestors that are healthy and whole come to visit you. Each day for several weeks, come to this space for a few minutes, and listen for any messages you receive. You may choose to bring more offerings or additional objects to the space.

🌱 EXERCISE: Learn an "ancestral skill" from your lineage and share it with someone in your life. This can be anything—food, hunting technique, art or craft, language, plant, family story. If you have trouble thinking of something, this may be a good time to enlist a family member's support.

A STORY OF MY PEOPLE

They say that my people lived on their lands for hundreds of generations, some for perhaps a million years. They lived in partnership with the forests, waters, stones, and animals, keeping their Beloved Dead close by and tending to the cycles of their lives and the world around them.

Then things began to change. Some say it was due to a curious biological adaptation, others say shifts in material culture. Whatever the cause, some began to specialize in raiding, pillaging, and hoarding. Their sky god grew above their other gods.

Generations passed as my ancestors endured waves of invasion. The Cimmerians, Scythians, Ostrogoths, Huns, Khazars, Mongols, Romans, Anglo-Saxons, Vikings—these were some of the invaders endured by my ancestors across the continent of Europe. Undoubtedly, some of my ancestors were the ones doing the invading, too.

Though each invasion showed differences, patterns remained the same. Conquering forces came in search of new lands and resources, in the name of a far-distant ruler. They demanded allegiance from local populations, who found themselves under economic and political control from outside forces. Some forces ruled more gently. Some were more repressive, physically enslaving local populations.

Despite these imperial efforts, village life remained close to the land, tied to traditional ways. People still lived with the cycles of the seasons, in relationship with the many beings of the lands and with their ancestors.

Christianity brought wholesale change. Over several hundred years, an alliance between the church, the state, and the merchant class consolidated in a series of religious decrees known as the Papal Bulls, giving birth to a worldview known as the Doctrine of Discovery. This provided the moral justification to conquer and seize lands and bodies, to extract and consolidate wealth in the hands of the elites.

The Crusades. The Spanish Inquisition. The Burning of the Witches. The Enclosures. These repressive efforts set the fate for my ancestors, driving neighbors against each other and into the wage economy, disconnecting them from their lands and their beliefs. Like many around them, my people became landless then, driven toward cities in search of work and facing religious persecution for their beliefs.

Soon they heard whispers of empty, wild, and fertile land, on a continent soon to be known as North America. My ancestors left England beginning in the 1770's, part of an escape valve quelling peasant uprisings by sending them off seeking a better life.

They landed in an area known as Lenapehoking, the lands of the Lenni Lenape people who had lived there peacefully for 400 generations or more. By the time my people arrived, the Lenni Lenape had been reduced by three quarters, mostly through disease brought by early waves of European colonizers.

This port city where they landed, now known as Philadelphia, grew rapidly. The Lenni Lenape were pushed further and further west. Some stayed and assimilated, others fled to Canada. Many were killed in violent assaults or from starvation or disease.

The violence quickly spread west. The Sand Creek Massacre, Battle of Greasy Grass, Wounded Knee Massacre: the list of horrors goes on, as methods of resource extraction in the form of land and labor, experimented upon with the lives and bodies of my European ancestors, were perfected and employed against the people Indigenous to Turtle Island. At the heart of this effort was the removal of children from their families, forcing them into residential boarding schools in a brutal attempt at wholesale cultural genocide.

Meanwhile, as settlers just a few miles from what would be known as the Mason-Dixon line, my ancestors soon found themselves the beneficiaries of the slave trade. Enormous prosperity came to the lands through the bodies of thousands of African peoples kidnapped and shipped across oceans, subject to unconscionable abuses and horrors.

Generations passed as new waves of my ancestors arrived to these lands, following stories of fortune and freedom. Eventually, family lines converged through my birth, in some ways as a result of the careers of my two grandfathers.

Though both men were born in the eastern US, their fortunes brought them west. They both settled in the sunshine and fertile landscape of California due to military expansion of the US about a hundred years previously. After a notoriously brutal war, the US seized almost half of Mexico. This expanded the young country to the Pacific Ocean; opened up trade with Asia; and provided access to mineral wealth in Arizona, agricultural wealth in California, and new sources of cheap labor for railroads. Soon, the US emerged as an Empire — eventually the most politically powerful in the world.

My grandfathers were part of these Empire-building efforts. One: a sugar broker made wealthy by an industry dependent on seizing Indigenous lands and turning self-supporting local populations into farm workers for small wages beholden to a global economy. The other: the son of an immigrant family who made his way into the white middle class thanks to military service, GI benefits available to him as a white veteran, and a long career for a private defense contractor.

This story is the backdrop for that day when I was 13, when I noticed a flier for a rite of passage journey. That chance encounter began the path I've followed ever since: a path, I like to believe, my ancestors offered me – a path back to their ancient ways, so long obscured and hidden from my people, a path that is somehow part of the redemption of my People.

> ⚘EXERCISE: Reflect on what you know of "the story of your People". What were their ancient ways, and what happened to them? What did they come to replace them with? And how might you reclaim and evolve them?

CARVED LIKE A LANDSCAPE: THE PLACES WE ARE FROM

"I am from a valley nestled amongst the Rocky Mountains of western Montana. The mountains, approximately 60 millions years old, extend from Canada to New Mexico and divide the state of Montana in half. The glacial Lake Missoula, formed between 15,000 and 13,000 years ago during the last deglaciation, is the valley of my birthplace. My body has ingested enough of my environment (through dirt filled cuts, locally grown food, my spirit swept up by the winds and my soul lost/found along its winding mountain paths), that I feel more related to this landscape than I do to my grandparents. I know this land's features, like a face of a loved one. I know it has impacted all of me and my life." –Gretchen, age 26

Traditionally, when Hawaiian children are born, part of their umbilical cord is taken and placed in a *puka*, a small hole, created in the rock. There is a place on Hawai'i Island where you can walk amongst thousands of these holes, created in ceremony to connect an infant to the lands where they are from. For the rest of their lives and beyond, a puka exists that is just theirs, a symbol of their connection to the island.

Many of us today had no ceremony to seal and affirm our connection to the land. Still, we each come from a very specific place on this planet. For some of us, though fewer and fewer as time goes on, we remain planted in the same landscape for our whole lives, perhaps on the same lands of our ancestors for generations. For others, there is constant motion in search of the right place. For some, survival means fleeing one's home and relocating. I even have friends that identify as global pilgrims; for them, home is wherever they find themselves on a given day.

As we consider where we belong, and how we fit in, key pieces of the puzzle include the ecosystems in which we were born, and the physical environments where we live, work, and play. Rite of passage guide and founder of Thriving Sun, Chris Quiseng, puts it very simply, "We are our landscapes."

Chandi, age 26, is quick to describe how much growing up in the Ka'u District of Hawai'i has impacted her. "I was raised in Hawaii my whole life," she says. "I was born here. I grew up in Ka'u, in the forests of Ka'u. I was raised where I was close to both the mountains and the ocean. That defined who I was. As a child I was raised in the natural world, building treehouses and forts, always outdoors and climbing trees."

"This place Ka'u means "the feed," like the life force. What feeds you. That is what it does to the people here, because we are so deeply rooted in the community. There are a lot of sacred sites in the area, so I was able to be a part of that growing up. And to live so much more of a natural world connection, rather than being absorbed in TV and shopping and all the social norms that are familiarized with the Americas. Hawaii is different. The Hawaiian culture is very much alive here."

Chandi's experiences in nature instilled in her a deep sense of belonging: "I feel truest and like I belong when I am in nature. When I am out exploring somewhere, when I am adventurous and free whether it is hiking somewhere to an amazing waterfall or in the ocean. In the ocean, I feel so at home, freediving, swimming just like where I am comfortable in. Pure, not thinking of anything or doing anything!"

Despite the fact that her parents themselves were not from the island, as a mixed-race woman with Oneida-German ancestry, Chandi feels the similarities in Hawai'i with her ancestry. She says, "I feel deeply rooted with my Native American culture being here."

Traveling to the mainland, she experienced cultural differences. She describes it this way: "Here [in Hawai'i] it is the *Aloha Spirit!* 'Hi, how can I help you? Can I carry your mail to the car? Or open the door for you?' I remember going to the mainland, and people don't have that eye connection, that warmth, that *Aloha*. Like 'Oh I will go out of my way to help you!' The people are very different.

It's important to understand and remember that we exist not just in relation to other human beings. The more-than-human world has shaped us as well.

I come from a land of big rushing rivers, giant cedar trees, and salmon, bordered by the ocean on one side and rugged snowy mountains on the other, from lands long-tended by Coast Salish peoples. Just as the glaciers carved out the landscape during the last ice age, my interior world has been sculpted by this ecosystem. It's the place on earth where I feel most at home.

I also come from the city of Tacoma, smaller step-sibling to Seattle, from a little cul-de-sac adjacent to a large overgrown field. Though it's been more than 30 years since I lived there, I still dream of the house, yard, and neighborhood where I had my first childhood adventures. In and amidst the houses and the concrete, my first encounters with the wild world took place, imprinting my body and psyche.

Indigenous scholar Vine Deloria, Jr. says, "There is a clear Indigenous understanding that it is the land that shapes the people, and that one cannot divorce the spirituality of the people from the spirituality of the land." No matter who we are, where we were born, or where we live, we come from the land. Taking time to appreciate how the lands that we have lived upon have impacted and shaped us is part of knowing where we are headed. This may take a very long time, and be hard to translate into words. We're not often asked to reflect on how we've been shaped by our physical landscapes.

⚘ EXERCISE: From the following sets of elements and environments, select where you feel most at home or what is most comfortable to you.

Saltwater / freshwater
Mountain peaks / valleys
Inland / on the coast
Open country / forest
Wet / dry
Warm / cool
Fur / feathers / scales / fins
Earth / wind / water / fire

⚘ EXERCISE: Think of a place that impacted you, either because you were there for a long time or because significant events occurred while you were there. This landscape can be sparsely inhabited by humans, very urban, or somewhere in between.

> First describe the landscape: its climate, geographical features, whatever you know of the geological forces that created the place. Second, reflect on how this landscape has shaped you. What did you learn by being in this landscape that you may not have learned elsewhere? What didn't you learn here that you might have elsewhere?

GOING GLOBAL

"This story of the universe is the story that the universe tells of itself. It is the story told by every being in the universe, by the stars in the heavens, by the mountains and rivers of Earth, by every wind that blows, by every snowflake that falls, by every leaf in the forest. To know this story of the universe as our sacred story is to have an adequate foundation for the task before us. This story tells us who we are and how we came to be here and what our lives are all about." –White American cultural historian and author Thomas Berry

Our particular place is important, but we also live together on this increasingly interconnected planet. Global crises, like the climate crisis or the COVID pandemic, remind us of this truth. We all call the Earth our home. So where did we, as a human species, come from? Answering this question means exploring *origin stories*.

Origin stories, a basic and fundamental part of mythology, have been part of human cultures since we could speak. They help us place our little, perhaps inconsequential lives, within a greater context. They give our lives meaning. Traditionally, a young person would never go through an initiation into adulthood without knowing the origin story of their people. In fact, they would have learned this long ago in childhood, when they received basic cultural training. For those of us from religious families or ones strongly connected to non-Western cultures, we may have learned an origin story very early on.

As science separated itself from spirituality and culture, our myths gave way to facts and figures, always in dispute. Yet there is perhaps nothing more fundamental to culture as a people's mythology. Thomas Berry, a cultural historian and self-described "geologian," devoted his life work to helping us understand where we find ourselves within a truly universal context—that is, the story of the whole universe. He saw "The Universe Story" as the story for our times, our origin story, the place where the full capacities of modern science transcend into the mystical. It's a Western conception of history, and not the complete truth. Western scientists learn more every day!

Still, as a Western educated person who doesn't resonate with the origin story coming out of the Bible, the story of the Big Bang helped me understand where I come from in the larger sense of things: as a human being, a member of the Earth community, and a being made of stardust just like all other matter in the universe. It's helped me understand that my life is truly a miracle. 4.6 billion years of amazing circumstances, in which infinite other possibilities could have occurred but did not, have led me to this moment, to this life, to this body.

As we've talked about, understanding and making space for our differences is very important. However, to be always in our differences is to neglect the unity that is also the reality. We *are* all one people, citizens of this planet we call home. We all eat, we all love, we all suffer. The suffering and joy of one are the suffering and joy of us all—all humans, and the more-than-human world as well. As we find ourselves increasingly interconnected through quickly changing technological, social, economic, and environmental realities, we must find a way to hold both our differences—and the similarities we share. We belong to humanity, we belong to the Earth, we belong to the universe.

AN ORIGIN STORY

In the beginning there was nothing. Then (who knows how or why) at some point over thirteen billion years ago, the universe flashed into existence. It expanded and cooled. Energy, time, and space began to exist. Energy organized into molecules of hydrogen and helium.

A billion years passed. Galaxies emerged. The first stars sprang forth and died. Supernovas exploded, spewing forth new elements like carbon, iron, and oxygen.

Observing the Unfolding Universe

Billions more years passed. As a supernova exploded, our solar system was born, bringing forth our sun. Matter spewed out, fashioning planets that soon orbited around the sun's explosive power, including the now-blue-and-green sphere we call home.

As Earth cooled, comets and meteors pelted the surface. A huge planetoid crashed into the Earth, spewing forth matter to create the moon, which was quickly pulled into the orbit of our precious planet.

Over time, Earth continued to cool, gradually developing an atmosphere and making possible the miracle of rain. And rain it did! Downpours deluged the planet for tens of millions of years. Soon, shallow seas peppered with islands covered the planet.

Billions of years passed. Eventually, life came forth in the form of one-celled beings. These cells, our ancestors, began to grow and divide. Hundreds of millions of years later, as their readily available food supplies began to dwindle, these cells turned to the sun for sustenance, evolving the capacity for photosynthesis. In this process, they released oxygen, which was toxic to them. Oxygen piled up in the atmosphere, threatening life on the planet.

Miraculously, cells that could thrive with oxygen emerged forth about two billion years ago. They developed a simple capacity for respiration, drawing in oxygen as sustenance. In this process they protected larger cells from the oxygen, giving birth to the nucleated cell and creating the possibility for the more complex life that would follow. Eventually, two cells shared their genetic coding, giving birth to offspring, and sexual reproduction was for the first time, possible. Their descendants began to merge into relationships with one another and multi-celled, sexual life became possible. All this happened in the seas.

Eventually, these beings evolved the capacity for sight, and the universe could see itself. Fish soon emerged, with a backbone, an encased nervous system, and sensory organs. Following close behind, plants and animals began to migrate out of the seas and onto land. Worms, mollusks, crustaceans, algae, and fungus were some of these early explorers. Mosses, the first plants, began to emerge.

Over one hundred million years later, forests developed. Over millions and millions of years, as trees grew forth, lived, and decomposed back into the earth, forests began to sequester the carbon they pulled out of the atmosphere which later fossilized as coal and oil. As the forests spread, some amphibians evolved into reptiles. For the first time eggs were carried internally. This allowed the reptiles to move further inland. Eventually, dinosaurs emerged. Some of them evolved into birds. Flowers bloomed forth on the planet, filling landscapes with color and attracting the insects flying through the skies.

Around 65 million years ago, Earth's fifth great mass extinction event marked the end of the dinosaurs. A huge asteroid struck, causing a severe drop in temperature.

The demise of the dinosaurs ushered in the age of mammals. A large variety of animals begin to inhabit the earth over the next tens of millions of years, including baboons, giraffes, bears, pigs, and the first hominids. Eventually, these humans evolved the capacity to stand on two legs, and ventured out of the forests and onto the savannahs.

Several million years passed. Sometime between 100,000-300,000 years ago, the species *Homo sapiens* emerged. Simple tools, control of fire, language as we understand it, art, and spirituality soon sprang forth, along with rites of passage and other cultural practices. These early humans migrated, pushing northward and eventually crossing water to inhabit lands across the globe.

Tens of thousands of years passed. Humans developed complex systems of shaping and tending the natural world around them. Civilizations flourished and died. Major religions sprang forth. The globe became increasingly interconnected through technology, warfare, trade, and commerce. Peoples the world over found strangers arriving to their homelands speaking strange languages, carrying guns and disease. Weapons of war increased in destructive power. Social stratification increased. Humans tapped deep into the earth's reserves, drawing forth the remains of ancient marine ancestors with the means to power machinery and change the climate. Humans, a bit of the earth, deeply affecting the whole...and so the story continues.

⚘ EXERCISE: Reflect on the origin story here and/or the origin story of your ancestors. What does this story teach you about our role as humans on the Earth? What warnings or instructions does it contain for how to live lives of purpose and meaning?

LEARNING HOW TO LEARN

"He who does not know where he came from cannot know why he came here and what he came to this place to do. There is no reason to live if you forget what you're here for...When you do not know who you are, you follow the knowledge of the wind." –Dagara Author and Teacher Malidoma Somé

This chapter has covered vast swaths of territory: relationship with our ancestors, our families, places that we are from and that have claimed us, even the whole Earth on which we live our lives! It's a lot of ground.

So what is really necessary for *you* to do to be ready to step into adulthood? Consider the following questions as possible benchmarks for stepping into adulthood. Are there any areas here that need your attention before you move forward?

1. Do you have a basic sense of who "your people" are, and where you come from?

2. Do you have at least one space where you truly feel that you belong (either a human space or a space in the wild non-human world, or both)?

3. Do you have a basic level of acceptance of the people and places you come from, and a commitment to ending legacies of harm?

4. Do you have a commitment to doing your part to support the well-being of your community?

These areas are important because they help us understand the people and places that have shaped us, those to whom we belong. Becoming an adult requires us to develop this understanding, to learn to be in relationship with the world around us as our relatives, our kin.* Seeing other beings of the world as our kin, in turn, makes it possible to withstand the pressures of a society more devoted to us as consumers and workers than as human beings.

To really begin to understand where we come from, the first task is *patience*. While there are many strategies to build a sense of rootedness and belonging, none of them are fast. Ancestral reconnection is not something that will provide instant gratification; nor is developing a relationship with place. This is painstaking work that takes a lifetime. After decades on this journey, I am still just scratching the surface.

There are many directions that this exploration can take you. Yet one of the things that we lack in Western culture are the stories that teach us what is important to remember. On my journey, I've learned that much of the information isn't very useful; it's the essence of things that is important. It's distilling ways to tell the stories so I can retain them, and pass them on. I try to engage in learning about the people and places I come from as reclaiming an oral tradition. I ask myself, "What can I *learn by heart* and draw to mind when I need it?"

On my ancestral pilgrimage, I started out in the same compulsive, addictive way that I scroll through my social media feeds. I was hungry for any and all information: facts, names, dates, all of that stuff. Quickly, I learned that this wasn't going to get me anywhere; it was too overwhelming. I began to pace myself so that I could take in relevant details in a way I could metabolize, and access deeper knowledge: context and patterns, stories. Finally, I began to find the deeper underlying arc: the essence of the stories. There is no way to force a relationship to come, whether it's with a living human, ancestors, or the river near my house. Relationships come through time, presence, care, and attention. This can be hard in comparison with the instant gratification kind of world I experience in many areas of my life, yet placing my attention here cultivates a long view of time, from ancient ancestors through far-distant descendents, that can help me put my life into context.

---

*Rarámuri author Enrique Salmon calls this kin-centric ecology.

🌱 **EXERCISE**: Reflect on the following questions:

- Who are your people? Where are you from?
- What is one place where you feel that you truly belong, and why?
- What about the people and places you come from brings pain or discomfort when you think about them, or feels hard to accept?
- What would support you to find a basic level of acceptance? What legacies of harm are you committed to ending? What would support you to end these legacies?
- Are you committed to taking responsibility to do your part to support the well-being of your community? What does this look like on a tangible level?

🌱 **EXERCISE**: In the last chapter you were asked to begin to identify words for a "Statement of Intent." You'll work on this statement in earnest in the next chapter. For now, you can add to your list by first reviewing your work in this chapter. Again, go back through the exercises, particularly the ones where you did some writing, and underline words that stick out to you related to who your people are, and where you come from (5 and 25 words total is great). These could be words that speak to your belonging in ways that feel particularly important, bring curiosity, are surprising or don't make sense, or feel like edges in your life. Add these words to the list you made before.

☾

Chapter Seven:

WHERE AM I GOING AND HOW DO I GET THERE?

"I seem to be going in circles. I got the message as a kid that as one grew up they were supposed to travel largely in a line...So I am still making peace with the idea of circles." –Izaac, age 28

A few nights before the ceremony, I had a dream. Four quart-sized canning jars, clean, well-polished, and full of blood, glistened down on me from a shelf above my head. I didn't know where the jars had come from, I didn't know what they were for, but I knew they were mine and I felt okay with that.

The weeks, maybe even months, leading up to the ceremony had been exhausting. I felt frayed around the edges, ready for rest and no responsibility. On the first day, I shared with my guides that all I wanted to do was dance beneath the moon. "If I could just dance in the moonlight for the next two weeks," I declared, "that would be perfect." I felt ready to lay down all of the old stories about who I was and what I believed, stories that felt like a bag of burdens dragging behind me and growing bigger everyday. I longed to let them go, and invite in guidance from the earth, the moon, the stars, and my ancestors.

A few days later, I walked off into the mountains alone, ready to do just that. I carried my backpack, sleeping bag, four gallons of water, and a simple but still-mysterious prayer, whittled down with the support of my guides for the journey: *I tend the blood with dignity, at home with my place in the family of beings.*

On a little bench below two rocky peaks with a rolling saddle between them, I made home for four days. An old pinyon pine tree offered me shelter and companionship. Over four days, I told her many stories. I shared about all the ceremonies I had experienced in my life, my complete sexual history, my story with power, my story with money. I prayed that the stories would stay here and feed her roots, or float away on the wind. I wanted to leave all of these stories in the mountains, and come home clean, unencumbered.

Each night, I slept beneath the stars, tossing and turning on a leaky camping mattress.

The last full day I awoke early and dressed in a traditional *vyshyvanka* embroidered dress I had brought for this occasion. I put on a beaded Slavic necklace I had just repaired the day before, and made my way up to the top of the steep rocky peak.

> "Ideals are like stars. You cannot touch them with your hands, but like the seafaring man on the desert of waters, you choose them as your guides and, following them, you reach your destiny."
>
> –German Revolutionary turned United States Senator Carl Schurz

There, I invited in my healthy and whole ancestors, those that were ready to be part of the healing, and asked them to share their stories with me. I made prayers and offerings, and shared with them my longings. I spoke of what I needed to let go of and what I was ready to call in. I found a little cave and after asking permission I crawled inside, seeking guidance and protection. I stayed up there for a long time, in an altered state from days without food or other humans, taking in the clouds and birds, the rock and trees, the feeling of my ancestors close by and paying attention.

After some time, I made my way back down to my pinyon pine home, ready to rest in preparation for a long final night. The next morning, I made vows of my commitments moving forward, gave thanks and water to the pinyon and the other beings of this place, and made my way back to my companions and guides.

I returned to my life lighter, clearer. I felt free of the stories about sex, money, power, who I was, that had burdened me. I felt clearer about what was important to me, and carried new images to anchor me to these insights. In the years since, I have carried this prayer, "I tend the blood with dignity, at home with my place in the family of beings" as my north star. Tending the blood: My blood, women's blood, the blood shed by my ancestors and the blood of those harmed by my ancestors. With dignity: In my worth and worthiness as a human and as a woman, standing in my power. At home with my place in the family of beings: At home in my social locations, in my geographical place, in my family and relationships.

And I know that sooner or later, this story, too, will need to be released or renewed. When it does, I'll return to the land again, to release, pray, and invite in what's next.

We've talked throughout this book about the reality of constant change in our lives. Whether we want things to or not, just as soon as it seems like we reach a state of equilibrium, something begins to shift—whether in the outer world, or in our interior world. Things that once worked for us no longer do.

Have you ever watched a little kid acting like they're younger than they are? Things that they had done just months, weeks, or sometimes days earlier to make people laugh are suddenly no longer funny. Often, they'll keep trying over and over, not sure what else to do. It's a remarkable thing to watch, painful because we've all experienced the confusion and frustration that comes from having outgrown your former self but not yet knowing what will replace it.

Luckily, there are time-tested tools that can help us navigate through these confusing "liminal" times with more grace and skill, and less confusion and angst. They help us to figure out where we are at and where we are going, critical to make the passage from one life stage to another. But be warned: learning these tools doesn't necessarily make our lives easier or happier! Change is often difficult, especially so in a culture that has taught us that control and certainty are both possible and desirable.

What these tools do provide are ways to find and make meaning when the ground is shifting under our feet. They help to increase our courage and resiliency in the face of crisis. The more practice we get applying tools to navigate life's transitions, the more skilled we get using them. The more skilled we get using these tools, the more confidence we gain that they truly work, and the more confidence we gain in our own deeper wisdom and knowing. With this comes deeper self-love and self-acceptance, which in turn allows for bigger and bigger risk-taking. We can put ourselves in unknown territory and accept high levels of vulnerability, because we can trust our capacity to ultimately soothe and care for ourselves, and know we will be alright. With ever deeper levels of vulnerability, we allow ourselves to be transformed through our encounters with others. We find that the identities that we once so tightly clung to are no longer necessary, and we can in fact survive without them. Our belonging no longer depends on these once so essential roles.

My mom said to me a few years ago that gardening taught her that there aren't four seasons, there are 365. Not long after, when she drove from New Jersey to Seattle, she observed that transitions across the landscape were marked by similarly subtle gradations. I see this in my own life, as well: how each passing day marks a subtle shift in who I am and how I relate to the world around me, an opportunity to cling and try to control, or to surrender and observe what unfolds. Or (as is usually the case) to do some weird contortion of both at once, a thoroughly uncomfortable and awkward dance.

As you continue to pack the backpack you'll carry into adulthood, this chapter offers a few more items that will be helpful for you. These are tools for you to use during big life changes to come, but they are also here to support you through the more subtle changes of the everyday.

INTENTION

"Intention is a really important aspect of any rite of passage or any ceremony, or our life! Conscious intention sets something out in the field, in the world, that I don't understand, and it is strong." –white American Rite of Passage Guide, Meredith Little

A powerful practice for navigating times of transition is setting an intention. In the field of medicine, the word intention refers to the *healing process of a wound*. As we find ourselves needing guidance about what's next, whether as a daily practice or during much bigger transitions in our lives, articulating our intentions helps to set forces in motion. For example, I might set the intention "to be open" or to "speak from my heart" as I begin my day. Inevitably, my day will give me opportunities to practice whatever I am setting forth, with my intention.

An intention is usually short and to the point. It may not yet be fully formed or clear, but if we take a deep breath, quiet our minds and open our awareness to our hearts and bodies, invariably there is something that we yearn to move towards. Depending on our belief system, we may understand this as something we want to move towards, or something that is asking us to move towards it (or both). We may kick and scream, resisting it, or we may rush full-heartedly into its arms. Either way, it lingers out there, on the edge of our vision, waiting for us to move towards it.

An intention is different from a goal. A goal is a clear endpoint you're trying to achieve. Intention is more subtle and open-ended. My favorite way of understanding intention comes from what I learned from white American yoga teacher Laura Yon, about a particular yoga sutra (short, Ancient yogic teachings, similar to proverbs in the Judeo-Christian tradition) that roughly translates as: we set our intention to cooking, and then we release the outcome, and observe what happens.

Developing a strong intention is key in a rite of passage. Traditionally, rites of passage mark transitions into clearly defined roles, well understood by the individual and the community. Yet in a culture with few intentional rites of passage and with such a focus on individualism, we must be clear for ourselves what exactly it is that we are stepping into and claiming at a particular time in our lives.

A statement of intent makes clear the transition you are marking in your life. It's the doorway you walk through. You let go of the old identity, step into your intention, and see what happens. Your intention carries you through the rite of passage process, and into your life beyond.

Corinne, 31, had been feeling the need for change for a long time, but found herself avoiding it. A childhood filled with social isolation and key traumatic experiences at the hands of loved ones had left her with an arsenal of defense mechanisms. Her heart was full of love, but her strong protective boundaries made this difficult for others to feel. She felt trapped in a prison inside herself: "For a fairly sedentary person, I sure am good at running. I run from the things that make me uncomfortable, I run when it seems like I might fail, I run from vulnerability, I run from things that remind me of all of the other things I'm running from. So why stop running now? A lot of reasons, really, but the biggest one is that I'm exhausted. My body is tired, my heart is tired, my mind is tired, and my soul is tired. I'm stuck in this rut—that I'm realizing I've been stuck in for a long time—and I know that I can't move forward in my life until I am able to confront the things I'm running from."

When she made the commitment that it was time for a rite of passage, Corinne knew that developing a statement of intent was part of the process, yet she found the process daunting: "When I think about what I would want out of something as powerful as an intent statement, it scares me, because I am afraid that deep down I don't have the strength to own who I am, let alone to find power and pride in it. I am afraid that I've spent so much of my adult life running, that I have no idea where I've wound up."

Corinne knew some part of what she needed to claim: her womanhood. For her, a woman meant being resilient, gentle, and brave. Constrained by her fears, she wanted to claim being "unafraid." As she explored further, she realized that it wasn't being free from fear that she wanted to claim, but moving forward despite her fears, with courage. She wanted to claim openness, but that too felt not quite right. Vulnerability was closer to the essence—honoring her tenderness. What was key for her was to claim her ability to express her love, to radiate it. With tears in her eyes, she spoke, "Courageous and vulnerable, I am a trusting woman who radiates love." As she said it, she smiled. "That's it," she said. "it's like I found the perfect wedding dress."

School of Lost Borders co-founder Meredith Little, who has guided people through the process of setting an intention for land-based rites of passage for over thirty years, says that rites of passage are essentially rites of confirmation—they *confirm* an inner shift that has already happened. She says that we must be careful that our statement of intention is something we're ready to claim, something that we've done the work to claim, not lofty far-off goals. She quotes one of her teachers, a Paiute elder, who would say to her and others, "You white people, you're so silly! You go out on a vision fast, thinking that just by going out there, Great Spirit will strike you and transform you, and you don't want to do any of the work. You go out asking for something you're not ready for...All that does is make you sick!" Meredith goes on to say, "Intention is about getting clear, what am I really ready to mark, that I've done the work for."

This can be hard for many of us. Lots of people feel the urge to make an intent statement like a checklist of all the things they wish they were, yet this is definitely a place where simplicity serves. As Andrea grappled with wanting to claim self-sufficiency, intuition, and more, she found that her intent statement carried more power for her when it was simple: "I am an adult who has purpose." That statement, easy to remember and concise, gives her lots of space to learn and grow, as she discovers what adulthood is for her, and what her purpose is as an adult in her family and community.

When thinking about intent, keep in mind that this isn't an exercise that's really about you, and what you want. It isn't about what will make your life happier, easier, more comfortable, or more successful. Your intent is about what the world needs for you to claim, in order to fully inhabit your niche. Elder Paul Hill says, "Intent is judged by answering the question: Is it in the best interest of the community?" Sometimes, this will include a component of healing, strengthening, caring for oneself. But the focus must always remain on the greater whole.

The heart of a statement of intent is most often the role that you are claiming. Who are you, as we discussed in the last chapter? Who are you becoming? What are you committing to be, for yourself and for your people?

This often has to do with life stage. It is a powerful and important thing for someone to consciously and intentionally step into adulthood. Claiming oneself as a man, or a woman, can also be very important, both defining a life stage and a clear gender role. Unless you identify as gender fluid or non-binary, these types of roles are important to consider, even if you find yourself shrinking away from the labels. I've worked with dozens of folks in their twenties who are initially repelled at the prospect of stepping into manhood, womanhood, or adulthood; these words were so heavy with cultural baggage that they had no interest in inhabiting them. And yet—we need initiated adults. We need adults of all genders. Embracing these words does not mean adhering to the cultural baggage that comes with them, but rather redefining what these words mean, dusting them off and remaking healthy culture by reclaiming them.

Claiming another social identity may be appropriate at this time in your life. When one young woman I was working with claimed her role as a lesbian, and took that intent into ceremony with her, she found that the doubt and shame about her sexual orientation that had plagued her for so many years began to finally fall away. Another friend and colleague claimed "settler" within their intent, and found that owning themselves as a settler on Turtle Island allowed for a very different way of relating to the lands and First Peoples.

Claiming a professional role or archetypal way of serving the community may also be what's called for. For those that lead rites of passage, there is a moment when they must claim the role of mentor or guide, and go through their own ceremony to step fully into the work. As Rachel crafted a statement of intent, she started with claiming her womanhood. Soon, she discovered there was another part of herself that needed to be named at that time. For Rachel, claiming herself as an artist marked a profound shift,

Word Cloud of Intents from Young People, 2013-2016

which required her to make room for her creative expression. She found that soon thereafter, opportunities for her art to be seen and appreciated by others began to appear.

Your intent should feel risky to claim. When you say it out loud, it might feel audacious: "Oh no, I might sound arrogant if I claim too much in my intent. Who am I to think that I could be described in that way?" But this is not a moment to hide your bright light, or your luminous darkness. Be real about where you are at on your developmental journey. No reason to get ahead of yourself. But it's also critical to step boldly into what life's asking you, and courageously move towards that which is terrifying. It's those things that seem risky that are worth working towards.

Over more than a decade, clients at Pacific Quest*, an organic gardening-based program for struggling young people with a strong rite of passage component, developed a statement of intent to carry them on their life after the program, and on their path toward adulthood. These statements reflected their individuality: the struggles they faced, what they were claiming as they moved forward, and what they felt Life was asking them to claim. The word cloud in this section, put together by Michael McGee, is the result of over 300 intent statements developed by young people ages 13-24, between 2013-2016.

> ⚘EXERCISE: Now it is time to craft your intent statement. This statement should be direct and to the point. Think of it like an essential oil. It takes 20 pounds of lavender flowers (that's more than an armful of lavender!) to make just one ounce of lavender essential oil. The oil is that potent. Your intent should be like that: distilled to the essence. Think 15 words maximum. Ten is even better!
>
> Begin by creating sacred space for yourself. Do something to clear yourself from mental clutter, like

---

*While many young people, families, and staff members been positively impacted by Pacific Quest and other similar programs in the Outdoor Behavioral Health Industry, many have had negative experiences. This book is not an endorsement of this or any other particular program.

dancing, taking a shower, or going for a walk. Once you feel a little clearer and more grounded, take a look at the list of words you've been collecting over the last couple of chapters. Underline a few key words or phrases from this list that stand out to you now: again because they are the most important, curious, confusing, or edgy. Start to pull these words together into a statement describing who you are and what you are ready to claim in your life.

As you continue with this process over the coming days, weeks, even months, continuing to refine your statement, balance *making* your *intent* and *listening* for your intent. Your intent may come through thinking about it, but it may also come in the moments between thoughts. Perhaps flashes of inspiration come to you in a dream, or in the shower, or even heard on the radio. Let words roll around in your mind and heart, and let them begin to click into place on their own.

Take the time to work it down to the essence. Keep writing drafts, giving yourself challenges—cut out one more word on the next go round. Then another. Then another. Remember, the simpler your intent statement, the more direct and powerful it can be.

WILD WANDERING

"I find that the most healing times for me are when I go out in nature by myself and cut myself off from the rest of the world. It's when I feel at peace and clear." –Micaela, age 25

On a day-long wander by herself, Katelyn, age 25, found an important lesson when she found herself face-to-face with a fence. "One side of the fence was forested, shaded, full of brush, mosquitoey and the view to the ocean blocked," she wrote several weeks later. "This is the side of the fence I was on. I spent the first half of my day here."

"The other side was an open, rolling pasture exposed to the warm sun and the ocean view. I wanted to be on the other side. I wanted to feel the sun, the breeze and the openness. I was on the property of a friend and knew both sides of this fence belonged to this friend, however the pastured side was being rented. I stood by the fence for a long time, wanting to be on the other side. The thoughts going through my head were of fear around getting hurt myself climbing over the fence, and mostly of fear around being confronted by the renter of the land, even though I felt that risk was very low. I have a lot of fear around making people feel uncomfortable and can often be confrontation-avoidant. I'm a people-pleaser to a fault and am working on it. I realized, 'This is my wall. I know clearly I want to be on this other side, yet I am limiting myself because of fear and because of fear of making another person feel uncomfortable. Yet I am uncomfortable on this side of my wall.'

I stood by the fence for what felt like a very long time. Eventually I crossed the barbed wire fence and I felt relief, relaxation and also consistently vulnerable being so in the open and some lingering fear of being approached by an unwelcoming man.

Katelyn's story shares a simple but powerful practice, that of wild wandering. The form looks like this: set an intention, move across a (physical or imaginary) threshold, and begin to move. Abstain from a few simple things: food,*enclosed human-made structures, interaction with other humans, and technological devices.

Letting go of these conveniences and distractions, you can open your senses to the natural world, and to yourself. You can notice where you're drawn, and where you avoid. You can rest when you wish to rest, lie down if you want, dance, scream, play, laugh. Throughout it all, you can observe what comes to you,

---

* In this book so far, I've made a few references to going without food, also known as fasting, as a part of my own or someone else's rite of passage ceremony. Fasting is common in many religious and spiritual practices. But it doesn't work for many people, for a variety of reasons, and it isn't a prerequisite in rites of passage. You can always engage in wild wandering and nourish your body with food! I'll get into this more in Chapter Eight.

whether it's a falcon, a rainstorm, an ant, or a bit of trash. The goal is simply to be present with what is.

Whenever our vision is unclear, or we wish to invite guidance from the world beyond our own selves, wild wandering can be helpful. In this simple practice, we step into a conversation with the greater world, and become characters in our own waking dreams. The breeze on my cheek, the hummingbird zipping into the bushes, the chattering squirrel…they are all siblings with whom I can communicate and share respect, remembering my place in the cycles of life.

A walk such as this may or may not be a time for silence. There is great freedom and opportunity in speaking to the spirits, to the ancestors, to the rocks and trees and birds. Storyteller Martin Shaw says, "Speech is how we taste our ancestors." Humans, with our ability to move our mouths in ways that can convey large and abstract concepts, that step beyond the moment, reaching into the past or into the future, can offer our gifts to the rest of creation through praise and prayer. We may offer our words in this way, or seek guidance by entering into dialogue, asking for a rock or a creek to speak to us, to share with us something of its own nature, to share with us some newfound wisdom or to draw forth our own.

This practice works best when we do not analyze what happens to find meaning, or use it as an opportunity to think really hard on something difficult. Rather, we simply enter into an unfolding story, and observe with curiosity what happens. The clarity that comes may not be in the form of words or ideas, but rather may involve a shift in our hearts, in our emotional world, or in our physical bodies. We allow the world to have its way with us, trusting that the end result will be just what we need.

Doing this is not necessarily easy, even if you have a lot of experience. "I walk daily," says Izaac, age 28. "I always have. Walking consistently grounds me in my body and being, helps to clear my mind, and connects me to the landscape that I am within." Yet despite returning to this practice intuitively in his life, when Izaac was asked to participate in an intentional wander in preparation for his solo fast, he found himself struggling. "I was 'trying' to accomplish something on this walk," he shared. "I became so focused on my intention of the day and staying open to the environment that I was walking within that I became all tangled up in my head. Once I gave up on this and decided to just go on a stroll my spirit opened back up and I saw what was going on."

Many offer this form as a full day's wander, from sunup to sundown. Wandering for this length of time is a powerful practice. But for many, a full day is out of reach. Several hours, or even a short walk, can stir the imagination and bring shifts and clarity. While beautiful remote locations are powerful, city parks or even vacant lots can provide deep insight as well. Ideally, somewhere you can avoid other humans is helpful. While walking amidst human activity can also be useful in this practice, it's more difficult to stay present, open, and receptive, while negotiating the fast-paced urban life. It can be easier to make your external environment less overwhelming, especially at first.

> ⚘EXERCISE: Go on a wild wander while holding the question, "What is life calling me to step into?" With this question, you are continuing to refine your statement of intent, inviting in information from the more-than-human world. Set yourself up well by blocking out the time in advance, determining the location where you'll do your wander, and asking someone to be your emergency contact. By doing these things, you are creating the container for your wander.
>
> As you begin, mark the threshold into this wander, perhaps setting down a stick or some stones you pass over, or noticing a landscape feature that creates a threshold you can move through.
>
> As you wander on your journey, remember that the goal is not to think your way through, or to find an answer to the question. It is simply to allow whatever comes, to come. Stay attentive to physical safety; "stay found" even amidst your wander.

Cross back over the threshold to mark the end of your journey.

Physical safety is the priority; as humans we are vulnerable and must take great care of our bodies as we engage in emotional and spiritual work! Learn the hazards of a location before you venture there, whether those hazards are humans, plants, animals, or elements like sun or rain. Take essentials with you: plenty of water, protection from the elements, a bit of emergency food. Tell your emergency contact where you're going and when to expect you back, and what to do if you don't contact them when you expect to. As you wander, pay close attention so that you can easily find your way back to your starting point.

This is an important place to practice drawing community into your process. Tell your story to your mentor, a friend, or a family member upon your return. Ask them to share reflections on your story—not to analyze your story and find the hidden meaning, but rather to mirror back what they noticed in your telling like words or images that stuck out, and what your body language was like at different parts in the story.

EMBODIED RITUAL

"Ritual is to the soul what food is to the physical body." –Bukinabe writer and teacher Sobonfu Somé

As I prepared for my trip to Europe to visit the lands of my ancestors, I considered what I might do to mark this transition time in my life. I was ready to let go of some of my recent struggles. My friend suggested I cut my hair, or perhaps even shave my head. I didn't feel ready. I left for England shaggy, badly in need of a haircut.

Shortly after I arrived, I mentioned this to the friend I was staying with. She told me about a hairdresser friend of hers, attuned to the spiritual dimensions of her work (ritual comes in all sorts of unexpected ways!).

I made an appointment with the hairdresser. When she came to the house, I told her about my last several years, and what my intentions were for this journey. In ceremony, she cut my hair, releasing the stories contained in it. I swept up the hair into a little bag, and offered it back to the land as compost and nesting materials for birds. I moved forward lighter and freer, having let go of some of what I had been carrying from the past.

This story is a simple example of what ritual looks like. Ritual and ceremony are key parts of all spiritual and religious traditions, frequently taking a set form that is repeated in specific, consistent ways. But they are not just part of religious life. As a culture, we have many rituals embedded within our institutions, as well as daily lives. Blowing out the birthday candles is just one example of a secular ritual that many people honor. Sporting events are rich with secular ritual, as well—full of symbolism, small details that are done in the same way each game, and specific roles that players, coaches, referees, and fans enact.

Yet often these types of rituals lack clear intention and the type of transformation we may want to bring into our lives. With clear intention, ritual can provide actual, tangible value, for us as individuals, for our communities, and for the earth around us.

Ritual is the creative, soulful embodiment of our intentions, that which we are making true in our lives. Embodiment is key. When we engage in a ritual act, we embody a different way of being in the world, and bring that change inside of our skin, into our limbs and cells. When I cut my hair, I didn't just think about how it was time to let parts of myself go. I embodied a transformation. Small parts of me were literally cut from my body.

Research in psychology and anthropology suggests that the reason why ritual forms, or what rite of passage scholar Ronald Grimes calls "spiritual technology," have so much endurance in human cultures is because they have an actual survival value for humans, as well as beneficial ecological consequences. Reviewing the research, Grimes concludes, "'...ritual practices may, in the

An Altar in the Forest

STEPS IN DESIGNING RITUAL

1. Identify your intention/outcomes and limitations/constraints (time, space, etc.).
2. Identify elements that will be included.
3. Gather your tools and resources.
4. Sanctify the space: clean, beautify, remove distractions/limit disruptions.
5. Prepare the people: instruct all participants in what they'll need, what to expect, preparations they need to bring.
6. Open ceremony: land acknowledgement, silence, invocation, other. Invite protection, and that only good comes from your efforts.
7. Engage in/perform ceremonial elements.
8. Close ceremony: gratitude, release, other
9. Set tone for what's next: celebration, silence, other.

INTENTIONS FOR CEREMONIES:

- Gratitude
- Grief
- Releasing/Severance
- Cleansing/clearing
- Making commitment
- Welcoming
- Honoring
- Beginning
- Forgiveness
- Celebration
- Establishing rhythm
- Many others!

SOME ELEMENTS OF RITUAL AND CEREMONY:

- Nature
- Location: inside, outside, in between
- Building an altar or centerpiece
- Sound: bell, drum, rattle, voice, music, silence
- Scent: herbal smoke, essential oils
- Meditation
- Prayer/Invocation
- Storytelling/myth
- Movement
- Sacred speech
- Four elements: water, fire, earth, air
- Taste: ingesting food or drink
- Sight: darkness, light, candles
- Artistic expression: painting, drawing, etc.
- Offerings, gifting
- The role of the unexpected
- Others?

long run, be more practical than 'our' practicality." He describes having a conversation with an archaeologist that helped him to understand how deeply ritual affects humans:

He was explaining how certain values and social practices can be inferred from ancient bone matter. An archaeologist can deduce from bone composition that the men of a particular society consumed more protein than the women. On the basis of bone size and shape, it may also be evident that in some cultures women habitually carried heavier loads than men. Certain social practices are literally inscribed in the bones. Even though we imagine bone as private, and deeply interior to the individual body, it is also socially formed.

Piercings, tattoos, and other ways of marking our bodies in permanent ways are further ways that ritual manifests on our physical bodies, changing us forever.

Rich with symbolism, ritual and ceremony* help us to make meaning out of our lives. Rite of Passage practitioner Elder Paul Hill, Jr. says that "A ritual is the enactment of a myth. By participating in a ritual, you are participating in a myth." When enactment of a myth is a practice shared by a community or group of people, a ritual will typically take a prescribed form, enduring over time. There is great power in doing things in precise ways, honed over time to meet specific intentions.

Yet still, rituals morph and change, based on changing needs. Especially for those of us living in cultures without deeply transformative, shared rituals, we need to get creative! We don't have a rich repository of ceremonies that have meaning helping us to navigate through our daily lives as well as larger seasonal shifts, so we must re-create and re-generate our own. Remember the question I offered back in Chapter 4: *What will serve in this place, with these people, at this moment?* At times the answer may

---

*You may notice that I'm using the words ritual and ceremony interchangeably. People have very different definitions for each of these words. Some distinguish strongly between the two, and sometimes in contradictory ways. This conflicting way of using the terms has led me to be flexible in when and how I use them, working to meet people where they are at. Whether you prefer the word ritual or ceremony, the important thing is to get comfortable with the type of intentional embodiment that helps us move into a different way of being in the world.

ARCHETYPAL RITUAL ACTIONS ADAPTED FROM VIRGINIA HINE

A reminder to the reader: you are navigating risky terrain when you engage in ritual practice, where you can invoke more in the inner and outer world than you intend or are prepared to hold. One way to ground your explorations is by sharing your plans with your mentor(s) and community before engaging in any of these ritual actions, and creating a plan to debrief after. Please be clear and specific about what you're inviting in, and make sure to fully close your ritual practice by releasing and clearing the space.

SEVERANCE

- proceeding to a sacred area
- crossing a threshold
- lighting candles or lights to sacralize a space
- exiting from familiar
- rending/tearing
- cord-cutting
- hair cutting
- knocking down
- smashing
- breaking
- burning
- burying
- setting aside symbols of status/role
- untying
- washing off
- veiling
- stripping away
- purification
- removal of symbolic clothing

TRANSITION

- touching sacred objects
- isolation/solitude
- vigils
- nakedness
- living in "communitas" without status or role
- symbolic death and rebirth
- name change
- lifting up/raising high
- fasting
- nurturing/rest
- ordeals/stress/tests
- making vows
- immersion in water
- enactment of change or transformation
- hair style change
- period of silence
- wearing masks
- altered states of consciousness

ARCHETYPAL RITUAL ACTIONS ADAPTED FROM VIRGINIA HINE, CONTINUED

INCORPORATION

- moving away from a sacred area
- re-crossing a threshold
- re-entry into familiar
- fusing/joining objects
- exchange of hair cuttings
- building up
- exchanging gifts
- mending
- accepting symbolic clothing
- taking lights from a common source
- sharing food/drink
- feasting
- hand clasps/embraces
- unveiling
- tying/knotting
- circular positioning
- group chanting/singing

lead you to set, prescribed forms that have endured over time; at times what will serve may be entirely new and emergent.

In this day and age, many of us try to think our way into change, with slow results. Ritual is truly transformative—for individuals, human communities, for places. It transforms by changing things for all parts of us as humans: body, mind, heart, spirit.

Ritual shifts our thinking. As we talked about in Chapter One, ritual provides new mental pictures to make sense of ourselves and our lives, new stories. New synapses in our brains get formed through these types of ritual acts, and as we continue to support those synapses in firing they begin to strengthen. Our minds can return to them as a new "story" whenever we feel doubt.

Through ritual, our emotions are evoked, and we can move through them and release them symbolically. Grief, rage, joy, fear, anger, gratitude—these emotions and so many more are an essential part of what makes us human, but we frequently do not have safe spaces to fully feel them. Often, we stuff them for a more convenient moment, but that moment never seems to come, so we begin to turn those emotions inward. Frequently, they turn into depression, anxiety, aggression, ambivalence, or disease. Done well, ritual creates a container where we can consciously and safely evoke our unprocessed emotions, let them cycle through us, and then be released or transmuted.

All of these provide the capacity for change. But there's also the spiritual impact of ritual. Ritual can shift things in dimensions far beyond the human world. German philosopher Frederich Neitzche wrote, "When one rows it is not the rowing that moves the ship; rowing is only a magical ceremony by means of which one compels the demons to move the ship." While you may or may not believe this literally, ritual invites us to step into a world in which we are no longer the powerful masters of the universe, but rather small conduits for powers much bigger than ourselves.

When one doesn't have ready access to time-tested, effective rituals (consistent with their values and beliefs), it can feel natural to turn to other traditions. But there is power in engaging in rituals of your own making, either as an individual or as a group. For those of us without rituals that make sense to us, this is how we re-create a culture that actually works for us.

If you're not practiced with ritual, your attempts may feel awkward and clumsy at first. Many of us are inexperienced when it comes to ritual; we simply haven't had the education and training needed to be skilled. Ritual requires humility and discernment, and the discipline to call in only what you're ready to handle! Experienced teachers and guides are invaluable here; seek them out. Yet this doesn't mean you shouldn't experiment. It means that you need to approach ritual as a cautious child, learning about how the world works through play, discovering what works for you and what doesn't. And like I shared in the story of my ceremony on the mountains, take time and care to ask for safety and protection.

⚚ EXERCISE: Using the above guide, create and enact a simple ceremony for yourself or for someone else. It doesn't need to be anything fancy or elaborate, or serious and somber. Experiment as you figure out what feels good and authentic to you, while also taking care not to exploit sacred practices from other cultures.

FROM ME TO WE: SERVICE AND ACTIVISM

"The ability to serve others has been a big motivator for me to learn and try new things. I have realized that being competent in a wide variety of skills and environments allows me to help more people, things, and nature. This makes me feel needed, accomplished, and connected. I can see and feel how my actions have contributed to the growth of something bigger than myself and it gives meaning and perspective to my life." –Gretchen, age 26

Another critical way that we explore the question of where we're going is through the practice of service. In stepping into adulthood, we are stepping into a time of serving the broader community. Our focus moves further beyond ourselves and our own personal interests, and towards the collective good. Clearly, we can't do this just by focusing on our own internal process! By getting out there, and contributing your gifts in service, the gifts that we each have to offer become clearer. We see how we fit in, and the purpose we can serve. Howard Thurman, a Black American philosopher and educator who fought to break down racial, ethnic, and gender barriers, said, "don't ask what the world needs, ask what makes you come alive, then go do that. Because what the world needs is people that have come alive." Yet for many of us, it can be difficult to identify what makes us come alive! Service and activism are opportunities to explore what draws you, and how that can contribute to the broader good.

Service can include taking on a formal role, like an internship or volunteer position in your community. It can also include seeking out informal opportunities to help out in your community: visiting the elderly woman in the apartment down the hall, for example, and helping her out with household tasks. It can look like political activism, upping your game as a supportive and available friend, or picking up trash in your neighborhood. It's less about what you do, and more about orienting toward the world as one who gives more than they take.

⚘ **EXERCISE**: Consider the ways that you've been of service in your family and community already. Write in your journal: What comes naturally, and brings you pleasure? What makes you come alive? What are the gifts that you feel you most have to offer?

⚚ EXERCISE: As you reflect on the service you've previously done, consider how you want to serve your community now. Perhaps this includes drawing on skills and interests that you already know you have; perhaps it means exploring new areas. Take a tangible step today towards offering this service to the world.

⚚ EXERCISE: A critical part of service is offering what others actually want, not what we think they need! Ask a person in your life, a mentor or a peer: how can you be of service to them?

THE ROAD AHEAD

You stand now at the threshold, about to turn toward shaping your initiation. Perhaps you've moved slowly along the journey so far, taking the time to savor the exercises and reflect deeply. Perhaps you've moved quickly, skipping over pages, feeling anxious for the moment of transformation you can feel is coming, wanting to just get on with things already!

In our fast-moving world full of instant gratification, it can be so tempting to move on to the next new thing, bright and shiny. The paradox of initiation is that it only comes to those who are sufficiently prepared, which can take weeks, months, or even years. I have watched many people feeling called urgently to a rite of passage ceremony, only to be asked to wait. When it is finally their moment, over and over I hear them express gratitude at the delay.

Your challenge now is to know yourself when it is time, to look for the signs and clues that it is the moment to leap. So before you turn the page toward initiation, take a moment to ask yourself: am I ready?

When you can answer a full-hearted yes, read on!

☾

*Walker, your footsteps
are the road, and nothing more.
Walker, there is no road,
the road is made by walking.
Walking you make the road,
and turning to look behind
You see the path you never
again will step upon.*

*Walker, there is no road,
only foam trails on the sea.*

–Spanish Poet Antonio Machado

PART III:
CROSSING THE THRESHOLD TO ADULTHOOD

Chapter Eight:

INITIATION

"I believe there is much to be learned from slowing down and dedicating time to oneself to seek and reveal the inner wisdom." –Chris, age 28

"I don't know why I want to do this, but something is urging me to." –Sarah, age 27

Reflecting on her life, Naila, age 21, says that she's had three initiations so far. The first was at menarche (her first menstrual cycle), when she was 14. Her mom organized a small ceremony with women from her community. "It was a bit secretive," says Naila. "Not secret in terms of hiding, but there was a magic to it." Naila was blindfolded, and the women, dressed in red, came to collect Naila. She was placed on a horse and led on a ride to a special place on the land. The older women shared what it was like to be a woman, and invited her to join them in womanhood.

She was given presents: "beautiful rings and so on." Summing it up, Naila shares, "this wasn't a big thing in a way, but it was very meaningful to mark that point in my life story."

> "Initiation evokes a revelation of the sacred and that is the primary means of making us fully human."
> –paraphrase of Religious Historian Mircea Eliade

Naila's second major initiation was described earlier in the book, in the section on virginity: for her first experience of lovemaking, she and her chosen lover were sent off with care from the community, had their time together, and then returned to a party and celebration.

Her third initiation came shortly thereafter, when she was 16 and traveled to the United States from Portugal on her own, for an intentional nature-based rite of passage experience. The initiation began even before she left home. "I had never done such a huge journey alone," she says. "I booked my flights by myself. I went on this journey, and my flight left without me and so it was really like: 'OK, try to get along!' "

After working with the airline to get on a new flight, Naila made it to her destination in California. There, she joined a group of young people for a guided four-day solo fast experience, with preparation time before and integration time after. "The main thing I gained from it was actually being able to feel at home wherever I am," Naila says, reflecting on it five years later. "I am always there, I always have something I can rest in. Wherever I go, there are people around me and I can look at humanity and see that we are all seeking the same thing in life. When I came there, I immediately had friendships with a lot of the participants. And I still have deep friendships with them. This whole journey was so empowering.

"It was also really about getting to know myself. Who am I? What do I want to do in this world? What could be my task for why I came to this planet? When I came out of the solo time I can definitely say that I knew more about who I am, on all levels. But I also knew, 'OK, I am simply 16. I'm a teenager, I can just be young.' Because in my life I behaved older than I was or than I am, like I try to seem more mature, and this was a moment of, 'Ah I am simply 16! I can ask as many questions as I want!' Of course, everybody can ask as many questions as we want, but it was such a release of knowing this is where I am in a whole life journey."

Naila was privileged to come from a community that recognized her need for initiation, and prepared her for it. Yet even for this young woman who grew up in a strong fabric of community, at some point she needed to leave the community behind, and travel far from home, on her own, for her initiation ceremony. In turning the page to this chapter, you have signaled that this is what is next for you as well.

So far in this book, we've been slowly building a foundation, exploring the role of rites of passage historically, and what they mean in our lives and communities today. Along the way, you've prepared yourself, building skills and diving deeply into a range of topics in order to develop a holistic picture of what's needed to step through the gateway into adulthood. This preparation work has been critical. Aristotle says the role of the guide is to help the initiate attain the "correct posture." This is what you've been doing: developing proper posture towards adulthood in order to successfully step through the threshold on your own.

Now we arrive at the key moment: initiation. Ultimately, no rite of passage happens without a "rite"—a ceremony to mark the passage. This ceremony marks the moment of confirmation, when you step fully into the next stage of life. Over the course of this chapter, you will explore some of the possibilities for initiation, as you put together the pieces to create your own powerful threshold experience to help you step fully into the next stage of life.

THE THRESHOLD WITHIN A THRESHOLD

"Thresholds are dangerous places, neither here nor there, and walking across one is like stepping off the edge of a cliff in the naive faith that you'll sprout wings halfway down. You can't hesitate, or doubt. You can't fear the in-between." –Science fiction writer Alix E. Harrow

Whenever I'm asked to design a rite of passage process, I begin by identifying the larger developmental transition happening for someone (like between childhood and adolescence, or between adulthood and elder years). Then I begin to apply the stages of a rite of passage from the 10 Essentials list: severance, threshold, and incorporation.

This chapter is all about the threshold stage, the place in-between. You have done the preparation work you needed to do to be ready to step into adulthood, and you've begun letting things go from your former self to make way for what is next. Now it's time to create the conditions where you can be fully in-between, "no-longer and not-yet."

For example, think of Naila's story, navigating the developmental transition from childhood to adulthood. She experienced a severance from childhood, marked and held in community, when she received her first blood. This ceremony honored the death of her childhood, and marked for her and the community that she was now in the liminal stage of adolescence. After this happened, she found herself in the threshold time of adolescence, making her way along the path toward adulthood. When she was 16, Naila found herself saying yes to a rite of passage journey far from home, all the way across the world. With this last adventure, Naila moved across multiple *thresholds within thresholds:* solo time in nature *within* a larger initiatory process *within* the life stage of adolescence. It was after this third initiation, where Naila took the time to honor and allow herself to "just be 16" that she was ready to return home, and take her first steps as a young adult within her community, beginning the work of incorporation.

This didn't mean that Naila always felt like an adult after her rite of passage in nature! Reflecting on this story a few years after I initially interviewed her, Naila wrote, "I did feel more initiated and 'adult'/grownup after this rite of passage, but I wouldn't say that from that moment on I felt adult."

Already on this journey, you have left behind the known world of your previous identity, and shed parts of yourself. You are very much in a liminal space already. Now you are preparing to cross *thresholds within thresholds* as you make the passage into adulthood. As you prepare, there are two important questions to ask yourself: *What will help me move into adulthood? What is left to be done before I can fully move into this stage of life?*

Threshold within a Threshold within a Threshold

❦EXERCISE: Before you can fully step into the liminal phase, there must be a marking of severance. Consider what it's time for you to let go of—what roles, habits, behaviors, relationships. Referencing the lists in the previous chapter, prepare for and create a "severance ceremony."

FINDING A GUIDED EXPERIENCE

When Nadia was around 24, she knew that it was time for some sort of change. She had lost both her parents in the years before this, and was living with her aunt in the capital of Madagascar. While her aunt was kind, this was a very rough time for Nadia. "I was kind of longing for home, longing for love, longing for that answer, you know, of what my future will hold for me," she recalls.

She reached out to a friend of a friend in the United States. Through a series of connections, she eventually connected with Surfing the Creative, the program mentioned earlier where young people come from around the world to dance together, in study and ceremony, as they move towards adulthood. Nadia immediately knew this experience was for her. "They sent me this video with all these young people who come from all over the world, who were being accepted as who they are and learning to be confident, to love themselves, and to face their future," she says. "The first time I saw the video I was crying and I knew that's what I needed! I needed that moment of: 'Ok, now I know what the way is even though it's not clear. I know what the tools I need to get to move forward.'"

Through a lot of hard work on Nadia's part and the support of the program, Nadia traveled to take part in the camp over the course of several summers. Coming from Madagascar to Boulder, the camp was a very new, strange experience for Nadia. "The experience was weird, because it was new and I didn't understand how things were working. I myself am not a dancer. I mean, I dance but not using dancing as a tool. So the first experience for me was really the new, the weird, the unfamiliar. However, the new, the weird, the unfamiliar brought a light into the answer of the question of who I am. It opened new doors, to who I am, to who the world is, to who the community is, to who I am as myself as Nadia, to who I am as a woman, to who I am as my role in my communities."

Nadia's story illustrates the power of seeking out an established rite of passage offering to support you on your journey. It's also an example of how the experience can come from unexpected places.

There are hundreds, perhaps thousands, of options available for guided, supported initiatory journeys available to young people today, from short weekend immersions to extended, multi-year journeys. These offerings employ dozens of different modalities as means of transformation: the arts, experiences in nature, political activism, cultural exploration, service, and more. Some focus on particular genders, religions, cultural background, or other social locations; others, like the one Nadia experienced, emphasize bringing together groups across broad differences.

Taking part in a guided experience of this sort creates an opportunity to be supported by mentors and guides who know what they are doing. This allows you as a participant to let go, and be fully immersed in the experience. It creates the possibility of gaining exposure to new things that you can't even imagine, often following a framework that has taken years, perhaps even decades or longer, to develop and refine. It also means surrendering your control and trusting others to lead you through a process. Humility, tolerance, and challenging your worldview are just some of the benefits that can come from that.

Additionally, in a program or community-based setting you're held within a community of peers who are going through what you are going through, as well. This shared lived experience can be valuable, both during the experience and in having a circle who understands what you've been through to support you upon your return.

This option is great as a means of setting yourself up for success. Without experiencing a model of what an effective rite of passage looks like, you're likely to do a lot of unnecessary flailing.

Last, a program provides accountability, which makes it harder to back out when the going gets tough. I've seen many folks try to design their whole experience and it just never quite happens.

By this point in the journey, you may have already caught notice of offerings that are out there. Take note of the things that have come into your awareness, even if they're subtle and not yet clear! To find what program or experience might be right for you is a deeply intuitive process. As always, there are suggestions in the Online Resources for places to get started.

It's important to note that there are programs out there that are not skillful or effective, and some don't have much awareness of cultural exploitation. If you see something that appeals to you, often programs make it possible for you to talk to the person guiding the experience, and to talk to someone who has taken part in the experience in the past. Be clear what you are looking for. Here are some questions to ask:

1. What is the lineage of your program? What traditions do you draw from, and how did they come to be part of your program?

2. What sort of training do your guides receive?

3. Do you provide support upon my return?

Oftentimes, the sticker price for these programs can feel quite expensive. Charging money for ceremonial processes is also a very sensitive, complex issue. The reality is that it can take a lot of resources to create experiences in today's modern world, especially ones that interface heavily with dominant culture. Insurance, outreach, legal requirements, permits: all of these things take money. There is also a lot of value in providing a livelihood for those leading the experience. If the prices feel outside of your reach, don't let that stop you! Strong programs will have generous financial aid, scholarships, lifeways back*, and/or sliding

---

*Lifeways back initiatives recognize that many Black and/or Indigenous people lack access to traditional cultural teachings because of colonization and chattel slavery, and offer their work for free or at a reduced cost as a means of returning these practices to the peoples from whom they were stolen.

scale options, and they want to share their work with any young people with a strong desire to take part.

In addition to support from the program itself, asking for support from your community (whether that be family, friends, local businesses, or more) can become a powerful part of your experience in its own right. When I did my coming of age trip at 13, I cleaned houses and babysat to earn the money I needed. Along the way, my parents' friends became invested in my experience, and I created a community interested in my story when I returned. I also noticed that I felt way more invested in the experience than my peers whose parents had paid for them (and sometimes even bribed them!) to participate. When I look back, securing the resources for the experience was part of what made the experience as valuable as it was for me.

⚘EXERCISE: Visit the Youth Passageways website and take a look at some of the offerings that are available.* What inspires your curiosity?

---

*As I said earlier in the book, Youth Passageways is the group I helped to start some years ago, and where I continue to serve as a member of the staff. Many of the stories from this book come from the efforts of others and myself in working to establish Youth Passageways as a diverse coalition supporting rites of passage in the world today. Some of the offerings listed on our website I think are amazing, some I have questions about. I offer it as a resource to you because I think it's a great place to start to see what's out there, and begin to follow your instincts to find what's right for you.

SELF-DESIGNING A CEREMONY WITHIN ONE'S COMMUNITY

Sometimes, there is not an experience out there that is quite what you need for the initiation journey you are on, or you are simply called to use your own initiation to develop a stronger community where you are. This is not ideal for your first rite of passage experience, but these are not ideal times. For a number of reasons self-designing may feel like your only option, or the right option for you despite the hazards. If this is true, your first task is to call together a group of people to support you on your journey. I'd suggest three to five people. This group will help you figure out what it is that you're marking, and then design an experience to effectively make that transition. If you go this route, at least some elements of the initiation should be placed in the hands of others, and remain unknown to you.

As you think about who to invite to support you, people who live far away may come to mind. There are definitely benefits of finding folks who live in physical proximity, with whom it's easy to meet in person. There are also benefits to including people who feel right to include even if they are far away. I suggest you trust your instincts while also challenging yourself to find one person, preferably more than one, who is in physical proximity. This helps to build local, in-person community, and provide immediate physical support if you need it.

People that you include don't need to have experience navigating the same sort of transition you're going through or come from a similar background. They do need to be people you trust and people who care about you. The group you select also needs to include at least some people you'd consider to be "mature adults," as well as folks that have the capacity to offer you some time and attention to support you on your journey.

The rest of this chapter includes critical information for you if you are going to design your own rite of passage ceremony. It will also be helpful for you if you ultimately choose a guided experience.

A FEW BENEFITS OF GUIDED AND SELF-DESIGNED RITE OF PASSAGE CEREMONIES

GUIDED	SELF-DESIGNED
Support from trained mentors and guides	Embedded in community of beings (people, places, elements of the more than human world) that are chosen by you
Design that has often been refined over time	
Others are going through the experience alongside you	Can be created to meet your own unique needs and intentions
External systems of safety and accountability	Can feel (and sometimes be) more accessible

⚘ EXERCISE: Reflect on the following questions: Why might you consider self-designing a rite of passage for yourself? What hazards do you see in this option, and what benefits? If you chose this route, what support would you need, and whom could you trust to provide it?

FOUR ELEMENTS OF A RITE OF PASSAGE

As you consider what your threshold-within-a-threshold will look like, there are four elements of a rite of passage that you'll want to attend to. After years of creating rites of passage for teens, Rite of Passage Journeys' Founder Stan Crow found that lots of people started asking him to explain how he did his work. What were the essential elements of a rite of passage? He looked back over the years of his work with youth, trying to articulate the central components that made what he did effective. As he reflected, Stan saw that there were four main elements key to providing

Four Elements of a Rite of Passage as described by Stan Crow

meaningful, transformational initiation experiences for the young people he served.

PRACTICAL TESTING

An initiation is a test. Like any test, it includes the possibility of failure; you might not make it to the other side. To me, this is part of what makes an initiation meaningful—it actually requires skill, preparation, and capacity.

It's important to emphasize the *practical* nature of this test. What is being tested is that you have the qualities and capacities needed to live as an adult among your People. While the physical courage to face down a lion may be a practical skill in one community, in another community the capacity to work together in a group to restore a stream may be far more relevant.

For many offering rites of passage in the risk-averse, litigious dominant culture, figuring out how to create meaningful tests with the possibility of failure is difficult work. It is a heartbreaking paradox that while programs are expected to ensure high levels of safety, countless young lives are lost through unprecedented high rates of suicide, substance abuse, and violence, not to mention the millions of young people who make it through their adolescence alive but emotionally stunted and traumatized.

Your task is to design for yourself an experience which pushes you to your very edge, where you are able to go beyond where you thought you could go and see your true capacity and limitations. At the same time, and I say this unequivocally: we need you! Please do not take unnecessary risks, and become yet another lost soul destroyed by our culture. Remember that to be alive in these tenuous times is a challenge in itself! In a world of climate crisis and radical social change, each creative, vibrant, young soul struggling to bring forth their gifts in the world is essential.

This is your daunting, perhaps seemingly impossible task: how do you weave a container around you so strongly that it ensures your emotional, physical, and spiritual safety, while at the same time pushing yourself harder than you ever have before?

MENTORED LEARNING

We've already spoken a lot about mentoring. At this stage, I want to reemphasize the importance of having a mentor or guide that has been through the initiatory journey, to successfully support you in your passage. This is not a journey that you can or should go through completely by yourself! While there are times in the initiation that you will need to navigate through without a mentor right there, it is essential to have at least one person holding the space for you while you are on your journey, acting as a touchstone throughout the experience.

Also, there are specific skills and qualities that need guidance in order to be learned, whether they be skills like leadership, problem-solving, and communication, or skills such as outdoor living, learning ancestral or spiritual traditions, or maybe even carpentry! A rite of passage is about helping you to bring forth your gifts in service to your community, and a mentor helps you gain the knowledge and skills you need to do so. If you still feel lost about where to turn for mentorship, please reach out to Youth Passageways for support and we will problem-solve with you. We are connected with people across the globe who might be available for support.

EMBODIED RITUAL

We've talked a fair amount about ritual so far. The *rite* in a rite of passage is essential; it's the physical embodiment of change and transition. Ritual pulls life transitions out of the mundane, daily world of our existence, and connects what is happening in our minds, hearts, and bodies with the creative forces at play in the world: the powerful elements of earth, air, water, and fire; the changes of the seasons; the movements of the stars and cycles of the moon. The forces involve high drama, and our rituals must, too. Through ceremony, we create a knowing in our bodies, not just our minds, that *things are different now*. A threshold was crossed, and there is no going back.

COMMUNITY CELEBRATION

The last essential component of a rite of passage is the coming together of a community, to mark and celebrate the transition. This is important both for the initiates and for the broader collective. Folks that have just undergone a challenging and difficult transformation are seen, honored, and recognized. The broader community is renewed, and their bonds are strengthened.

Storytelling is often a significant component of this element of a rite of passage. The stories that someone carries back across the threshold can be powerful: raw, elemental, unfiltered, and soulful. They can carry simple yet profound truths. The stories contain *medicine*, not only for the person sharing their story, but for the broader community. Because of their power, it's also important that these stories are told at a sacred time and in a sacred manner, to help them retain their potency.

For many years at Pacific Quest, groups of select staff had the opportunity to participate in a 72-hour fasting solo on the land, utilizing a lot of the elements found in this book. When they returned from their solo time, all the former participants of this experience were invited to come hear the stories. Each time, a circle of caring community members gathered to hear the stories that the six folks who have just been fasting bring from the land. Coming together in this way, participants were witnessed and supported by a broader community who could relate to their journey. Their experience was strengthened and affirmed while they were given valuable insights into the challenges of bringing their experience from the land back into their daily lives.

At the same time, former participants are reminded of their own journeys and gain new insights into how they want to further incorporate the experience, sometimes even years later. They also give back some of their hard-won insights, and provide guidance and mentorship. Together, a truly remarkable, deeply connected community grew out of a professional workplace, where a small group of people got to know and support each other intimately.

A FEW EXAMPLES OF THE FOUR ELEMENTS OF A RITE OF PASSAGE

MENTORED LEARNING	PRACTICAL TESTING
Apprenticeship for a job or trade. Studying a particular craft or artistic form with a master teacher.	Performing or presenting your learnings in a formal setting.
Learning camping skills.	Time in nature—solo and/or in a group setting.
Working with a coach or therapist to develop skills to support relational healing.	Organizing a community action on behalf of an issue you care about.
Engaging in activist training.	Traveling to a place very different from your own.

EMBODIED RITUAL	COMMUNITY CELEBRATION
Routines of daily acknowledgement: greeting the sun, greeting the moon, meal blessings.	Feasting on a meal created by the initiate for the community, or by the community for the initiate.
Severance ceremonies.	Storytelling circle where the initiate shares their rite of passage experience.
Ceremonies to honor and gift your community.	Gifting to the initiate and/or from the initiate to their supporters/community.
Donning new ritual clothing to mark a transition.	Seasonal gatherings to mark ongoing transitions in the lives of community members and renew commitments

SOLO TIME IN NATURE

"In the past, the times I have felt most empowered and connected to myself are those spent in nature. In the desert, at the bottom of giant canyons, protected by sandstone walls and accompanied by cheerful cacti, I first discovered my power. In the Adirondack mountains, I practiced. In Hawaii, I have learned about how to let go, to be, and to trust myself." –Veronica, age 24

We've already explored the importance of connecting with the more-than-human world through time on the land in your homeplace, and through the practice of a wild wander. Hopefully so far, you've created opportunities to be in nature and are experiencing the benefits. These benefits include nervous system regulation, since time in nature has been scientifically shown to help us cope with and recover from stress. Hopefully, your time in nature has also helped you deepen your relationship with the broader, more-than-human world around you, coming to see other beings as your kin. Maybe it's provided insights and clarity as well, and helped you discern next steps in your process.

In this day and age, with the vast disconnect of many humans from the rest of the natural world and the speed with which things move, solo time in nature is an invaluable, if not critical, part of a rite of passage experience. While it's not one of the four elements that Stan identified, for me it provides the ground-cloth on which all the models, frameworks, and theories lie. If you are comfortable outside, nature provides a refuge and a training ground for you to continue to deepen into relationship with the world around you and draw the lessons that will allow you to best serve your people. If you are uncomfortable in nature, with a strong container and good preparation, time on the land provides testing, challenge, and opportunity for healing; a threshold into a deeper level of trust in the world around you; and a chance to affirm your birthright of connection to the more-than-human world.

Even with all of the technology and amazing brain capacity that we have as humans, a fundamental truth is clear: we can't control nature despite centuries of trying. This is true of ourselves as well; we as humans are one part of nature. Time on the land, in communion with the elements, other beings, and our own doubts and fears and insecurities: there is simply nothing that replaces it.

Of course, I am biased. My journey with rites of passage began with 24 hours alone by the ocean, and nature has been my solace when times are rough ever since then. It is different if you haven't grown up with ready access to wild nature. For many, nature is a place of hazard, as well, where animals or humans may harm us. This is connected with skin color, gender, the unique needs of our body, ancestral trauma, and more.

As Katheryne, age 26, prepared for solo time in nature, she shared that "as a young Black woman, for a long time I believed that nature and the outdoors did not exist for me. It was not safe for me. Those grand adventures to forests and waterfalls and oceans were not for me." Challenging these messages in herself and in the outer world was both part of what drew her to participate in the experience, as well as one of the barriers she faced.

With regard to solo time in nature, as with all of the elements of rite of passage, you need to discern how it fits into your journey, and where you need support in designing and implementing your experience.

FASTING AND OTHER SACRIFICES

A few times in this book I've mentioned fasting, a common practice in relation to solo experiences, but haven't yet provided much context. A common, and often important element of rites of passage is going without certain things. On nature-based solo experiences, for example, food, an enclosed shelter, and human company are frequently given up for the duration of the solo time.

There are great gifts that come from giving up one or more aspects of your day to day life as part of this process: making *sacrifices*. The roots of the word *sacrifice* mean "to make sacred." When we give something up, we make what we are doing sacred. As rite of passage guide Will Scott puts it, "we make our intentions more real by showing that we mean it: we are willing to give up comfort in service to our longings." This is part of the purpose behind many religious traditions, like the Muslim practice of fasting from dawn until dusk during the month of Ramadan, or the Catholic practice of giving something up during Lent, the 40 days from Ash Wednesday to Easter. There are all sorts of things we can sacrifice in our lives today: food, human contact, watching TV, time on screens or social media specifically, creature comforts.

To speak more specifically about food, fasting offers a number of benefits. That's why it's a common practice in spiritual traditions the world over. Fasting is a physical challenge, brings heightened consciousness and awareness, shifts our daily rhythms, and can heighten our senses. It also allows us to empty out our bowels, clear toxins, and reset our digestive system.

Fasting is definitely *not* for everyone, however. People with certain health challenges, difficulty maintaining body fat, on medications that need to be taken with food, and/or with a history of disordered eating will usually not be served by fasting. I've worked with many people who choose to bring food while on a solo experience. Sometimes this is as basic as simple snacks or fruit to be taken with a medication, sometimes people make simple one-pot meals once or twice a day, and sometimes people decide to eat normally. It is a very common practice for folks to ingest electrolytes while fasting, and everyone I work with carries emergency food as a safety backup. I have often seen people turn food preparation and ingestion into a powerful, healing aspect of their ceremony. As with every other aspect of this book, please focus on making healthy, safe, and body-affirming choices. Especially if you have any of the risk factors named earlier, deciding whether or not to fast is a great conversation for you to have with your medical care provider, mental health support people, and your body.

While abstaining from creature comforts (whether food, screens, or a tent that you can zip up from the elements) can be a powerful aspect of your ceremony and an important part of practical testing, this isn't necessary or even healthy for everyone. Especially for people that experience a lot of hardship in their day to day life, choosing to bring a little extra—a snuggly warm blanket, a nourishing special hot beverage—can be an empowering gesture of self-honoring and care. This is a great place to reflect on your intentions, your edges, and what will truly serve you at this time.

And please, no matter what, tend to your physical safety first and always. Remember: we need you!

PLANNING A SEND-OFF CEREMONY

Whether you embark on an experience through a program or you self-design your own threshold experience, you'll want to have some sort of send-off in your community. Whether you invite a few people or host a larger community gathering, I suggest you include the following parts:

1. Invite your mentor to be part of the planning, and incorporate anything they want to include that resonates for you.

2. Include some sort of sharing from you, about your learning journey so far, where you're going, and what your intentions are for your threshold time.

3. Invite any questions, advice, or blessings, anyone wants to offer.

4. Ask for whatever support you wish for during this time from the guests (you might, for example, give a candle to each guest, and ask that they light it at a certain key time).

5. Be witnessed in making a prayer of gratitude and calling on your ancestors, your Higher Power, or whatever forces feel supportive for your journey.

6. Formally lay down former roles and relationships.

7. Make a vow of safety: how you will care for yourself while you are away.

8. Share food together as a nice way to close/transition.

BUILDING A PLAN FOR RETURN

In the next chapter, we'll explore the Return: what it's like to come back into your daily life after a transformative experience, some common challenges, and some strategies to support you in the process. But before you even embark on your threshold experience, you'll want to lay some groundwork to come back to. Similar to your send-off ceremony, you will want to have a return ceremony, where you invite the same people to come and celebrate your return. Elements of a return ceremony might include:

1. Invite your mentor to be part of the planning, and incorporate anything they want to include.

2. Again share your intentions for your time, and share the story of your journey.

3. Invite reflections that anyone wants to offer.

4. Express gratitude for the support you've received from the community. Gift-giving can be an effective way to express gratitude.

5. Be witnessed in offering a prayer of gratitude and release for your ancestors, your Higher Power, or whatever forces you called in at the beginning.

6. Formally pick back up roles that will continue, and name/embody changes and new roles you are claiming.

7. Definitely sharing food here as a way of marking and celebrating!

In addition to planning this event to happen shortly after your return, it's also wonderful if you can create some open time in the first few weeks after your return for reflection and integration. This time will be as essential as your time in the initiation experience itself.

☽ **EXERCISE**: In communication with the peers and mentor you identified for support early in the book, explore the pros and cons of a Self-Designed versus Guided Initiation. Do the research you need to do to make a decision. If you decide to engage in a guided experience, do the work of finding the right match and securing your spot on it.

If you decide that a Self-Designed Rite of Passage is for you, fill out the worksheet in Appendix II and begin to brainstorm your experience. Don't judge, evaluate, or censor at this time, just continue to dream! Invite guidance and help from your support team. You can pause on your reading—and go back and review sections that feel important—until you've completed your initiation.

☾

Chapter Nine:

RETURN

"Incorporation is this life-long thing. I go through phases where I feel really connected with my intent and others where it seems like a long way away. It's an intentional process where you need to be gentle with yourself, but it's so helpful when I can touch back into my experience."
–Katheryne, age 29

Katheryne knows a lot about the challenges of incorporation. In her first solo ceremony when she was 27, she went out to claim, "I am me. An irrepressible force of power and freedom and love." While her experiences out there gave her a sense of her power, coming back into her day-to-day life, and especially at work, almost immediately she felt pushback from the world around her. Returning back from this experience she felt the challenge of living as herself, "an irrepressible force," especially at work. She described the experience as "pretty monumental, because it really set the scene for how I would exercise my power and my voice. After my fast, I was not afraid of putting myself out there, and exploring my leadership and my power. Power has been an important part of these last few years, and recognizing how I do have power, even if you look at it historically and statistically [as a queer Black woman] I don't have power."

Growing up in a military family in the suburbs, Katheryne learned early on how to get along, especially in primarily white contexts like her high school. But she noticed the many inequities in her workplace, and there were a lot of things which made her uncomfortable. Before her fast, "I had a lot of hesitancy in how I put myself out there in naming my opinions, and naming when I was uncomfortable. I was sort of a doormat. I kept my mouth shut and just went along." Friends and colleagues encouraged her to speak up. "I was told that I needed to trust my power and trust my voice," she shares.

She found that when she returned from her solo time, she began speaking up, and the reaction wasn't positive. "All of that turned into me challenging people to have difficult conversations when I found myself being scapegoated, which was hard as a Black woman. I didn't feel like I could keep quiet and allow things to continue anymore. Soon I found myself in a situation where I was told I needed to turn down my voice."

Katheryne found that her time on her solo both catalyzed these changes in her, and supported her in navigating the changes. "It was difficult, but I trusted myself, and I was more in tune and able to care for myself first. It became really empowering to understand that my voice has weight and value, my words have meaning. I can use them to protect myself and others."

As Katheryne reached the end of her time with the company, and prepared for a big move, things grew particularly acute. "I was trying to understand my legacy, and feeling the limitations, and all this stuff coming at me. I felt this energy coming through my hands and surging through my chest. It felt like my ancestors coming through me like, 'We're here, what are you going to do?' It felt like rage, and it felt like passion. I felt a lot of passion toward the end." Katheryne found herself fully inhabiting her intent: being herself, an irrepressible force of power and freedom and love.

CROSSING BACK OVER THE THRESHOLD

In the last chapter, you built a plan around your threshold experience, and you took time to envision what your return might look like. Of course, a plan is just a plan. Remember: you, as the initiate, are not solely in charge of this experience. Mystery is ultimately the one moving you through this journey.

Sometimes, there can be a lot of desire to linger at the threshold. It can feel so alluring to stay where things often feel clearer, away from the mundane details of life. Sometimes folks feel impatient to return as soon as possible, and begin to apply the insights they have had. However you feel about it, it's important to take clear, decisive steps back over the threshold, and return to the world you left behind. Here is where you can truly begin incorporating your vision, insights, and newfound skills into your life as you assume a new role on behalf of your community.

Returning from a rite of passage is a time of ripe opportunity, but it's also probably the trickiest part of the whole thing. The process of incorporation has never been easy, since it requires someone to inhabit a life they've never lived. Yet the task is particularly challenging in communities without shared initiatory rites. No clear pathway for return exists that others have walked before, no shared models that returning individuals and their loved ones can draw on for what is happening.

This means that returning from an initiatory experience can be deeply lonely and isolating. Some days, it might feel like the world is conspiring to undermine any changes you are trying to make. Other days, your initiatory experience is likely to feel impossibly far away, like a dream that has no bearing on reality. When I bring back folks from time on the land, invariably someone makes a comment about returning to "the real world." I remind them that their time on the land, in intimate connection with the elements and the pace of the rocks and trees, is as real as the world gets. This is one of the challenges in a cynical world: remembering that our moments of clarity and insights are not fanciful naivete, but are actually encounters with truth in a world filled with noise.

Community support is essential in returning back from a rite of passage. When Tarek, age 30, experienced difficulty returning from a powerful initiation at a holistic sexuality mystery school a few years ago, staying connected with others that had been part of his experience was foundational for his return. "I remember coming out of the experience, and still being in a foreign place," he says, reflecting back. "I remember still being raw, but also in my body and in my heart in a way I hadn't been before. There was a way of feeling uncomfortable because I was leaving everyone, after spending this intense time together, and having to go into the world without those people. That was one of the most difficult parts. A key part of my incorporation, even now, has been having check-ins with some of the people I did the course with. This has been super vital. So many of the things that are happening in our lives we can continue to relate back to our experience. It has been a challenge having to incorporate without any of the people I had the experience with."

Of course, you might have created your own initiation experience, and not had a community that experienced the same initiatory journey you did. This is why I urged you to create a community of support before you even went out: so you'd know who to call on when you return! No matter your circumstance, the task is the same for us all: return to the lives we left behind, and find ways to inhabit new ways of being each day.

How to do this difficult task can be found in the word "incorporation" itself. The root of the word is *corpus*: body. To incorporate is to literally *bring into the body*: to embody the new you. Think about a newborn baby who isn't quite sure what to do with their body right away. They are learning how to move their limbs and get their biological needs met, building muscles, and developing skills in coordinating the will of their brain with their actions.

In the same way, someone returning from a rite of passage is learning how to match their new role with the wider community around them, and learning how to inhabit a new form. This is part of why we've spent so much time talking about the importance of weaving a strong community around you to support you on this journey, whether your initiation was of your own design or you sought out a guided experience. Now, the community you've drawn around you are people that can support you in your return.

THE GIFTS YOU CARRY

To be human is to become visible
while carrying what is hidden as a gift to others.

—David Whyte, white American poet

Incorporation is where the rubber meets the road, and it becomes very clear that all the work you've been doing is not about you, at least not mostly. It's about the community, and how you can truly show up and be of service in a world that needs you and needs your gifts. Storyteller Martin Shaw says you are ready for incorporation when you're carrying a gift useful for your people. Rite of passage guide Will Scott agrees, and indicates that this is one of the hallmarks of passage into adulthood: "Once the rite of passage into adulthood has been completed...her sense of priority shifts from asking 'what are my gifts?' to 'how can my gifts serve the world?'" This is where you are at now, and there is no going back!

Tarek's initiatory experiences helped him bring back the gift of being more fully and authentically himself. "Around people that know me, they can tell right away the massive transformation I've had. The reflection that I receive from people that I know was an important recognition for me to feel seen, for them to see the things that I have moved through and the things I've let go of. The gift was coming back into the world in a way that was more true of who I am. Being able to share myself in a more authentic way in life. This gift has helped to inspire other people to have that journey for themselves as well."

Sharing your gifts may not be easy, and they may not always be well-received, like in the story of Katheryne at the beginning of the chapter where she began to speak up more at work. Still, reflecting back, she is very clear that the gift she brought back to her community was her challenging of the status quo:

"I was able to ask questions and pose challenges that helped to shape the community in ways that served everyone. It felt more...holistic. I would ask, 'what does it look like to look out for everyone and not just yourself right now? And what does that look like in a way that brings power and freedom and love, and not just power?' I brought an invitation to share that love and compassion across all cultural backgrounds. I felt this desire to put myself out there, knowing I had backup (both tangible and spiritual) to create the community I know is possible—more beautiful and sustainable."

Your gifts do not need to be fancy or flashy. They do not need to be 100% clear, either. As you return to your community, articulating simply that you have something to offer, and how you're committed to bringing these gifts forward in service to the community, is an important part of the process. The incorporation stage is less about unearthing your gifts and more about simply offering whatever you can and seeing how the world responds.

SHARING YOUR STORY

One gift that you definitely carry, to be shared with your people, is the story of your journey. It's important to remember that your experience, however unexciting, mundane, boring, or nonlinear it may seem to you, is a present you can offer. It is truly a *medicine story*: a story that can bring healing and wellness to those with whom you share it.

Many folks, when they return, don't feel they have a story at all, never mind one worth sharing. In situations where a broader community of folks gather to hear stories from those returning, there is always palpable anxiety in the circle before the sharing begins. Watching this process, and experiencing it myself, is part of what has helped me understand how valuable it is to share one's story in community and be witnessed. I commonly offer twenty minutes for the sharing of three or four days of solitude in nature, which is enough time for a bit of back story and much of what happened on the land, but not enough time for every little detail. There is something magical about both what is shared, and what is not.

An Initiate Returns

Before you share your story, there is an opportunity for it to continue to "cook" inside you. One guide describes it like a pot of rich stew simmering in an earthen pit, where the flavors meld together until it's ready. "You don't want to take it out too early, when maybe it's undercooked!" he warns. And just like a pot buried in the earth, it's hard to tell what's happening while it's in there. I have had many uncomfortable days, waiting until I could share my story, feeling that cooking and wondering what on earth I was going to say: was it enough? Was it silly? Was there really anything meaningful in what I had to share?

What I can tell you is that after years of listening to hundreds of stories, I am grateful for every time I get to feast on a rite of passage story someone offers from their heart, and I always find myself completely falling in love with the storyteller. Your story, shared from your heart, offers a glimpse into your deepest essence and the way you live that essence in the world.

There are many important reasons to take the time to tell your story. One, it allows others to see and know you intimately. It is an opportunity to practice vulnerability, an important quality of healthy adulthood that we often hide from one another. Parts of your story are likely to resonate with those that you share it with, providing new insights or reminders of important truths about being alive, and being human, in the world today. Your story is not just for you; it may have insights in it that others need to hear.

Your story also helps build a culture of recognizing and taking time to honor life's transitions, and gives others inspiration, emboldening them to honor their own life's transitions as well. I am often surprised and humbled how powerful it is for people, even those who have never done anything like this, to hear someone else's story of initiation.

Sharing your story also creates accountability for you to bring forth your new insights and commitments. As you publicly name your vows and intentions, you can deepen your own resolve. At the same time, new doors will often open synchronistically simply by you sharing, and your path forward can unfold in unimaginable ways.

Through receiving your experience, your community has the opportunity to affirm your insights and to challenge them when needed.* In many traditions, initiation between childhood and adulthood is a time of seeking visions. Those visions are typically messages from the spirit or more-than-human worlds regarding one's unique purpose, or gifts to the community. But young people in such cultures do not come back and proclaim, "This is what I am to do!" Instead, they bring back images and stories, which others with lots of experience are able to help them make sense of and figure out how these visions relate to the human world.

Gaining perspective from trusted mentors and community is essential. It's sometimes difficult to discern our wishes and projections from messages from the more-than-human world, especially for those of us who haven't received training in how to do this. Sometimes we might downplay or miss things out of a sense of smallness; other times hubris might get the best of us. Wisdom from spiritual realms has been used by individuals in pursuit of self-interest time and time again, and continues to underlie religious conflict the world over today. These stories stand as sharp cautionary tales. Community provides important checks and balances to our own internal grandiosity, self-diminishment, and wishful thinking.

While sharing your story is a critical part of the incorporation process, it's also important to be discerning about where, when, and with whom you share your story. Sharing too casually can diminish the power. In some traditions, people don't share their stories with anyone for a year or sometimes ever; in others, stories are only shared with a few trusted advisors. In the tradition that I was raised, there is important power in the sharing, and it is seen as part of what is helping to re-weave healthy communities. But it is still essential to exercise care. Some of my fellow guides liken the stories we carry back from rites of passage to newborn babies: you wouldn't just pass around your newborn for anyone to hold, any time! When I share my story with friends or family, we create a specific time, often over a meal or a walk, and I am

---

*In her book *Ancient Spirit Rising*, Pegi Eyers describes the phenomenon of unverified personal gnosis (UPG), which she describes as "insights received from spirits, deities, dreams, visions, ancestors, and intuition." Eyers says that while cultivating capacity to access wisdom and insights in this way is important, "having a community to validate UPG is crucial."

clear with them what I am asking them for. Do I want them to just listen? Am I open to questions? Do I want reflections at the end? My answers to these questions vary by person, as well as what is happening for me at the moment.

The further outside the realm of shared community experience, the more likely it is to be difficult to share. This was true for Tarek, whose journey included sexuality in ways that are very foreign in the Western paradigm of many of his friends and peers. Luckily, he was prepared for this by his guides while in the experience. They recommended that participants are very discerning about sharing the details of the specific rituals and ceremonies because it's hard for folks to understand it without having experienced it. Instead, they suggested participants share about the impact, and what participants learned about themselves. Tarek was glad for this advice. "Sharing with folks that haven't done it was really difficult," he reports. "What I found is that instead I held it within myself and allowed it to continue to inform me. I continued to share the story with those that I had shared the experience with, because of course the story continues to grow as life experiences outside bring new perspectives. Sharing my story with those with whom I shared the experience has been and continues to be an important part of the story still developing. A lot of chapters are still coming through!"*

Spending solo time in nature was easy for Katheryne to share with her immediate community, since many in her social and professional world had experienced the ceremony already. But this didn't mean it was easy for her to share with everyone in her life. "My biggest hesitation was to share my story with my family," she says. "I gathered them to share the story, and it went over really well. My brother shared about his own ancestral healing, and my parents spoke about what it's been like to share their power and their voice. It was really beautiful for all of us."

---

*It's important to note that Tarek's guides did not say that he shouldn't share his experience, but that he should be cautious about it. Secrecy has been misused by people in power, including spiritual teachers, in ways that can be deeply harmful. If guides or teachers are asking you to keep things that they do or say private, this is a warning sign that they may be abusing their power. This is a good time to turn to a trusted friend or mentor outside of the community, to help you discern if power is being used in ways that aren't healthy for you.

Her second time around, her family was able to be even more supportive. Her parents lit a candle while she was out, and wrote prayers for her that they shared when she returned. This time, she shared her story with her dad while on a road trip from Virginia to Savannah, Georgia, 8 hours away. Her intent, proclaiming herself as a powerful queer Black woman, became the backdrop for a conversation they hadn't ever had in any depth before. "He asked me lots of questions about what it meant to be queer, and living as a queer Black woman." She had come out years before, but this experience proved to be "the opportunity to really dive into what queerness looks like for me."

Katheryne felt like this was really big for her, and for her family. "I got to connect with my parents differently after that," she says. "It felt like it was trickling into my lineage. I come from a southern Christian family, and they wanted to talk more with me about my queerness. I heard from them, 'We've always thought you were special, and these are the ways we've tried to show it, but it didn't always come out this way.' Reconciliation came out of that."

PHYSICAL MARKERS

At Rite of Passage Journeys, when young people come back from their wilderness journeys, their friends and family come to witness and celebrate their return. The community gathers in a ceremonial amphitheater, and the returning initiates share the story of their journey, typically through skits, simple rituals, songs, and stories.

Before the returning initiates enter the amphitheater, the families assemble, eagerly anticipating the greeting of their young person. Before they see the young ones, the families are given instructions: your child may look the same, but you must remember that they are not. In fact, no children will be returning at all. The staff share with the families that in many cultures around the world, initiation tattoos, piercings, and other physical changes are common in large part because they serve a practical purpose: they remind the initiate and everyone they come in contact with that things are different now. They say that in communities without shared practices of physical markers as symbols of life transitions, the task is different. We must witness the transition, hear the story, and embed the physical marker in our imagination even if we don't see it on the outside.

Meanwhile, the young people gather a small distance away, hidden by trees. Anxiety builds in the air, as they know their families have arrived, but they haven't yet seen them. They hold a final circle, where they, too, receive instructions. "You have experienced many years of living with your family," their mentors might say, "and in certain ways you see yourself through their eyes. Over the course of this journey, you have consciously stepped into new commitments, had insights, made decisions about how you want to move forward. Over the coming hours, days, and weeks, you will undoubtedly find it hard not to slip back into old patterns and habits with your family. Your challenge now is to hold firm to your commitments, even when our time together in the mountains feels impossibly far away, like it was perhaps even a dream."

How will you bring back any new insights and clarity about you, and really live your intent, when you look the same and others may treat you exactly the same? You have more freedom than the young people and guides in this chapter; you can consider what physical changes you may want to undergo to mark this transition and share it outwardly with the world.

Many people will make, find, or purchase a piece of jewelry as a physical marker. This serves both as a reminder for them every time they see it, as well as a chance to display something to the rest of the world. You might also consider changes to your room or home space: adjusting the furniture or displaying a photo, drawing, or other piece of art that reminds you of your journey. I have a photo of a special tree from a fast years ago that I hang above my altar, that connects me to that place and ceremony.

If this journey has been particularly potent for you, you may consider some way of physically marking this on your body, in a safe, ritualized manner. Tattooing, piercing, cutting of hair, and scarification are common practices around the world, including in Western culture today, both for purposes of forging individual identity as well as signaling group membership. Many people cut their hair while they are in the threshold phase, or when they cross back into incorporation. Tattoos—especially designs that connect with your ancestral lineage—are another way that people bring back into their daily lives reminders of their rites of passage.

Clement, mentioned earlier in the book, has utilized their body as a canvas through their initiatory journey of gender identity. After their first fast, as they stepped away from identifying as a female and toward embodying the "third way," they got a tattoo to mark the transition. This permanent reminder of their experience is something they can look at every day, to remind them of who they are in the world, and can be a jumping off point for sharing about deeper parts of themselves when the right opportunities come along.

Of course, be thoughtful before you get anything permanently on your body! Work with someone safe, skilled, and experienced. There are beautiful artists out there who see their work as a craft and as a spiritual practice; working with someone who brings ceremony into their work in a conscious way can deepen the meaning.

NAVIGATING THE TURBULENCE

"I went to the first experience of Surfing the Creative and came back to Madagascar. I realized that I have a community now, someone to whom I can turn to, someone who guides me into that process, into that journey. That was really a great support for me coming back. I felt energized, I felt ready to go to my next stage of going deeper into what's next. I think that is always the question after each Surfing the Creative: What is next? It doesn't have to be something big, but what is next? We'd get resourced, we'd know where we belong and who is there for us as resources, and to see and to question what is next. I think that was really important for me." –Nadia, age 30

It's very easy, in the integration stage, to feel like you're "doing it wrong." You're not! The important thing is to keep going, to keep moving forward. There are many stumbles and tumbles, as you live into your new ways of being in the world. The task is not to avoid falls or missteps, but rather to get yourself back up, dust yourself off, and keep going.

For Katheryne, being in the mystery of it all has been the biggest challenge. "The hard work of incorporation," she says, "has come from wanting power and control. I've had to fight the urge of wanting to know every little thing, and it's made it hard to let loose and just let life offer me what it wants to offer."

A big challenge can also be feelings of isolation and alienation. It may feel like few around you understand what you're going through. You no longer fit into your old life, but you may not yet have found a space right-sized for you to inhabit. Katheryne has experienced this as well: "This thing about being a queer Black woman—wanting to embody and keep that intent and mind—I have felt hesitancy to do that because I'm like, 'I don't know if that's okay right now, and I'm a little scared to show it.'" This has led Katheryne to seek out spaces where the person she is now has room, particularly among other Black folk in her community where she can experience the joy of fully inhabiting her being.

Very commonly, people will experience a "crash" that comes after a peak experience like a rite of passage. This often leaves people chasing the next peak experience. Please avoid this temptation! Incorporation, with all of its mundane challenges, is an essential stage of the process. Give yourself at least a year in the incorporation phase. Marking the closing of this stage on the other end is often very helpful, even essential.

Practical skills that you learned in the threshold stage can be drawn on for support. This is part of why mentored learning is such an important element of a rite of passage! For Tarek, this came in the form of a "tool belt" he was given by his guides to use in their lives beyond the program, a way to work through feelings that may create blocks, specifically around releasing fear, guilt, shame, and trauma. "Continuing to utilize these tools has been an important part of my incorporation," he shares.

Just as there's no one right initiation experience for everyone, there is no one right way to navigate incorporation. I have found that what is most useful is to create space for folks to share what works for them.

Here is a list of a few recommendations from folks that I have guided over the years:

1. Post your intent statement where you can see it every day, like on a bathroom mirror.

2. Say your intent statement every day (tooth brushing is a good time).

3. Reach out to your community of support to remind you of insights you had.

4. Build an altar with symbols from your journey.

5. Write down your whole experience, so you can go back to it even years later.

6. Share your story.

7. Rearrange your physical space to reflect the person you are now.

8. Live your intent in daily life.

9. Spend time in nature, with the intention of connecting with your rite of passage.

⚘ EXERCISE: Pick three strategies from the list above, or add your own, and commit to engaging in these practices over the next year on a consistent basis. Share this commitment with your mentor, and ask them to check in on how it's going.

☾

Chapter Ten:

LIVING AN INITIATING LIFE

"*Being an adult means setting an example for, and teaching the younger generations through, conscious actions. Being an adult is continuing to grow, and creating an environment in which others can grow as well.*"
–Zach, at age 22

I wrote the first draft of this chapter in early March 2020. I had blocked out nine days for a book retreat and was thrilled to be able to finally focus after months of distraction. But focusing on my book was not what that time had in store for me—just like everyone else who had plans that changed during that tumultuous season.

Do you remember that time? Every day the world changed a little more, as normal lives receded and COVID became the focus of the whole planet. Things that had been unthinkable just days before suddenly became our new reality: school closed and sports seasons got canceled; people were ordered into lockdown; food and toilet paper were suddenly in short supply; health care workers, grocery store staff, and workers in food processing plants risked their lives just going to work; frightening daily death tolls overwhelmed hospitals and mortuaries.

> "Initiation is the beginning – it means to begin or to initiate – and it's never over."
> –Michael Meade

Globally, a massive severance was underway. The world that we lived in, or thought we lived in, suddenly disappeared. We were cast out into liminal space as the world we'd known evaporated, and what was to come remained a mystery. A doorway into transformation and change on a global scale had appeared.

I found it both heartbreaking and frustrating to hear all of the talk of getting back to "normal." So many things about "business as usual" didn't work in our world, and I felt the possibility for real change.

Over the years since the pandemic began, I've reflected a lot on the strength of desire to maintain the status quo, individually and collectively. Humans do a lot to keep change from happening or to go back to how things used to be. Yet the world *is* changing. Social inequity, polarization, massive population growth, climate chaos: these are the realities of our species at this time.

As you come to the end of this book, big questions await you about how to actually live, on a day to day basis, as an adult in this world. How do you attend to your own ongoing changes—and the changes of others—while consistently and intentionally moving forward?

We are at a powerful moment in history, in the midst of the "Triple Rite of Passage" we talked about in the Introduction. Our whole planet is undergoing initiation through massive human population increases, extinction events, climate catastrophe, and more. In the midst of these large-scale shifts, initiated adults are needed to support and care for their communities on all levels. And these initiated adults need to tend to ongoing changes, inner and outer, that call forth new responses and capacities all the time. We need to *live an initiating life*.

Here's a simple truth: it's really difficult to consistently live in this way. We live in a society that celebrates and encourages adolescent behaviors. There are a lot of forces in the world pushing you to maintain a status quo that is clearly not in the best interests of future generations. The pressure is often strong to stop paying attention, to "go along to get along".

Living an initiating life requires something like what Mi'kmaq Elder Albert Marshall calls *etuaptmunk*, or two-eyed seeing: "learning to see from one eye with the strengths of Indigenous knowledges and ways of knowing, and from the other eye with the strengths of Western knowledges and ways of knowing, and to use both these eyes together, for the benefit of all." While two-eyed seeing informs researchers integrating Indigenous and Western research methods, it is also a helpful orientation for how to live and survive under systems of domination while committing our lives to a future where humans live in balance and reciprocity with one another across cultures and species.

This final chapter of the book offers a few strategies and practices that have helped me and others do our best to live joyfully and with integrity, even when there are pressures to conform with unhealthy, adolescent cultural norms. Hopefully, you can draw on this chapter as a resource and support for you as you continue your journey.

RESPONDING TO THE CRISES OF OUR TIME

In the book so far, you've gone on a journey into the deepest recesses of your life: those experiences, qualities, relationships, which define you. In this chapter you are asked to hold a much broader perspective. While you are still tending to yourself and your own needs, it is time to really take responsibility for the world outside of yourself, as well. As we zoom out, here are two important frameworks to understand where we're at and how we can respond in ways that serve the broader world. They come from white American Buddhist scholar and systems theorist Joanna Macy. In her nineties now, she created *The Work that Reconnects* to help people connect with each other and with the web of life, transforming despair and grief into action.

Macy spent years as an anti-nuclear activist. Anti-nuclear activists are constantly working to prevent environmental catastrophe that could last hundreds of thousands of years. Trying to process overwhelming devastation, and losing important battles to industry, can burn activists out quickly. Macy and others experimented with methods to help activists and affected communities express their grief, rage, fear, and numbness, and found that these tools built resiliency to remain engaged.

THREE STORIES OF OUR WORLD

Macy articulated three stories she found common in the industrialized world today. All three of them are being embodied and enacted right now, today, and so in a sense they are all *true*.

Business as Usual is what most people encounter throughout their daily lives in the "Industrial Growth Society." Rooted in colonialism and Empire-building, this mode is driven by industrialism and measures success by growth and growth in terms of money. This view, frequently reinforced by corporations and politicians, holds that the resources of the Earth are infinite, our environmental problems can be solved with technological advances, capitalism will allow for prosperity for all, and Western culture's reach into the far corners of the globe is a good thing. Business as Usual is very seductive, and its marketing efforts make it almost impossible to get out of its grip.

The Great Unraveling is the worldview of many scientists, journalists, and activists immersed in documenting and fighting the destruction and violence humans perpetuate against the Earth or against each other. This is often where people resisting the seduction of Business as Usual find themselves overwhelmed by the things harming us and the rest of life on the planet – like the climate crisis, toxic air and water, loss of habitat and destruction of beautiful places, the decimation of languages and cultures, increasing wealth concentration, political polarization, and more. This is a very scary, often paralyzing or enraging, worldview to inhabit.

The Great Turning holds that a new form of human existence is emerging, where the urgency of the problems that we face are calling forth an entirely different face of humanity, a shift from Industrial Growth Society to life-sustaining civilization. The notion of The Great Turning is mirrored in many Indigenous prophecies from across the globe that point to times of cataclysmic change leading to a radical re-orienting of humans toward the world around us, and towards how we treat one another.

As Macy points out, no one knows how things are going to turn out. Can humanity save itself in time? How many species will go extinct in the process? How many cultures, languages, waterways, will be lost? How many humans, if any, will be left to face the new reality? We do not know the answers to these questions. But that is not the point. The point is to partner with Life toward The Great Turning, and then witness in wonder what unfolds.

❦EXERCISE: Consider which is your default story: Business as Usual, The Great Unraveling, or The Great Turning? As you go about your daily life in the next few days, observe which one of these worldviews is most common in the media you encounter, in what other people share with you, and in what you think and say.

THREE DIMENSIONS OF THE GREAT TURNING

In our attempts to heal our brokenness and give The Great Turning a chance, Macy identifies three dimensions of The Great Turning, all important in the struggle to create a just, sustainable world.

Holding actions are activities designed to limit or mitigate the damage we're doing to ourselves and the planet. Wet'suwet'en people and their allies working to stop the Coastal GasLink pipeline going through their territory is an example of this. So is someone volunteering at a food bank to help make sure people are fed.

Analysis of structural causes and creation of structural alternatives are efforts to develop and employ new technologies that are supportive of life. Efforts to reduce fuel consumption and increase energy independence, such as shifts to curb air travel and decrease the movements of goods across the globe, are examples of this.

So is someone helping to create a mutual aid support system to ensure everyone in their neighborhood has enough food to eat.

The final dimension of The Great Turning is called *shifts in consciousness*. These are attempts to fundamentally change the way we look at and understand the world. Developing an ethic whereby the sovereign rights of Indigenous peoples is a top priority, and the health of ecosystems is more important than cheap oil, involve a shift from the consciousness currently driving political decision-making throughout the Western world today. So does coming to believe that an economy that allows for massive wealth for a few and tremendous poverty for many is unacceptable.

> ⚘EXERCISE: Consider the three dimensions of The Great Turning. Which of these seems like the "best" to you? Are there any that seem less valuable? Where are your gifts best suited? Consider an issue that is important to you, or a social movement of which you are a part. Where do you see these three dimensions showing up in efforts to address this issue?

PRACTICES FOR LIVING AN INITIATING LIFE

The purpose of initiation into adulthood is to help you bring your gifts forward for your family (chosen or blood), your community, and the broader world. These levels are all interrelated. We are, as author adrienne maree brown points out in her book, Emergent Strategy, fractals of a larger whole. Our efforts on small scales mirror and impact changes on larger systemic levels. This means that every step we take to address those challenges becomes a healing not just for us but also for the collective, and every step we take in addressing larger systemic issues becomes an opportunity for our own healing.

One of the main benefits of investing energy to bring awareness to these levels is that we can start to see our challenges not as our own, but as challenges for the broader collective.

Resilience is perhaps the most important capacity we need, individually and collectively, as we navigate a changing climate

LIVING AN INITIATING LIFE

Practices for Living an Initiating Life

and human world in crisis. Coming from a root word meaning "to leap back," resilience is our capacity to recover from difficult circumstances. Like a sapling in the forest that is able to bend with a big windstorm and avoid cracking or getting blown down, it helps us navigate what comes our way — financial insecurity, facing injustice, health issues, death or loss, or any other change. Well-adapted and resourced adults have the capacity to bend and shift during times of change. And, sometimes we're not well-adapted nor well-resourced, and we need some time to breakdown, fall apart, and then put ourselves back together. This is a form of resilience too.

Think back to Chapter Two, and what we discussed about trauma: how trauma is the result of something that overwhelms our capacity to respond. Many communities have been intentionally cultivating strategies for resilience for generations due to ongoing trauma and harm they've experienced, helping them to persevere and find joy in the face of adversity and challenge. It's the same for individuals. While those that have endured childhood trauma may suffer from ongoing impacts of the harm, they may also experience an inner fortitude that comes from what they've survived. This resilience is strengthened through intentional healing work in a safe, therapeutic container.

The final part of this book offers a specific set of practices to cultivate your resilience, and help you live an initiating life as you journey forward.

ESTABLISH A DAILY PRACTICE

A few months before COVID hit, I moved to a house about a ten minute walk to the river. After COVID arrived, that walk became essential. Each day, to escape the confines of my little home, I would find myself out traversing that path to the river. I would put the same song on replay on my phone and dance on the rocky shores. As the world around me shifted, I found solid ground in my body, dancing by the river, watching the play of light and shadow as the trees began to bud and then leaf out. I would let fear, grief, and outrage move through my body, making sense of it all on a somatic level.

Instead of the whirlwind travels that I had planned for the spring, my world grew small. The changes of the path from snow-covered to a carpet of green life is an image that will forever be burned in my mind, indelibly tied to COVID; the budding of the cottonwoods will always be connected with George Floyd's murder. This simple daily routine became my most basic survival tool, my lifeline in a time of chaos, heartbreak, and confusion.

Daily practices, whether exercise, meditation, prayer, reading inspirational or sacred texts, journal-writing, spending time outdoors, engaging creative arts, or many other things, are foundational to our resilience. Even when times seem to be going well, we need them to connect with ourselves and what's really important to us, beyond our to-do lists. This commitment to daily rhythm helps build stability, discipline, and stamina.

When things are not going well, they can become our anchors in the chaos, a place of refuge and sanctuary even when the world around us is spinning out of control. Whatever you choose to do as a daily practice, start simple, short enough for you to do every day (you may include more practices, or for longer, when you have time), Let your practices shift and adjust over time and as you discover what works for you and is most helpful. The important thing is to show up each day, whether it's for 5 minutes or an hour.

CULTIVATE PATIENCE

This book took more than ten years for me to write. Ten years! Why would I keep putting so much life energy into something that was taking so long?! The best explanation I can give is that on a soul level, I had to do it; my ancestors told me to.

Along the way, I have been incredibly impatient. Impatience, it turns out, didn't get the project done any faster. It just increased my suffering.

When we are impatient with ourselves and with others, it can cause a lot of pain. We get frustrated, angry, resentful that things aren't going at the pace we want them to. But change takes the time it takes.

This doesn't mean accepting injustices or abuse. It is important to stand up and say enough is enough. Our planet is burning, our people are dying. Holding the urgency of the moment with the long arc of movements is critical.

> "Wisdom is understanding how long things take...Sometimes, because of the culture that we live in, that favors an individual perspective over a communal perspective, we think that what we see in one lifetime is all that we can see. But other cultures can see multiple lifetimes because they're sharing what they're seeing in a lineage. There are some things that you cannot see in a hundred years, that you must see in five hundred or a thousand."
>
> —Activist and founder of Ayni Institute, Carlos Saavedra

But as you know from your work over the course of this book, change doesn't come easily. One way to build stamina for the long haul and resist the ongoing attempts of the dominant culture to lure you back into complacency is by staying focused on larger time horizons. Dakota/Salish author, artist, and cultural practitioner Philip Red Eagle says that it took seven generations of losing their lifeways for his people to get where they are, and it will take seven generations more to recover. For those of us whose people began living under colonization more generations back, the path may be longer yet.

EARN A LIVING

Life under capitalism is complex. We need money in today's world, whether we like it or not, and most of us need to work in order to have money. Yet this system creates paradoxes that are in many ways irreconcilable.

As white American labor journalist Sarah Jaffe points out in her book *Work Won't Love You Back*, "many features of what people used to consider "employment security" are gone, melted into the air. Instead, as a thousand articles and nearly as many books have told us over and over, we're all exhausted, burned out, overworked, underpaid, and have no work-life balance (or just no life)." Yet at the same time, we receive a constant bombardment of messages that tell us that "work itself is supposed to bring us fulfillment, pleasure, meaning, even joy. We're supposed to work for the love of it, and how dare we ask questions about the way our work is making other people rich while we struggle to pay rent or barely see our friends." It wasn't always like this, Jaffe says. From the days of feudal systems until recent decades, "it was assumed, to put it bluntly, that work sucked, and that people would avoid it if humanly possible."

Safe and healthy working conditions, sufficient financial resources, and the ability to devote your life energy to contributions that feel meaningful to you are all reasonable expectations when we talk about *work* and *jobs*. Yet too rarely are all three of these conditions available. This means that each of us need to find ways to survive while also working together to create long-term societal changes toward health, well-being, and access to basic needs for all of us.

For some, this means creatively resisting cultures of overwork. Recent challenges to the status quo have gone viral, like the Chinese former factory worker Luo Huazhong's viral post in 2021 "Lying Flat is Justice," and the gospel preached by Tricia Hersey, founder of The Nap Ministry. "My rest as a Black woman in America suffering from generational exhaustion and racial trauma always was a political refusal and social justice uprising within my body," Hersey says about the roots of The Nap Ministry. "I took to rest and naps and slowing down as a way to save my life, resist the systems telling me to do more and most importantly as a remembrance to my Ancestors who had their DreamSpace stolen from them."

As Huazhong and Hersey have modeled, part of how we build our own resilience is by recognizing that many things commonly taught about money and work are just not true, like the idea that worth and value is determined by our productivity or how hard we work. Challenging the notion that money reflects actual intrinsic value (an hour of my time is less valuable than a doctor's, say, or more valuable than the time of a bagger at a grocery store) helps me to separate my sense of value from what I produce or how much money I have in the bank, which in turn helps me make conscious choices about where to put my time.

Our beliefs and values around money and work are informed by the messages we receive growing up. We each carry complex money stories, influenced by family, schooling, media, and more.

For example, in many middle-class American families, parents aspire to provide support for their children throughout their childhood and often into young adulthood, taking out loans if they can to fund college. Once grown, the ideal is that family members make financial choices independently. Young people become economically self-sufficient, and parents save for retirement so that they aren't dependent on their children in old age. In many poor, working-class, and immigrant families, the values are different. Economic interdependence among family members may be higher, with young people striving to provide support for their caregivers and working to contribute resources to the family. Meanwhile, for those who have traditionally had resources stolen or withheld from them, and who are impacted by poverty in their own families or communities, finding ways to be financially secure can be an act of resistance against a dominant society that says their lives are less valuable.

This context makes choices about jobs, work, schooling, and more very difficult. It can be challenging to discern how much we need, how much we are able and willing to make choices that stand in contrast to societal norms, and consider seriously the benefits and challenges of living on the financial edge.

"Money is like water. Water can be a precious life-giving resource. But what happens when water is dammed, or when a water cannon is fired on protestors in subzero temperatures? Money should be a tool of love, to facilitate relationships, to help us thrive, rather than to hurt and divide us. If it's used for sacred, life-giving, restorative purposes, it can be medicine. Money, used as medicine, can help us decolonize."

–Activist and author Edgar Villanueva

Luckily, there are really creative folks out there challenging the status quo around how we think about money, and working to transform our economic paradigms. Two related concepts on the periphery of mainstream discourse about money today that are challenging the status quo are efforts toward mutual aid and the gift economy. Both of these frameworks re-orient away from notions of competition and scarcity, and towards notions of abundance and exchange. Mutual aid networks often spring up in communities in crisis, supporting the movement of resources (food, water, money, labor) in ways that honor the inherent dignity and contribution of all members of a community. A gift economy framework shifts away from paradigms of "purchasing goods or services" towards offering them freely and inviting reciprocity.

As you navigate your own path forward, figuring out how to earn a living that meets your needs and values as best you can, you can draw on the tools in the Online Resources.

CENTER THE MOST VULNERABLE

A couple of years ago, I helped coordinate an organizational leadership retreat for my work. The group of about 15 people was very diverse in terms of race, gender, class, culture, and age. For three days, we came together, sharing food, stories, ceremony, and laughter as we envisioned next steps for our organization. Sharing in this way strengthened trust, connection, and intimacy between us as a small group.

The second evening we were together, about 50 more people, mostly white, from around the region came to join us for a larger gathering. This large influx of people, who weren't sufficiently prepared for the sort of space they were stepping into, was quite overwhelming for members of our original small circle. This was especially true for the People of Color in our circle who knew few of the arriving guests. The next morning, several members of the circle shared tenderly about what it was like to suddenly find themselves surrounded by so many white people they didn't know after being in a small group they were growing to know and trust, and with whom they had opened their hearts vulnerably.

This event reminded me of something I had learned many times before, yet can be easy for me to forget: the importance of centering the most vulnerable in my decision-making and planning. In this circumstance, centering the vulnerable would have meant considering the gender, age, racial dynamics, life experiences, abilities, temperaments of this smaller group to plan the gathering, making sure that what we planned truly worked for everyone, and building in contingencies to help people feel safe when conditions changed.

Centering the most vulnerable means reflecting deeply on who or what feels threatened by choices that are made. I can look at this on an intrapersonal level (inside myself): there may be something I really want to do, but I have to admit that a vulnerable, wounded part of me due to childhood trauma might not be ready for it. I can look at it interpersonally, carefully considering the vulnerabilities of others due to their life experiences, social locations, and other factors, and considering the impact my actions will have on them. I can also look at it globally, understanding that the communities most vulnerable to catastrophic climate events are disproportionately Black, Brown, and economically disenfranchised, and advocating for policies that help mitigate climate change and support climate refugees.

Of course, when we think about who's vulnerable, we also have to think about the many beings of the more-than-human world, who are profoundly vulnerable to our choices as humans.

When we look at larger, society-wide levels, there can be contention about who is most vulnerable, or impacted by systemic oppression, or marginalized. But it doesn't have to be a competition. By seeking out perspectives different from our own, and patiently creating space for the voices that are often silenced, we can learn about what it means to create a world that works for all.

BE VULNERABLE YOURSELF

Part of how we center the most vulnerable is by practicing being vulnerable ourselves. Our vulnerability makes space for vulnerability in others, and helps us slow down our pace by acknowledging tender spots, insecurities, and places where we need support. Far from being a sign of weakness, vulnerability is a sign of strength.

As we talked about earlier in the book, many of the messages we receive as young people about what it means to be an adult don't make space for vulnerability. Adults are supposed to know what they are doing. Yet the truth is, most of the time we don't. Mostly, adults are doing the best they can, working to take care of themselves, the people they love, and hopefully clean up messes they make as best as they can. The more we can show this to one another and to young people, the more that we can build resilient communities based on trust, cooperation, and solidarity with one another. It's a strange but true paradox that when we hide our vulnerability, we make ourselves harder to trust.

Perhaps no one is more famous globally for helping people understand, appreciate, and embrace vulnerability than researcher and author Brené Brown. Brown conducted thousands of interviews in her efforts to understand vulnerability, widely sharing her results in best-selling books and some of the most-watched TED Talks of all time.

Brown's work started with this basic premise: we are all searching for connection. As she dove more deeply, she discovered that in order for connection to exist, people must let themselves be seen, which makes them vulnerable. Fear and shame block us from letting ourselves be seen, which in turn blocks connection.

What do vulnerable people have in common? Brown's data on thousands of people boiled it down to a few traits that these people share: a sense of courage, compassion (first for self and then for others), and connection as a result of authenticity. She calls people who exhibited these traits "whole-hearted." When folks aren't able to be whole-hearted, Brown says, they numb vulnerability, which in turn numbs gratitude, joy, and happiness. Brown offers a prescription for vulnerability: love with your whole heart, practice gratitude and joy, and believe that you are enough.

Vulnerability does not mean the absence of boundaries. In fact, setting a boundary with someone can be a deeply vulnerable act. It means admitting your limits and stating your needs even when doing so might lead to shame, blame, anger, disappointment, or rejection from people we care about or depend on.

Whether it's by opening ourselves up or saying "This is as far as I can go," vulnerability is not easy. Yet it strengthens the resiliency of our relationships, allowing others to see who we really are, and making space for them to do the same.

LIVE IN PARADOX

The world today is filled with black and white thinking, and attempts to fit things neatly into categories of *good* and *bad*, *right* and *wrong*. But in reality, most things defy these easy boxes, existing somewhere in the middle or containing elements of both.

Take COVID, a source of incredible suffering, hardship, and tragedy. At the same time, COVID also presented opportunities for our societies and industries to slow down, build connections with loved ones and the more-than-human-world, and establish new mutual aid networks. We saw what is possible in a short time when nation-states put their mind to something: how quickly relief for the people can be distributed, prisoners can be released back to their loved ones, and clear air returned to our communities.

One of my mentors, Gigi Coyle, jokes about making a t-shirt with the phrase "Both/And" on it that she can point to whenever someone presents her with a binary choice: something that is "either" one way "or" the other. She often talks about finding "the third way." This is such a common refrain around her that anytime I hear myself framing something as a binary choice, I immediately begin searching for a third option, one that integrates some elements of the two.

As you move forward, notice your attempts to categorize things into easy binaries, and instead practice holding complexities and tensions. Being an adult requires making difficult choices, often with unknown outcomes and consequences for both yourself and others. Accepting that there may not be a clear right or wrong choice can liberate you and help you see your options more clearly.

OBSERVE PROTOCOL

Living in Hawai'i, I quickly learned to never wear shoes inside. When I arrived at someone's doorstep, I would slip off my footwear. This common and expected custom in Hawai'i, as well as many other places around the globe, was a gesture of respect for my hosts. It was a form of local *protocol*.

Protocol can be thought of as learning manners, behaviors for basic respect, and can often be quite subtle. What is protocol in one cultural context can be deeply offensive in another setting, as I experienced when I was researching Indigenous belief systems regarding wolves among the Ahousaht, a Na-chuh-nahlt nation in Clayoquot Sound, British Columbia.

For this project, I was privileged to interview Ahousaht Tyee Hawiih (Head Hereditary Chief of the Ahousaht Nation),

LIVING AN INITIATING LIFE 325

Cross Cultural Protocols as described by Youth Passageways

Maquinna (Lewis George). When we arrived at the end of the interview after his sharing of many great stories, I asked him how he would like to be referred to in the chapter I was writing. I felt rather proud of the question, thinking it showed how sensitive and aware I was, in my desire to represent him in the way he wanted to be represented. He very gently explained that I did not understand Ahousaht protocol. If I did, I would have known that I was putting him in an uncomfortable position because protocol dictates humility among the Ahousaht. He couldn't tell me his title as Head Hereditary Chief; that could be seen as bragging. I needed to talk to others to understand his role.

This definitely made my job harder. I had to do internet research, talk with other people, and send him a copy for his approval, hoping that the way I explained his role in the community was accurate. But I learned a lot from it, and I am grateful for the lesson.

Not long after I completed this task, I was asked by an employer to compose a bio for a website. As I wrote the bio, making myself sound as good as I could, I reflected on the different cultural values that underpinned this Ahousaht protocol compared to the Western orientation towards talking ourselves up.

Mainstream Western culture often shirks away from rigid sets of social morays. Given the highly repressive contexts that many people come from, expression of our wildness and freedom is essential. At the same time, there are many gifts that come from protocol as a way to honor and respect one another. This is one of the paradoxes of being human in the world today. It is our responsibility to navigate cultural contexts very different from our own. It's like being a good guest in someone else's house. It is also our responsibility to create shared protocol in our families and communities in ways that reflect the values that are important to us.

At Youth Passageways, as a community coming together across many lines of difference, one of the first tasks we undertook as a community was to outline our protocols. You can read them in Appendix II as an example of how one community created a set of protocols to guide our work together.

BE HUMBLE

As the story of Maquinna in the last section illustrates, in some cultural contexts humility is a deeply cultivated trait. In Western culture, it's generally less valued and in fact often stigmatized.

Humility and human share the same root word, *humus*, which means soil or from the earth. When we come from a place of humility, we recognize that we are nothing more, and nothing less, than soil.

How simple and humble is soil! Dirt underneath one's fingernails, that's how small we are in the cosmic sense of things. And how powerful: from soil, food grows to nourish and sustain us; without soil, there is little life.

Humility means recognizing our own limitations. It means being honest about what we don't know, and being open to learning new ways. It also means acting when we are called upon to act, even when we know there are others who could do things more gracefully or effectively, or that with more learning we could do things better. It means trying our hardest, being open to feedback and criticism, and learning to do things better the next time. Sometimes it means recognizing our own limitations in the area of humility, and accepting that we might not always take criticism gracefully.

PUT RELATIONSHIPS FIRST

As a newly-initiated adult, you have important responsibilities toward your community. Some of these may be familiar; others less so. First, it is your responsibility to support your peers in finding their way toward meaningful adulthood. You can help them find the support they need while also recognizing that their journey will necessarily be very different than your own! Sharing your story in an open and honest manner, but not in a way that implies you have the answers, is a challenging and important responsibility.

Second, it is your responsibility to cultivate an intergenerational community. Drawing in older adults often left on the margins, and inviting them to be part of your life, can be an important support for folks that are told that aging means you are increasingly less valuable and relevant. Similarly, you have gained the experience now to support younger folks on their journey into and through adolescence. Creating opportunities to draw folks out of their daily lives and into spaces where all of them are welcome is a very important task in preparing us to weather challenges in our communities.

Third, it is your responsibility to strengthen your skills and capacity to work across differences. Age is an important one, as discussed above, but so is race, class, ability, religion, politics, interest, and experience. In this historical time of extreme polarization, skills in coming together across differences are some of the most valuable gifts we can offer our communities (and an easy area to experience practical testing!). You can help build what Martin Luther King, Jr. called "Beloved Community," a society based on justice, equal opportunity, and love of one's fellow human beings.

TAKE ACCOUNTABILITY

A few months ago, I had a falling out with a close friend and working collaborator who was going through a really stressful time in their life. The stress they were experiencing, combined with their trauma history and neurodivergence, was more than I could adequately support. I tried, but my own trauma history, lack of skillfulness, and inconsistent boundaries kept making the situation worse. Finally, we had a painful rupture that really hurt both of us.

Since then, we've kept our contact to a minimum while we sought support to unpack what happened and figure out how to move forward. Despite the rupture, we both care about each other and remain committed to learning and growing through our relationship. Now, as we start to come back together, we're beginning by sharing honestly and non-defensively what happened for each of us that caused us to make those choices and taking responsibility for how we've impacted each other. The process we are in—taking accountability—is the final practice that I want to share with you.

Widely credited to The Northwest Network, an organization providing advocacy-based counseling and community education for queer and trans survivors of abuse, the simplest definition for accountability that I have heard is *"being responsible for your choices and the consequences of your choices."* This means sitting with uncomfortable feelings of guilt, shame, resentment, and more, in an effort to make sense of what has led to our actions (or inactions), doing what we need to do to really understand the impact this has had on others, both directly and indirectly, and then doing our very best to clean up whatever messes we've made. According to Mia Mingus, a writer, educator, and trainer for transformative justice and disability justice, three key aspects of accountability are *apologizing, making amends,* and *changing your behavior so the harm doesn't happen again.*

Taking accountability is not easy, especially because we don't have a lot of healthy models of what it looks like. Systems of (in)justice based on good/bad binaries of "victim" and an "offender," as well as social media dog piles and cancellations, create conditions that don't reward acknowledgment of our mistakes. This situation is made even harder when we don't trust that other people are going to take their share of accountability. When we feel (or are) mistreated, why should we do the uncomfortable work of taking responsibility for our piece in it?

When we step outside of dominant culture, healthier models of accountability abound, contained in bodies of work like restorative justice and transformative justice (there are some good links in the Online Resources). Restorative justice is rooted in traditional Indigenous practices of accountability. Transformative justice is rooted in queer, trans, and femme communities of color navigating abuse and trauma in situations where institutions like the police and social services are further threats to safety and dignity. Both center the needs of the person harmed and focus on healing, support, and accountability.

It makes sense that these important bodies of work have emerged among communities living on the margins and facing violence, where finding ways to address violations; support health, safety, and well-being; and repair relationships is work necessary for basic survival.

Whatever our background, taking accountability is critical to our own internal resilience, as we learn how to bounce back from the mistakes we make. It's also critical to the resilience of our friendships, families, projects, and communities. It's definitely part of being an adult in the true sense of the word.

As my friend and I navigate through the difficult time we're having with each other, and both take accountability for the ways we've hurt each other, our friendship grows stronger and we increase the effectiveness of our collaborative working relationship. This in turn strengthens the groups that we are part of, where we can show up in cooperation with one another as opposed to asking others to choose sides between us.

Taking accountability at these internal and interpersonal levels further strengthens our capacity to be accountable as larger and larger groups of people, as organizations, communities, even whole nations. Part of taking accountability means looking for where I can help groups that I'm a part of take responsibility for harms we've caused, historically and in current times. For me, this means advocating for return of lands and lifeways back to Indigenous peoples of the lands where I live and work, and reparations for the descendants of those enslaved here on Turtle Island.

As you've read throughout this book, cultural practices like rites of passage are deeply indebted to First Nations peoples of Turtle Island, and the traditions and wisdom that they have maintained despite persecution and genocide. I recognize further the economic benefits to my family line that comes directly from enslavement of African people, and their continued marginalization through Jim Crow laws, redlining, and more. That Black and Brown communities continue to suffer violence, land theft, displacement, environmental racism, police brutality, disproportionate rates of poverty, and so many more injustices in the name of people that look like me is unfathomable. For me, taking accountability as a rite of passage guide and US citizen requires doing what I can to help achieve full sovereignty and self-determination of Black and Indigenous communities. I understand that there are many challenges with how this can practically occur. However, the challenges are often named without understanding how much time, energy, and creativity has been invested by Black and Indigenous communities and their allies for how to return resources to communities that had them stolen, in ways that will build toward healing and reconciliation. I've included links in the Online Resources to learn more about decolonization, rematriation, and reparations.

"Accountability is a fierce, radical, amazing way to choose to stay in relationship to each other," says Sonya Shah, founder and Co-Executive Director of the Ahimsa Collective, "while acknowledging that harm can happen, and that actually we're all going to hurt each other sooner or later." She paints a picture of a world where accountability is the cultural norm, where we take responsibility for the ways we've impacted each other as often and as easily as we put on a seatbelt. As initiated adults living an initiating life, we have the power to create that world.

⚘ EXERCISE: Write down the *Practices for Living an Initiating Life* in your journal, and create one actionable step for each. This may include research you need to do, paying attention to how it shows up in your life, or reaching out to other people. Which one of these seems like the easiest one to implement? Which seems the hardest or least inspiring? Make a commitment to focusing on one of these a week for eight weeks, starting with the one that seems easiest, and each week take some notes on how it goes.

⚘ EXERCISE: At the end of eight weeks, come back to the list. How did you do? Consider what you want to carry forward. What additional practices for living an initiating life do you want to add for yourself?

MOVING FORWARD

"Nothing less than the most radical imagination will carry us beyond this place."
–Poet Adrienne Rich

Welcome to the end of this book—and the beginning of the rest of your journey. You made it!

Not long after I began writing this book, the verdict came down in the case of the murder of Trayvon Martin. Martin, an unarmed African-American teenage boy, was killed by George Zimmerman, a mixed-race Hispanic neighborhood watchman. Zimmerman was found not guilty under Florida's "Stand Your Ground" law, sparking a national conversation about race and giving rise to Black Lives Matter.

> *"I'm on a 500-year clock right now. I'm right here knowing that we've got a hell of a long time before we're going to see the end. Right now, all we're doing is building the conditions that will allow the thing to happen."*
>
> –Activist, grassroots organizer, and Mariame Kaba

Almost a decade has passed since then, and as I write these final words, I watch and read about Ukrainian cities being pummeled by rockets and mortar shells, two weeks into the Russian Invasion. These are hard times in the world, and things aren't going to get any easier as resources get tighter, the climate changes faster, and forces pull us apart.

Yet as so many wise leaders point out, our fate is not yet sealed. As you come to the end of these pages, hopefully your skills and capacity to navigate changes have grown. Hopefully you feel clearer about who you are, where you come from, and what you have to give. As you venture forth from these pages, may you be gentle and kind with yourself and with your loved ones. May you cultivate your wildest imagination of the world you want to create, and throw your life into creating it. May you surround yourself with people who care about you and treat you well, and may you hold tight to them whatever comes. And may you remember that no matter what, the earth is always there beneath you, holding you firm on this wild planet, a source of strength to support you.

☾

Appendix I:

BIOGRAPHIES OF YOUNG PEOPLE

These interviews were conducted over about 6 years between 2016-2022. Some people were interviewed more than once. Throughout the text I've offered ages at the time of interview. Biographies were written by the participants themselves.

Alyson (she/her) was born and raised in a small farm town in central Illinois. She currently resides in Bloomington, Indiana where she is working to earn a Master's degree in Environmental Health. Alyson is a white middle-class woman. With her degree in Environmental Health, Alyson will work to promote environmental justice through research that will inform policy.

Cameron (he/him) comes from a white, middle-class background and has lived in and around Seattle, WA in Coast Salish territories for nearly all of his life. Journeying into mountains and into Latin America – both inspired by his older brother– brought him alive in his late teen years, and set the stage for work in wilderness rites of passage and Indigenous solidarity.

Chandi (she/her) is from the district of Ka'u, Hawaii. Identifying as both white and Native American, her ancestry ties back to Germany and the Oneida Indian tribe. Her upbringing and ancestral roots have instilled a fascination of the interplay between wild places and the human condition. Chandi is a passionate learner and teacher of the relationship between humans and the natural world. Chandi is committed to help others heal by tapping into an individual's relationship with self and nature, supporting one's deep inner wounds, and building one's self-awareness.

Clement (they/he) is a white, transgender/non-binary human that was born and raised in the British Isles and now resides in the Pacific Northwest of the United States. When initially interviewed for this project, they worked as a guide for Pacific Quest Wilderness Therapy. Now, Clement is a public school social worker, narrative therapist, LGBTQ+ consultant, and Queer rite of passage guide. They guide cisgender teachers and administration in understanding and building authentic relationships with transgender and non-binary youth in the public school system. In the summers, they spend lots of time at the river with their partner and sweet dog.

Corinne (she/her) originally hails from the Bay Area and Central Valley of California, and currently resides on the Big Island of Hawaii. Corinne is passionate about mentorship, stewardship, and being a lifelong learner.

Dani (she/her) is originally from Michigan, of German, Polish, and Irish descent. Identifying as both white and middle-class, she now lives in The Kingdom of Hawaii, and is dedicated to art, conserving the ocean, her own self growth, and being a supportive community member. Rites of passage changed Danielle's life at the age of 25.

Dante (they/them) is originally from Tongva land, also known as Los Angeles. Their ancestors came from Italy, Germany, and Poland in the early 20th century and connection to ancestral cultures and traditions bring them a lot of joy. They currently live in Duwamish land known as Seattle in Washington state. Dante came from a tight-knit white middle class family and they spend much of their time building with others and learning from wise people.

Gloria (she/her) is a Mother and Latina community organizer in South Central Los Angeles. Her passion revolves around youth development and ending the school-to-prison pipeline and criminalization of BIPOC youth and people.

Gretchen (she/her) was born and raised in western Montana on the traditional land of the Salish and Kootenai people, currently known as Missoula County. Identifying as a woman, daughter, sister, and loving partner, she also claims animism as her spiritual perspective, and Caucasian of European descent with ancestors from Germany and Scotland. She now lives nomadically between southern Utah, western Montana and southeast Alaska, working as a Rite of Passage and Backcountry guide.

Izaac (he/him) is a man of mixed European ancestry who was born and raised in the rural midwest of the United States. He grew up on an acreage in Iowa within a middle class family that cultivated an ethic of care for others and the natural world. After many years of his early adulthood spent living, working and exploring on both coasts of the US, Izaac returned to his home state and life's base camp where he now resides in Des Moines. Izaac fosters a life that is steeped in nature, spirituality, creativity, family and work, play and service in community.

Jess (she/they) is a black, queer, gender nonconforming person with a working middle class background from Western Washington and currently resides in Seattle. They are a licensed cosmetologist and creative who enjoys working with people from all walks of life. The most important part of Jess' life is sharing love and acceptance to every person they meet.

Kay (she/her/ella) is originally from the lands of the Okanagan people, also known as Tonasket, Washington. She identifies as Chicanx and is a proud daughter of immigrants with her ancestors including ties to Indigenous Mexicans, Afro-Mexicans, and Spaniard Conquistadors. She lives in Northern Colorado, the unceded lands of the Ute, Cheyenne, and Arapaho peoples. Rites of passage have been part of Kay's life since she was a child.

Karla (she/her) is a community organizer from Boyle Heights/East LA. Her organizing journey began in high school, when she was encouraged to participate in a Gender Based Violence leadership training with the East Los Angeles Women's Center. Karla first discovered her voice and power at the age of 15 and has been a force to be reckoned with since then. At a very young age, Karla has been vocal about ending Gender Based Violence and empowering young leaders to find their voice. Today, Karla works as a Case Manager with at risk communities to assist them to live independently.

Katelyn (she/her) is an only child and introvert of an Irish-English-Ukrainian, middle-class household raised in Rhode Island and Massachusetts. Unlike the rest of her New-England-for-life family, Katelyn moved to the Appalachian Mountains for University to expand her knowledge of psychology, environmental health, anthropology, art and nutrition. Following graduation, she spent 15 months working in Wilderness Therapy with teens in these mountains, continually inspired and challenged. Now, she resides in Hawaii working and growing within an Outdoor Behavioral Health program as a guide to adolescents, support to field guides, as well as working as a coach with individuals and small groups. In her unstructured moments, she enjoys freeform dance, swimming like a sea lion, hiking, watching leaves gently move in the wind, and fostering treasured friendships.

Katheryne (she/her) is originally from the lands of the Muscogee/Creek, Yamassee, and Seminole (Georgia and Florida), but currently resides on the lands of the Multnomah, Clackamas, Tualatin, Chinook, and many others now known as Portland, OR. She feels empowered in her identities as a queer Black woman. She is currently studying mental health counseling and ecopsychology to help youth foster a sense of environmental stewardship in efforts to build a sense of belonging and purpose within the minoritized communities that are often left out of the outdoors narrative.

Lauren (she/they) is a Japanese American born and raised on the land of the Ohlone, Awaswas, Tamien, Muwekma and Amah Mutsun, (California). They now live on the land of the Snoqualmie people in Washington state. They love coastal prairies, big mountains, clear sunrises and flowing water.

Micaela (she/her) grew up in Olympia, Washington and currently resides in Portland, Maine. Micaela identifies as white, cisgender, and middle-class with Western European heritage. Micaela is currently attending graduate school for occupational therapy and hopes to continue working in adolescent mental health upon finishing her degree.

Nadia (she/her) was born in Antananarivo, Madagascar and now lives in Kigali, Rwanda. Nadia has an MSc in Education, Power and Social Change from Birkbeck University of London and believes in the power of education to be a tool to make an impact for children, youth, and women (education of self and others). She loves volunteering and helping others. She has taken the opportunity to share and bring her contribution through volunteering in the last couple of years before she moved to Rwanda. She envisions a world where youth and children are aware of their values and worth to make a difference around them.

Naila (she/her) is a 25 year old woman living in the Tamera Peace Research and Education Center in Portugal. She grew up in community and still lives in community, with the deepest motivation to be part of creating spaces where the true and humane in all life can become visible again and find acceptance.

Scott (he/him) is originally from the lands of the Odawa and Anishinbewaki people, also known as the state of Michigan.

Identifying as both white and middle-class, he comes from a strong Polish and French heritage. He now lives seasonally between Southeast Alaska and Michigan. Scott holds a deep admiration for nature and the interplay of life within it. He works to share his admiration through his work with at-risk youth.

Serena (she/her, he/him) was born and raised on Kānaka ʻŌiwi land on the island of Oʻahu in Hawaiʻi. She has a Bachelor's in English from the University of Hawaiʻi at Mānoa. She has been a spoken word poet for twelve years and writing is the medium she uses to explore queerness, gender, and what it means to be Māori.

Tarek (he/they) was born on Duwamish land, also known as Seattle, Washington. He now lives a nomadic lifestyle calling many places home and works as a rite of passage guide, produces music festivals, loves traveling and learning about cultures. He identifies as a cis-male pansexual, whose ancestry carries threads to Turkey and Mexico.

Tim (he/him) is from Portland, Maine. Recently, he moved aboard his sailboat, Wayfinder, and is currently cruising the east coast of the U.S., with the intention of sailing around the world soon. After graduating high school, he joined the Marine Corps, spent a year in jail, and continued a cycle of relapses for years that almost ended with his suicide. Today, he is in recovery, and constantly working towards becoming a better version of himself than he was yesterday. He finds himself most at home in the wilderness, challenging himself by pushing the boundaries of his mental and physical limits, and seeking spiritual connection with the world around him.

Vicki (she/her) is a white, straight, cis-gender, sober, Jewish, woman from Philadelphia. She currently resides in Palm Beach, Florida where she works at an Eating Disorder Treatment Center. In her spare time, she spends as much time as she can in the ocean and connecting to nature.

Zachary (he/him) was born in Ballard, Washington at Swedish Hospital. He grew up in a middle class household in Shoreline, Washington and is a current resident of Seattle, Washington. Zach identifies as a white male. He is a son, a brother, a friend and a coach. He is passionate about destigmatizing mental health and mentoring youth through athletics. He feels that his purpose in life is to make a positive impact on his environment through his ability to connect with people.

Appendix II:

WORKSHEET FOR A SELF-DESIGNED RITE OF PASSAGE INTO ADULTHOOD

WORKSHEET FOR A SELF-DESIGNED RITE OF PASSAGE INTO ADULTHOOD

INTENT STATEMENT:

Elements of a Rite of Passage

Using the following questions as starting points, brainstorm possibilities for your rite of passage ceremony with each element of a rite of passage. Go through each element a couple of times to make sure that what you include in one section is accounted for in other sections (for example, if you include a practical test of undergoing a solo backpacking trip, make sure you've included any mentored learning that's required for you to safely travel by yourself in the backcountry).

Practical Testing:

- What skills, qualities, or capacities need to be tested in order to fully inhabit my intent?
- What needs to be sacrificed or given up for a period of time?
- Who can help me assess these tests to match my skills?

Mentored Learning:

- What do I need to learn in order to safely and successfully undergo whatever practical tests feel right to me?
- What skills, qualities, or capacities do I want or need to develop in order to fully inhabit my intent statement?
- Who can I call on for support, training, and mentorship?
- Who are the Indigenous peoples of the lands I'll be on, and how might I give back and honor them?

Embodied Ritual:

- What elements of ritual and ceremony from the last chapter will support me in making this passage?

- What archetypal ritual actions from the last chapter will support me in making this passage?

WORKSHEET FOR A SELF-DESIGNED RITE OF PASSAGE INTO ADULTHOOD, CONTINUED

- What needs to be gathered in order to do this?
- How will I honor and include my ancestors?

Community Celebration:

- How can the community send me off in ways that are supportive for me and strengthen the community?
- How can the community support me while I'm away?
- How can the community welcome me home in ways that are supportive for me and strengthen the community?
- What gifts will I offer to the people who have supported me on this journey?

Timeline and Flow

Now look back over your brainstorm on the elements of a rite of passage, and begin to organize this in a chart for yourself, using what's offered here as a template.

PHASE OF THE PROCESS	WISHES, HOPES, AND INTENTIONS	WHEN, WHERE, WHO?	NEEDS/ ACTION STEPS	ADDITIONAL NOTES
Preparation				
Sendoff Ceremony				
Initiation				
Return Ceremony				
Reunion Event				

Appendix III:

YOUTH PASSAGEWAYS' CROSS CULTURAL PROTOCOLS IN RITES OF PASSAGE

Youth Passageways has adopted these principles to guide its operations. It is our hope that this document may support affiliated organizations in creating their own working agreements, standards, and relations capable of addressing and caring for the needs that arise through their good work. This is a living document, which will be regularly updated. Please submit feedback, comments, and stories about how this document is being used to: info@youthpassageways.org

CONSIDERATIONS

These protocols and approach outlined in this document can bring difficult dynamics to the surface, within individuals and communities. This document came into existence through a painful process, involving the blood, sweat, and tears of many. Navigating it may similarly require difficult soul-searching for you and your community/ organization. We are still learning how to best support others as they navigate this process. A couple of considerations we suggest: 1) assess investment/buy-in from members of your team, and their relative level of power and influence, before starting the work of unpacking this document. Don't go it alone! 2) consider the social positioning (both within the organization and in a broader societal context) of those leading the process. 3) Take stock of your resources (time, money, emotional energy, expertise) before diving into these protocols. Realistically consider if now is the right time, as exploring the document is likely to bring core issues into the light before it helps resolve them. Please contact info@youthpassageways.org if you'd like more support in this process.

CONTEXT

Rite of passage ceremonies are both old and new, and can be learned, inherited, gifted, created and experienced, in many contexts. It has been the experience of many in this network and beyond that there is a tremendous gift and beauty in this, and also that disputes can arise in the construction, use, and sharing of ritual practices and language.

Many of these disputes have their roots in the centuries of violence, genocide, and intentional cultural destruction. Continued inequities reinforce deep wounds within and between cultures. These dynamics occur between indigenous and settler cultures, and diasporic communities and "dominant" cultures. In unique ways, each of these groups has suffered from uprooting and historical trauma. The circumstances by which each of us have lost or been ripped from our indigeneity constitutes a specific history, and carries specific wounds and responsibilities. Because of the complex fabric of history we may play the roles of both colonizers and colonized, the under/over privileged, depending on the context. All of these factors influence what is possible and what is challenging in the delivery of rite of passage ceremonies and processes.

The contemporary rites of passage movement stands indebted to many cultural traditions which have in best-case scenarios gifted practices and in many cases suffered theft or appropriation. Particularly important to acknowledge are indigenous societies for their centuries- and millennia-long cultural practices in human development. They have provided a formative influence on contemporary movements theoretically, aesthetically, and in terms of actual ritual practices. We also recognize that human beings, regardless of cultural background or connection to tradition, have painstakingly fought to reclaim lost cultural traditions, and by direct communion, inspiration, and intuition, have created new forms of initiation and other cultural rituals and ceremonies that have validity for their communities and beyond. The intersection of these truths needs particular care and attention, especially for a national youth rites of passage network. With discernment, we respect both established and emergent practices with all of the attendant complexities that this entails.

Our movement exists because the "THE HOUSE IS ON FIRE!", and our young people are in a state of desperation on an international/global scale. Working through and learning from the inter-cultural conflicts in our movement and building toward reparations and restoration is an integral part of creating the ceremonial processes that allow communities to be renewed by the fires of transformation crossed by their youth. It is also an integral part of the world of justice, peace, purpose, mystery and abundance into which we seek to initiate our youth. Many well intentioned people do unintended harm when they mean to do good. Our hope is that through learning from one another and through practice, our intentions, actions, and effects as a movement can be aligned. Our goal is not to offer an exhaustive document or settle issues once and for all, but to provide context, background, starting points for consideration, and a deepening and softening into the issues and questions. We recognize what we propose to do here is many lives' work and we enter with humility and desire to learn. May these principles and questions draw on the wisdom of our ancestors and teachers, serve as a next unfolding and point of reference, and support future generations.

ASSUME GOODWILL

We enter with a spirit of goodwill. We strive to trust that others are doing the same.

HISTORICAL CONTEXT, HEALING AND RECONCILIATION

We acknowledge historical context and historical relationships of peoples and place, recognizing that many cultures have been subjected, and continue to be subjected, to deep violations. This context affects access to power and justice and is embedded in relationships between peoples. We strive to educate ourselves and others about these dynamics, open ourselves to the pain, help sensitize others to it, and contribute to healing and reconciliation.

THE RIGHT TO EARTH AND SPIRIT

We recognize the rights of all people to deep relationship with Earth and Spirit, and that we all have the right and innate ability to receive information from the more-than-human world.

CULTURAL HUMILITY

We commit to a practice of cultural humility and cultural self-awareness. We strive to increase skillfulness communicating across cultures and deepen awareness of our own and other's cultural norms. We take responsibility to deepen our understanding of our own cultural and ancestral practices and ritual forms, and those of others. When we share teachings/artifacts from cultures other than our own, we do so with discernment, and provide context. We strive to become aware of and name the lenses through which we see the world, and recognize that others may see things differently. We ask rather than assume as much as possible.

RELATIONSHIP TO PLACE

Both in our home communities and when entering into a new place, we strive to educate ourselves about the land, the historical and contemporary and political context of the peoples of that land, build relationships with the people of that place, and follow local protocols as best we can. This includes seeking permission to conduct ceremony or other activities in that location.

ADDRESSING AND GROWING THROUGH CONFLICT

We are committed to ongoing Cross-Cultural relationships, and strive to develop and support mechanisms and processes for working with conflict, reconciliation and forgiveness. We believe that justice and healing are central to each undertaking, rather than secondary benefits or distractions.

SEXUALITY AND GENDER

We recognize the essential nature of sexuality and gender in the work of rites of passage, and openly explore the dynamics of masculinity, femininity, and queerness (as archetypal energies, social dynamics, and deep cultural wounds) in our work together. We recognize that binary thinking is a product of patriarchy and colonization, and seek to bring balance by honoring and making space for all genders inside and outside of this binary. We strive to create inclusive spaces where LGBTQIA+ folks (Lesbian, Gay, Bisexual, Transgender, Queer or Questioning, Intersex, Aasexual, plus) feel seen, heard, recognized, and honored, and to recognize and mitigate our own privilege in order to create safe spaces to center the voices of those often marginalized.

DIFFERENT PERSPECTIVES/PERCEPTIONS OF TIME

We strive to become sensitized to different perceptions of time within and between different cultures. We recognize that ceremonial time differs from linear time and our work and schedules are designed with that awareness. We strive to set and keep to agreements of time and space, including agreements that at times, time will be fluid and processes will last as long as required. We commit to holding a long view of time, which holds in our awareness many generations of ancestors as well as future generations to come.

LEGAL CONSIDERATIONS AND FREE PRIOR AND INFORMED CONSENT (FPIC)

We recognize that many aspects of culture, including dress, symbols, ritual and language, may be subject to intellectual property laws. Additionally, some indigenous peoples have their own norms, customs or legal systems associated with the use of their cultural ways. We strive to become aware and abide by these norms, customs and laws and practice Free Prior and Informed Consent.

EXCHANGE OF MONEY/COMMODIFICATION

Many issues exist around the commodification of spiritual traditions and cultural symbols of indigenous and diasporic peoples. We strive to educate ourselves on these issues, and to act with consciousness and transparency around the exchange of money in our work. We support practitioners having sustainable means as they assist communities and pursue right livelihood in these transition times. We strive to make initiatory work accessible and equitable for all that need it.

LEGACY

We honor our teachers and seek blessing to operate alongside of our mentors, teachers and elders in the use of ceremonial and ritual processes. Our work is inherently inter-generational, therefore we seek out participation from all generations. We are accountable to future generations for what we model by what we teach and how we teach it - today.

GRATITUDE, GENEROSITY, AND CELEBRATION

We celebrate, acknowledge, and give thanks for every step toward right relationship. It takes courage to face these conversations directly; even having them is cause for celebration. We water the good along the way.

ENDNOTE REFERENCES

INTRODUCTION

p. 10 **recent study** by Harvard: "Harvard Youth Poll." December 1, 2021, https://iop.harvard.edu/youth-poll/fall-2021-harvard-youth-poll

p. 12 **He used the term to refer to:** Arnold Van Gennep, *Les Rites de Passage* (Paris: A. et J. Picard, 1909).

"If the fires that innately burn": Michael Meade, *Men and the Water of Life: Initiation and the Tempering of Men* (New York: Harper San Francisco, 1993).

p. 14 **It offers a roadmap:** Amanda Ayling, personal communication, 2007.

p. 15 **"rites of passage are a cultural antihistamine":** Paul Hill, Jr., *Coming of Age: African American Male Rites-of-Passage* (Chicago, Illinois, African American Images, 1992).

p. 17 **"psyche gets pulled through:"** Luis Rodriguez, personal communication, 2020.

p. 18 **"there may be no time:"** Michael Meade, "Rites of Passage at the End of the Millennium," in *Crossroads: The Quest* for Contemporary Rites of Passage. (Peru, Il: Carus Publishing Co, 1996) p. 27.

p. 18 **Triple rite of passage:** Joshua Gorman, personal communication, 2008.

p. 22 **Western culture:** "Western culture." Wikipedia, last modified December 30, 2021, https://en.wikipedia.org/wiki/Western_culture

CHAPTER ONE

p. 31 **My mom, an educator:** This section draws heavily on Edith Kusnic, Fostering Thriving Communities through Rites of Passage: A Manual for Getting Started (Bothell: Rite of Passage Journeys, 2016), p 21.

Yuuyaraq, The Way of the Human Being: Harold Napoleon, Yuuyaraq: The Way of the Human Being (Fairbanks: College of Rural Alaska, Center for Cross-Cultural Studies, 1996).

p. 34 **"the sum total of ways:"** "Culture." Dictionary.com. Retrieved January 2 2021, https://www.dictionary.com/browse/culture.

p. 38 **"our place on the land:"** Jeanette Armstrong, "Sharing One Skin: The Okanagan Community," in Jerry Mander and Edward Goldsmith (eds.) The Case Against the Global Economy (San Francisco: Sierra Club Books, 1996), p. 465.

"No one is going to give you the education:" Assata Shakur, Assata: An Autobiography (Italy: L. Hill, 2001).

p. 40 **A Few Differences between Indigenous and Western worldviews:** This chart draws on a number of sources, including: "What are Indigenous and Western Ways of Knowing? Canadian Research Institute for the Advancement of Women," https://www.criaw-icref.ca/images/userfiles/files/Fact%20Sheet%202%20EN%20FINAL.pdf; Kindred Media, "Dominator and Indigenous Worldview Manifestations," https://www.kindredmedia.org/wp-content/uploads/Worldview-Chart-Black-Background-12-2020.pdf; First Peoples Worldwide, "The Indigenous World View vs. Western World View," https://www.youtube.com/watch?v=hsh-NcZyuil&t=319s; Nelson Education, "What is the Aboriginal Worldview," https://vimeo.com/113924147; as well as feedback from J. Miakoda Taylor of Fierce Allies and Rebecca Chief Eagle of All Nations Gathering Center.

"There is no single Indigenous or Western way of knowing:" Jane Stinson, "What are Indigenous and Western Ways of Knowing?" Factsheet, Canadian Research Institute for the Advancement of Women, 2018. https://www.criaw-icref.ca/images/userfiles/files/Fact%20Sheet%202%20EN%20FINAL.pdf

p. 41   **"creative maladjustment:"** Dr. Martin Luther King, Jr. "Creative Maladjustment." (Keynote Speech, Annual Conference of the American Psychological Association, September 1967).

p. 43   **who coined the term rites of passage:** Arnold Van Gennep, *Les Rites de Passage* (Paris: A. et J. Picard, 1909).

p. 46   **intuitive knowing that survivors of violence often report:** Gavin De Becker, *Gift of Fear*. (United Kingdom: Bloomsbury, 2000).

p. 48   **Whether your access to nature is big or small:** Inspired by David Moskowitz, "The Earth Speaks, if We Care to Listen," *ICA Journeys*, December 2001.

p. 55   **It was with Melissa on the dance floor:** For more about Golden Bridge and Melissa Michaels' work, see Melissa Michaels, *Youth on Fire: Igniting a Generation of Embodied Global Leaders* (Boulder, CO: Golden Bridge, 2016).

p. 56   **Animals have ways of dealing with this:** For more on this subject, see Peter Levine, *In an Unspoken Voice: How the Body Releases Trauma and Restores Goodness* (Berkeley: North Atlantic Books, 2010).

p. 58   **Children of parents with addiction issues:** Lauren Chval, "Children with addicted parents face difficulties in adulthood, including a higher risk of addiction," *Chicago Tribune*, April 30, 2018, https://www.chicagotribune.com/lifestyles/ct-life-children-addicted-parents-0430-story.html.

p. 59   **ways that we can resource ourselves include:** This is adapted from Hala Khouri, *Peace from Anxiety: Get Grounded, Build Resilience, and Stay Connected Amidst the Chaos.* (Boulder: Shambala Publications, 2021).

p. 59   **Short list of sensations:** For a more in-depth exploration of this, and a more robust list of sensations, see Melissa Michaels, *Youth on Fire*, 2016, Chapter Six : Embodying Life's Rhythms.

p. 61   **"People who use their minds to reflect on the inner nature:"** Dan Siegel, *Brainstorm: The Power and Purpose of the Teenage Brain* (New York: Jeremy P. Tarcher/Penguin, a member of Penguin Group USA, 2015).

p. 66   **dreams are our "personal mythology:"** Martin Shaw, "Rogue Bards" Workshop presented at Schumacher College, Dartington UK (July 2016).

CHAPTER TWO

p. 77 **Developed by Steven Foster and Meredith Little:** Steven Foster and Meredith Little, *The Four Shields: The Initiatory Seasons of Human Nature* (United States: Lost Borders Press, 1999).

p. 81 **Killing the child:** Steven Jenkinson, "The Skill of Dying in a Death Phobic Culture" Interview with Jesse Mendes (2014). https://soundcloud.com/orphan-wisdom/sets/stephen-jenkinson-the-skill-of-dying-in-a-death-phobic-culture

p. 83 **"I feel like you can make your own life:"** "Cade Quigley, interview with Byron Odion", Voices of the Methow, podcast audio, (August 4, 2018) https://www.youtube.com/watch?v=ZrF4FStIM9k

p. 83 **boys as young as ten:** Thomas Hine, *The Rise and Fall of the American Teenager: A New History of the American Adolescent Experience* (New York: HarperCollins, 1999): p. 16.

p. 84 **"sturm und drang:"** G. Stanley Hall, *Adolescence: Its psychology and its relations to physiology, anthropology, sociology, sex, crime, religion and education*, Vol. 1. (New York: D Appleton & Company, 1904).

"to be normal during the adolescent period:" Anna Freud "Adolescence" *Psychoanalytic Study of the Child*, 13:1 (1958): p.255-278.

p. 85 **new insights about what is happening during adolescence:** Dan Siegel, *Brainstorm: The Power and Purpose of the Teenage Brain* (New York: Jeremy P. Tarcher/Penguin, a member of Penguin Group USA, 2015). This section draws heavily on Seigel's work.

p. 89   spent decades taking people on the land in ceremony: Bill Plotkin, *Nature and the Human Soul: Cultivating Wholeness and Community in a Fragmented World* (United States: New World Library, 2010).

p. 90   "fabric for us to refashion:" Ibid.

p. 92   primary breadwinners: Thomas Hine, *The Rise and Fall of the American Teenager: A New History of the American Adolescent Experience* (New York: HarperCollins, 1999): p. 75-94.

large portion of their waking hours: Ibid., p. 203-224.

p. 92   Puberty is coming biologically earlier: "Human Development- Development of the Reproductive Organs and Secondary Sex Characteristics" *Encyclopedia Brittanica Online*, Accessed Jan 14 2022, https://www.britannica.com/science/human-development/Development-of-the-reproductive-organs-and-secondary-sex-characteristics

p. 93   In the geographic heart of India: This story is based on my personal notes from an educational visit to Mendha Lekha in January 2005.

p. 95   In the 1950's: Herbert A. Bloch and Arthur Neiderhoffer, *The Gang: A Study in Adolescent Behavior* (New York: Philosophical Library, 1958), p.17.

many of the key elements of a rite of passage: Dadisi Sanyika, "Gang Rites and Rituals of Initiation," in Louise Carus Mahdi et al (eds), *Crossroads: The Quest for Contemporary Rites of Passage* (Chicago: Open Court Press, 1996), p. 117.

p. 98   "the principal reason:" Thomas Hine, *The Rise and Fall of the American Teenager: A New History of the American*

Adolescent Experience (New York, HarperCollins Publishers, 1999).

CHAPTER THREE

p. 104 "power is at play:" J. Miakoda Taylor, personal communication, February 25, 2022.

p. 105 "power has such a bad reputation:" Ibid.

three types of power: Starhawk, *Truth or Dare: Encounters with Power, Authority and Mystery* (San Francisco, Harper San Francisco, 1988).

p. 108 "Social (in)justice framework:" This framework, initially developed by Kruti Parekh, was further developed by Kruti Parekh, Pınar Ateş Sinopoulos-Lloyd, and Darcy Ottey for a workshop series titled "The Ecology of Power and Privilege: A nature-based approach to anti-oppression work," 2017 See https://youthpassageways.org/the-ecology-of-power-privilege/.

p. 110 be careful where you walk: Sindelókë, "Of Dogs And Lizards: A Parable of Privilege," Sindelókë,Wordpress Blog, December 16, 2021, https://sindeloke.wordpress.com/2010/01/13/37/ as quoted in Pegi Eyers, *Ancient Spirit Rising: Reclaiming Your Roots & Restoring Earth Community* (Canada: Stone Circle Press, 2015).

p. 112 exploited native cultural symbols: Philip Joseph Deloria, *Playing Indian* (United Kingdom: Yale University Press, 1998).

p. 114 spiritual bypass: Tina Fossella and John Welwood, "Human nature, buddha nature: an interview with John Welwood" *Tricycle: The Buddhist Review*, Spring 2011.

p. 114   "taking the gifts of the ancestors:" Starhawk, "A Recipe for Diversity," November 26 2010) https://starhawk.org/a-recipe-for-diversity-or-a-bunch-of-diverse-things-and-a-recipe/

p. 115   "cultural appropriation is violent:" Brandi Douglas and Steph Viera, "Disrupting Rainbow Capitalism," NDN Collective, June 22, 2021. https://ndncollective.org/disrupting-rainbow-capitalism-we-will-not-be-commodified-or-erased/

p. 122   Ways People Engage Across Cultures: Chart inspired by Richard A. Rogers "From Cultural Exchange to Transculturation: A Review and Reconceptualization of Cultural Appropriation." Communication Theory 16(4), November. 2006, p. 474 - 503.

p. 118   "Due to lack of reciprocity:" Carlos Saavedra & Fhatima Paulino, "Decolonization & the Long View of History," Irresistible podcast, February 2018. https://irresistible.org/podcast/15

p. 119   the realm of Tibetan Buddhism: Christopher Koch, "Neuroscientists and the Dalai Lama Swap Insights on Meditation," July 1, 2013, https://www.scientificamerican.com/article/neuroscientists-dalai-lama-swap-insights-meditation/

p. 125   danger of emphasizing "rights:" Sakej Ward, "So you want to be an ally?" Lecture at Surrey City Library, June 18, 2017.

p. 127   What Indigenous nation(s): Some of these questions are adapted from: Catalyst Project, "Indigenous Resistance Homework," https://collectiveliberation.org/wp-content/uploads/2018/10/Indigenous-Resistance-Homework.pdf

CHAPTER FOUR

p. 133 **"The erotic is a measure:"** Audre Lorde, *Uses of the Erotic: The erotic as Power* (Brooklyn, N.Y.: Out & Out Books, 1978).

p. 134 **"radically alter consciousness:"** Michael Pollan, *How to Change Your Mind: What the New Science of Psychedelics Teaches Us About Consciousness, Dying, Addiction, Depression, and Transcendence*, (United States: Penguin Publishing Group, 2018).

p. 141 **"more-than-human-world:"** David Abram, *The Spell of the Sensuous : Perception and Language in a More-than-Human World*. (New York: Pantheon Books, 1996).

p. 142 **Find someone who you trust:** I first participated in this activity with Lizz Randall of Body Trust Circle. Melissa Michaels also offers a helpful description of this activity in *Youth on Fire* on p.126.

p. 148 **A pleasure goddess:** Betty Martin, "The Wheel of Consent," retrieved March 23, 2022. https://bettymartin.org/videos/

p. 150 **Like illicit drugs and alcohol:** For more information on dopamine, serotonin, and other neurotransmitters, their effects, and safe, healthy, non-addictive ways to promote their release, check out the website www.naturalhighs.org, or see Hyla Cass, MD, and Patrick Holford, *Natural Highs: Feel Good All the Time* (United States: Penguin Publishing Group, 2003).

p. 151 **"boys' brains are being rewired:"** Philip Zimbardo, "The Demise of Guys.," TED Talk, February 2011, Long Beach, CA, 4:18. https://www.ted.com/talks/philip_zimbardo_the_demise_of_guys?language=en#t-8646

p. 160 simple formula for "relational communication:" Dan Siegel, *Brainstorm: The Power and Purpose of the Teenage Brain* (New York: Jeremy P. Tarcher/Penguin, a member of Penguin Group USA, 2015).

empathy is measurably diminishing in our society: "Empathy: College students don't have as much as they used to," Michigan News: University of Michigan, May 27, 2010, https://news.umich.edu/empathy-college-students-don-t-have-as-much-as-they-used-to/.

p. 165 **addressing our addictions:** Bill Plotkin, *Wild Mind: A Field Guide to the Human Psyche* (United States: New World Library, 2013) p. 181-205

CHAPTER FIVE

p. 184 **The aim of soul work:** Thomas Moore, *Care of the Soul: A Guide for Cultivating Depth and Sacredness in Everyday Life* (New York, HarperCollins, 1992), p. Xvii.

p. 186 **"Only to the extent that we expose ourselves:"** Pema Chödrön, *When Things Fall Apart: Heart Advice for Difficult Times* (United States: Shambhala Publications, Incorporated, 2005). p. 9

p. 190 **who often held (and hold) venerated positions:** "Indigenizing Love: a Toolkit for Native Youth to Build Inclusion" Western States Center, Portland OR, September 2019, https://www.healthynativeyouth.org/wp-content/uploads/2019/09/IndigenizingLoveToolkitYouth.pdf

p. 190 **There had been increasing challenges to these rights:** Sylvia Frederici, *The Caliban and the Witch* (Brooklyn, Autonomedia, 2004).

p. 191 **gender doesn't define a person as much as it used to:** Shepherd Laughlin "Gen Z goes beyond gender binaries in new Innovation Group data" Wunderman Thompson, Mar 11, 2016, https://www.wundermanthompson.com/insight/gen-z-goes-beyond-gender-binaries-in-new-innovation-group-data

p. 195 **The Gender Unicorn:** Trans Student Educational Resources, 2015. "The Gender Unicorn." http://www.transstudent.org/gender. The Gender Unicorn is licensed under Creative Commons Licensing; no permission necessary.

p. 197 **"race is the child of racism:"** Ta-Nehisi Coates, *Between the World and Me* (United States: Random House Publishing Group, 2015),p 7.

p. 199 **class is a social system that divides people:** "Class Markers" Showing Up for Racial Justice, retrieved April 6, 2022, https://surj.org/why-class-matters-in-organizing-for-racial-justice/.

p. 201 **unique challenges that African-American women endure:** Kimberlé Crenshaw, "On Intersectionality" Keynote Address, WOW, 2016, https://www.youtube.com/watch?v=-DW4HLgYPIA.

p. 205 **National Rites of Passage Institute:** Paul Hill, Jr., *Coming of Age: African American Male Rites-of-Passage* (Chicago, Illinois, African American Images, 1992), p. 94.

p. 207 **"the more individualized and isolated our sense of self is:"** Dan Siegel, *Brainstorm: The Power and Purpose of the Teenage Brain* (New York: Jeremy P. Tarcher/Penguin, a member of Penguin Group USA, 2015) p. 301.

p. 212 **Social isolation literally kills people:** Jessica Olien "Loneliness is Deadly" Slate, August 2013 https://slate.

CHAPTER SIX

p. 217 **Pod Mapping Exercise:** This Pod Mapping Worksheet was developed by the Bay Area Transformative Justice Collective and is included under Creative Commons Attribution 4.0 International License. Mia Mingus, "Pods and Podmapping Worksheet," https://batjc.wordpress.com/resources/pods-and-pod-mapping-worksheet/.

p. 228 **A Story of my People:** This story draws on many sources, and is particularly indebted to the Kevin Stroud, *The History of English* podcast; Sylvia Fredici, *The Caliban and the Witch*; and Roxanne Dunbar-Ortiz, *Indigenous People's History of the United States*.

p. 231 **"We are our landscapes:"** Chris Quiseng, personal communication, 2012.

p. 233 **From the following sets of elements and environments:** This activity is adapted from "Identity Mapping: Your Identity Map," Teach Indigenous Knowledge, retrieved January 15, 2022, https://teachik.com/identity-mapping/

p. 235 **the story for our times:** Brian Swimme and Thomas Berry, *The Universe Story: From the Primordial Flaring Forth to the Ecozoic Era—A Celebration of the Unfolding of the Cosmos* (United Kingdom: HarperCollins, 1994).

In the beginning there was nothing: This section, particularly the first half of it, draws heavily on a ritual known as "The Cosmic Walk" which was created by Sister Miriam MacGillis and Larry Edwards of Genesis Farm, NJ, and is based on the work of Thomas Berry and Brian Swimme. See "Cosmic Walk, an Interactive Ritual" https://worshipwords.co.uk/the-cosmic-walk-sister-miriam-therese-mcgillis-usa/

p. 239 **learn to be in relationship with the world around us:** See "Wildness - Enrique Salmon on 'kincentric' ecology" Center for Humans and Nature https://youtu.be/8SFzfBgJOi8

CHAPTER SEVEN

p. 249 **"that I've done the work for:"** "Meredith Little interviewed by Clinton Callahan," *School of Lost Borders*, March 2013, https://vimeo.com/78215782

"Intent is judged by answering the question:" Paul Hill, Jr., *Coming of Age: African American Male Rites-of-Passage* (Chicago, Illinois, African American Images, 1992), p. 92.

p. 251 **Word Cloud of Intents from Young People:** Michael McGee, "Word Cloud of Intents of Pacific Quest students," created 2016. Reprinted with permission.

p. 255 **"Speech is how we taste our ancestors:"** Martin Shaw, "Rogue Bards" Workshop presented at Schumacher College, Dartington UK (July 2016).

p. 261 **"more practical than 'our' practicality:"** Ronald Grimes, *Deeply into the Bone: Reinventing Rites of Passage* (Berkeley and Los Angeles, University of California Press, 2000), p. 7-13.

"A ritual is the enactment of a myth:" Paul Hill, Jr., *Coming of Age: African American Male Rites-of-Passage* (Chicago, Illinois, African American Images, 1992), p. 72.

p. 262 **Archetypal Ritual Actions:** These lists are modified from Virginia Hine, as quoted in Meredith Little, "Self-generated Ceremony", http://138.197.207.151/content/self-generated-ceremony-meredith-little

CHAPTER EIGHT

p. 272 "Initiation evokes a revelation of the sacred:" Mircea Eliade as paraphrased in Ronald Grimes, *Deeply into the Bone: Reinventing Rites of Passage* (Berkeley and Los Angeles, University of California Press, 2000), p.100

p. 281 Stan saw that there were four main elements: To learn how Stan Crow's Four Elements of a Rite of Passage have lived on and developed at Rite of Passage Journeys, please see Edith Kusnic, *Fostering Thriving Communities through Rites of Passage: A Manual for Getting Started* (Bothell: Rite of Passage Journeys, 2016). You can access this manual through www.riteofpassagejourneys.org.

p. 288 "willing to give up comfort in service to our longings:" Will Scott, personal communication, December 1, 2021.

CHAPTER NINE:

p. 297 when you're carrying a gift useful for your people: Martin Shaw, "Rogue Bards" Workshop presented at Schumacher College, Dartington UK (July 2016).

p. 300 challenge them when needed: Pegi Eyers, *Ancient Spirit Rising* (Otonabee, Ontario: Stone Circle Press, 2015) p. 81.

CHAPTER TEN

p. 311 etuaptmunk, or two-eyed seeing: Cheryl Bartlett, Murdena Marshall, and Albert Marshall, "Two-Eyed Seeing and other lessons learned within a co-learning journey of bringing together Indigenous and mainstream knowledges and ways of knowing," *Journal* of *Environmental Studies and Sciences*, 2 (November, 2012), pp. 331-340.

p. 311 **The Work that Reconnects:** Joanna Macy and Molly Young Brown, *Coming Back to Life: The Updated Guide to the Work That Reconnects* (Canada: New Society Publishers, 2014) p. 5-6.

p. 312 **Three Stories of our World:** Molly Brown and Joanna Macy, "Choosing the Story We Want for Our World, "https://workthatreconnects.org/choosing-the-story-we-want-for-our-world/ (Jan 9, 2018).

p. 313 **mirrored in many Indigenous prophecies:** "Apocalypse Prophecies: Native End of the World Teachings," *Indian Country Today*, September 13, 2018, https://indiancountrytoday.com/archive/apocalypse-prophecies-native-end-of-the-world-teachings

Three Dimensions of the Great Turning: Joanna Macy and Molly Young Brown, *Coming Back to Life: The Updated Guide to the Work That Reconnects* (Canada: New Society Publishers, 2014) p. 6-18.

p. 314 **fractals of a larger whole:** adrienne maree brown, *Emergent Strategy: Shaping Change, Changing Worlds* (United Kingdom: AK Press, 2017).

p. 318 **"Wisdom is understanding how long things take:"** Carlos Saavedra & Fhatima Paulino, "Decolonization & the Long View of History," Irresistible podcast, February 2018. https://irresistible.org/podcast/15

p. 319 **work sucked, and that people would avoid it if humanly possible:** Sarah Jaffe, *Work Won't Love You Back* (New York: Bold Type Books, 2021).

p. 319 **The Nap Ministry:** "Rest is anything that connects your mind and body," The Nap Ministry, February 21, 2022, https://thenapministry.wordpress.com/2022/02/21/rest-is-anything-that-connects-your-mind-and-body/

p. 329 **"being responsible for your choices:"** This definition is widely credited to The Northwest Network, an organization providing advocacy-based counseling and community education for queer and trans survivors of abuse.

three key aspects of accountability: Barnard Center for Research on Women "What is Accountability?" Oct 13, 2020, https://youtu.be/QZuJ55iGl14

p. 331 "Accountability is a fierce, radical, amazing way:" ibid.

p. 345 Cross Cultural Protocols in Rites of Passage: "Cross-Cultural Protocols in Rites of Passage," Youth Passageways (April 15, 2015) https://www.youthpassageways.org/ccp/ The Cross Cultural Protocols are licensed under a Creative Commons Attribution-ShareAlike

INDEX

Note: Page numbers in *italics* indicate figures, **bold** indicate tables in the text, and references following "n" refer notes.

A
Abrams, David, 50
accountability, 120n, 140, 215, 277–78, 300, 328–31
adolescent/adolescence, 77, 79, 82–83
    antiquated stories about, 83–84
    brain development, 84–87, 92, 95, 150, 174
    changing times and perspectives, 91–93
    cultural norms, 311
    ESSENCE of, 86, 88
    facing challenges during, 8
    life stages of, 98
    as liminal stage, 96–97, 274
    puberty, 92–93, 192
    transition into adulthood, 165
    soul development during, 89–91
    in Western culture, 13
addiction, 58n, 132, 165
    to cell phones, 9
    drug, 152, 173
    to food, 148
    hereditary nature of, 58
    physical, 150
adulthood, 5, 75–76, 79, 89, 99, 186
    benchmarks for stepping into, 239–40

independence of, 99–100
  initiation into, 13–14, 66, 81, 207, 314
  responsibility of, 99–100
  worksheet for self-designed rite of passage into, 342–43
alienation, feeling of, 15, 158, 306
Ahimsa Collective, 331
American culture, 33, 36, 83, 124–25
American Indian Religious Freedom Act, 115, 134
Ancient Spirit Rising (Eyers), 301n
ancestry/ancestral
  importance of, 218–22
  inheritance, 226
  recovering connection with, 211–14, 222–30
  trauma, 58
anxiety, 9, 11, 57, 60, 97, 134, **150**, 174, 224, 263, 304
archetypes, 66, 191, 193, 194
Aristotle, 273
Armstrong, Jeannette, **38**
arts, healing power of, 53–54, 165
assimilation, 93, **116, 122**, 224
authenticity, 90–91, 205, 323

B
Baker, Carolyn, 18
Battle of Greasy Grass, 229
Bay Area Transformative Justice Collective, 216
belonging, 14–15, 205, 212, 232
"Beloved Community", 328
Berry, Thomas, 183, 234–35
bias, 22, 154, 189
Bill of Rights, 124–25
Black communities
  Black Liberation movements, 38, 197, 332
  impacts of COVID, 187
  reparations to, 330, 331, 347
  violence facing, 57, 329
Black Liberation movements, 38, 197, 332
Black Lives Matter movement, See Black Liberation movements

brain development, 84–87, 92, 95, 150–51, 155, n174
bullying, 9, 12, 194
Bound, Outward, 154
boundaries,10, 138–42, 159, 176, 248
brown, adrienne maree, 314
Brown, Brené, 323
Burgess, Puanani, 181, 182
"Business as Usual", 310, 312

C

capitalism, 312, 318
Case, Pualani, 101–2
centering, 59 See also nervous system regulation
centering the most vulnerable, 321–22
ceremony, 5, 10, 13, 33, 51, 101–2, 113, 120, 134, 257–64, 273–74, 276, 279–81, 290, 304, 347. See also rites of passage.
 distinction from ritual, 260
childhood, 75, 77, 79, 89
 to adulthood transition, 13–14, 274
 end/death of, 80–82
 trauma, 125, 316, 322
 vulnerability in brain development during, 86–87
Chodron, Pema, 119, 186
Christianity, 121, 228–29
class, socioeconomic, 7, 8, 198–200
climate change/climate chaos, 8, 56, 97, 211, 310, 322, 332
Coates, Ta Nahesi, 197
colonialism, 12n, 117, 120n, 182, 312
colonization, 228-230
 impacts of, 40, 56, 97, 112, 134, 211, 346-350
 responsibilities of settlers, 126, 278n, 346-350
coming of age ceremony, 5, 10, 33, 51, 101–2. 120, 279
community celebration, 285, **286**
community, role in rites of passage 68, 93–97, 103, 135, 157–62, 199, 280, 285, **286, 296**, 301, 316
consciousness-shifting plant medicines, see mind-altering substances
consent, 10, 135–45, 163, 350
consumerism, 117, 135, 205

COVID-19 pandemic, 15–16, 44, 57, 187, 234, 309, 316–18, 324
Coyle, Gigi, 324
creative/creativity, 53-54, 66, 71, 88, 91, 105, 133, 166, 174, 252, 258, 317, 330
Crenshaw, Kimberlé, 201
Cross-Cultural Protocols, 324–26, 325
cross-cultural relationships, 349
Crow, Stan, 2, 69–70, 281, 282, 287
Crusades, The, 229
culture/cultural, 31–43, 76, 95–96, 115, 211, 324, 327
    American, See American culture
    appropriation, 111–18, **122**, 135. See also cultural exploitation
    assimilation, 116, **122**
    cross-cultural relating, 36, 29, 345–350
    iceberg, 36, 37, 39
    habitat restoration, 103–4
    humility, 43, 327, 348
    Indigenous cultural practices, See Indigenous peoples and cultures
    Indigenous vs. Western worldviews, 39–40, **41–42**
    emergence, 121, **123**
    exchange, 119–20, **123**, 127
    exploitation, 120n, 135, 278
    identity, 203–5
    misappropriation. See cultural appropriation
    recovery, 120–21, 120n, **123**
    values, 96
    unlearning 39–40
    Western, See Western worldviews and cultures
    white, See white culture

D

daily practices, 316–18
Dalai Lama, 119
de Becker, Gavin, 46
decolonization, 40, 320, 331
Deloria, Jr., Vine, 233

Deloria, Philip, 112
depression, 9, 55, 57, 134, **150**, 172, 263
Descartes, Rene, 206
Doctrine of Discovery, 229
dopamine, 86, 148, **150**
Douglas, Brandi, 115
drugs. See mind-altering substances
dysregulation, See nervous system

E

Eagle, Philip Red, 318
Earth's initiation, 18, 19
eco-tourism, 225n
Ecology of Power and Privilege, The, 206
ego, 64, 176
elderhood, 77, 79, 89–90
El Día de Los Muertos, 220
Eliade, Mircea, 272
embodied/embodiment/somatic, 63, 100, 258, 261n, 284, 316
    ritual, 257–64, 284, **286**, 342
Emergent Strategy (brown), 314
emotions, 61–63, **61**
empathy, 141, 160–61
Empire, 230, 312
Enclosures, The, 229
entitlement, 117–18
eros/erotic, 133
ESSENCE of adolescence, **86**, 88
etuaptmunk, 311
evolution of species, 237–38
Eyers, Pegi, 301n

F

false narratives, unlearning, 39–40
family 214–16
    chosen, 214, 215
    of origin, 212, 214, 215, 225
    relationship with parents and caregivers, **73**

fasting, 288–90
fearfulness about future, 10
femininity, 193
fihavanana, 139
Floyd, George, 187, 317
Foster, Steven, 77, 78
Four Shields model, 77-80
Free Prior and Informed Consent (FPIC), 350
Freud, Anna, 84

G

gender, 189–95, 349
Generation Z, 191
genocide, 38, 97, 112, 119, **126**, 182, 229, 330, 346
George, Lewis, 326
Ghotul, 93–94
gift economy, 320
Gift of Fear (de Becker), 46
Global Passageways, 209–11
Golden Bridge, 139, 276, 305
goodwill, spirit of, 348
Gond tribal members, 93
Gorman, Joshua, 18
Great Death, The, 32
Great Depression, The 92
Great Turning, The, 312–13
Great Unraveling, The, 312–13
grief/grieving, 32, 48, 55, 63, 69, 135, 220, 225, 263, 312, 31
Grimes, Ronald, 258, 261
grounding, 59, 91, 142. See also nervous system regulation
guided rite of passage ceremonies, 276–79, **281**

H

haka (Māori ceremonial dance), 112
Harrow, Alix E., 273
Hartshorne, Mary, 226
Hartshorne, Samuel, 226
Hawaiian people and culture, See Kānaka Maoli

healing, 53–54, 103–04, 114, 125, 153, 164, 174, 247, 314, 316, 348
Hersey, Tricia, 319
Hill, Jr., Elder Paul, 15, 211, 249–50, 261
Hine, Thomas, 98
Huazhong, Luo, 319
human development, 5, 77, 77n, 89, 138, 347
humanity, 18, 98, 235, 272, 313
humility, 43, 127, 264, 277, 326, 327, 348

I

identity, 169–70, 186
    and physical appearance, 171–75
    the Self, 176–81
    and social locations, 187–203
    and social roles, 185–86
    and soul, 181–85
imperialism, 38, 211
incorporation, 44, **263**, 291, 293–94, 296–99, 300–7
Indian Religious Freedom Act (1978), 115, 134
Indigenous peoples and cultures
    cultural worldviews and practices
        etuaptmunk (Mi'kmaq concept of two-eyed seeing), 311
        fihavanana, 139
        Ghotul (Gond gathering place), 93–94
        haka (Māori ceremonial dance), 112
        oli (Kānaka Maoli chant), 140, 210
        Turtle Island (Anishanaabe and Haudenasaunee), 22, 112, 17, 228, 250, 330
        ubuntu (Zulu), 206
        yuuyaraq (Yupik law), 33
    Gond, 93-94
    impacts of boarding schools, 229
    Kānaka Maoli (Hawaiian people), 101–2, 140, 209, 210–11, 231
    Māori, 40, 112, 196
    removal from homelands, 188
    solidarity with, 125

sovereignty, 204, 330
survival, 15, 65, 114
vs Western worldviews, 40, **41–42**
Sylix, 38
Xhosa, 218–19
individualism, 213, 247
Industrial Growth Society, 312–13
inequities, 346
initiation, 12, 17–18, 68–69, 207, 266, 271–76, 280, **281**, 290, 295–96, 299, 301, 310, 314
  elements of rite of passage, 281–85, 282, **286**
  finding guided rite of passage, 276–79, **281**
  sobriety as, 164–65
  solo time in nature, 287–88
  types of, 18
injustice, 40, 316–18
  social, 201
  systems/systemic, 56, 330
intention in rite of passage, 247–53, **260**
intergenerational communities, 68, 199, 327
intersectionality, 201–3
intimacy, 130, 133–34, 140, 321
intuition, 45–47, 61, 193, 249
isolation, 9, 72, 212, 248, 306

J

Jaffe, Sarah, 318
Jenkinson, Stephen, 81
Jesson, Clara, 226
Jesson, Jeremiah, 226
Jim Crow laws, 330
Johari window, 176–77
Journey of Soul Initiation (Plotkin), 207n
Jung, Carl, 64
justice, 84, 86, 103, 189, 197, 328, 329, 330, 348, 349. See also social justice, restorative justice, transformative justice

K

Kaba, Mariame, 332
Kānaka Maoli (Hawaiian people), 101–2, 140, 209, 210–11, 231
King, Jr., Martin Luther, 39–40, 104, 328
kinship, 41, 134, 139, 204, 211-13, 220, 223, 225, 240
Kusnic, Edith, 6, 31-33, 246
Kuzniak, Katarzyna, 226

L

Lamborn, Emma, 226
land, connection to, 231. See also nature; more-than-human-world
land acknowledgement, 260
language, relationship to worldview, **38**
Lenni Lenape, 229
LGBTQIA+ folks (Lesbian, Gay, Bisexual, Transgender, Queer or Questioning, Intersex, Aasexual, plus), 349
Lifeways Back initiatives, 278n
limbic system, 85
liminal stage. See transition
liminality, gender, 193. See also queerness
Little, Meredith, 77, 78, 249
Lorde, Audre, 133
love, 40, 53, 64, 98, 114, 125, 133–34, 158, 160, 163, 193, 214–15, 293-94 322, 323

M

Machado, Antonio, 268
Macy, Joanna, 311–12
Māori, 40, 112, 196
Maquinna Lewis George, 326–27
Marshall, Albert, 311
Martin, Betty, 147–48, 149
Martin, Trayvon, 332
masculinity, 152, 193, 194
Mason-Dixon line, 229
Meade, Michael, 12, 12n, 18, 252, 310
Medicine wheel, 77–78, 77n
#MeToo movement, 138

Mendha Lekha, India, 93–94, 96
mental health, 9, 15, 33n, 135, See also anxiety; depression; healing; isolation
mentors/mentorship, 68–71, 132, 164, 284, **286**, 304
menstruation/menarche, 93, 271
Michaels, Melissa, 55, 59, 139, 185
mind-altering substances, 34–35, 129–33, 150, 152–53, 156–59
Mingus, Mia, 329
money, 10, 201, 318–21
mood-altering medications, 33n
Moore, Thomas, 184
more-than-human-world, 14, 46, 47–51, 77, 79, 130, 141, 144–45, 158, 182–84, 212, 225, 232, 235, 238, 254, 256, 274, 277, 287–88, 301, 302, 322, 324, 348
mutual aid, 320, 324
myth/mythology, 65–67, 96, 234

N

Nap Ministry, The, 319
Napoleon, Harold, 31–33
National Rites of Passage Institute, 205
natural world, See more-than-human-world
nature, See more-than-human-world
Neitzche, Frederich, 264
nervous system, 148
    dysregulation, 57, 59
    regulation, 9, 59
niche, 206–7
Northwest Network, The, 328–29
novelty, **86**, 88

O

oli 140, 210
oppression, 58, 97, 201-2, 114, 188, 189, 197, 322
origin stories, 234–39
Outward Bound, 154
oxytocin, 146, 160

P

Pacific Quest, 252, 285
Palmer, Parker J., 183
Papal Bulls, 229
parents, 12, 20, 21, 69, 73, 119, 133, 186, 279, 319
Parekh, Kruti, 107, 206
Parish, Ramon, 197
patience, 240, 317–18
peers, 12, 72–73, 186
permission, asking for, 119, 140–42, 144, 244
Pesach, Shlomo, 220n
physical appearance, 171–75
physical markers after initiatory journey, 303–5
place, 23, 59, 96, 203, 212, 231–34, 240, 257, 304, 348–49
Playing Indian (Deloria), 112
plant medicine, 132, 134–35, 165
pleasure, 85-86, 135, 145–52
Plotkin, Bill, 89, 90, 207n
pod mapping exercise, 216–18, 217
pornography, 151
power, 104–7, 140–41
practical testing, 283, **286**
psychotherapy, 33, 33n, 63
privilege, 107–11, 188, 197, 213, 224
projections, 64, 115
puberty, 92–93, 192
puka, 231

Q

queerness, 7, 189–90, **192**, 213, 303, 329, 349
Quiseng, Chris, 231

R

race, 7, 8, 22, 107, 108, 196–98, 210
rage, 57, 63, 225, 263, 312
reconciliation, 348
relationships
      importance of, 327–28

relational communication, formula for, 160
shifting with parents or primary caregivers, **73**
rematriation, 331
reparations, 329–30, 347
resilience, 105, 314, 316, 319
resourcing, 55–60, See also nervous system regulation
responsibility, 5, 20, 79, 99, 100, 125, 126, 133, 142, 199, 215, 311, 326, 327, 328–31, 348
restorative justice, 329
returning from rite of passage
    building plan for, 291
    carrying gifts after, 297–98
    crossing back over threshold, 295–97
    navigating difficulty after, 305–7
    physical markers, 303–5
    sharing story of journey, 298, 300–303
Rich, Adrienne, 331
right to earth and spirit, 348
Rise and Fall of the American Teenager, The (Hine), 98
risk management 154–55, 157
rites of passage, 1–5, 10–11, 14–17, 20–22, 33–34, 51, 68, 94–97, 101–2, 111–18, 120, 124, 130, 243–46, 282, 285–86, 279, 330
    adapting to life without, 97–99
    ceremonies, 346
    cultural practices, 243–46
    definition of, 11–14
    "echoes" of, 16–17
    elements of, 281–83, 282
    in Mendha Lekha, 93–94
    guided ceremonies, 276–79, **281**
    for millennial, 212
    movement, 347
    phases of, 43–45
    self-designed, 342–43
ritual(s), See ceremony
Rodriguez, Luis, 16–17, 124
Rohr, Richard, 27

S

Saavedra, Carlos, 118, 318
sacrifice, 288–90
sacred(ness), 112, 113, 125, 131–35, 153, 161, 165, 288
safety, 135, 152–57
security, 90, 213, 318
Salmon, Enrique, 240n
Shakur, Assata, **38**
Sand Creek Massacre, 229
#SayHerName movement, 197
scarification after initiatory journey, 304
Schurz, Carl, 244
Scott, Will, 288, 297
self-compassion, 175
self-designing rite of passage, 280, **281**
self-initiation, 12, **16**
self-love, 175, 195, 246
self-regulation, 9 See also nervous system regulation
send-off ceremony, 290
sensations, 45, 59, 60–62, **60**
serotonin, **150**
service, 265–66
settler, 112, 120, 127, 229, 250
    culture, 346
    responsibility of, 126–28
severance, 44, **262**, 274, 276, 310
sex/sexuality, 130–34, 165, 302, 349
    and brain function, **150**
    conflicting messages about, 10
    connection, 157–59
    exploration, map of, 135–57
    hazards and benefits of, 156
    influence in adulthood, 129–33
    love and, 133–34
    pleasure and, 145–46
    and reproductive freedom, 190
    safety in, 152–53, 156–57
    well-being, 145

safety, 135, 152–57
shadow, 64–65, 115, 147
Shah, Sonya, 331
sharing stories of a rite of passage, 120n, 298, 300–303
Shaw, Martin, 66, 67, 297
Siegel, Dan, 60, 85, **86**, 87, 160, 207
Sinopolous-Lloyd, Pınar Ateş, 206
slavery, impacts of, 182, 224
Smith, Lillian, 31
sobriety, 64
    as initiation, 164–65
social engagement, **86**, 88
social identities, 185, 189, 220, 250. See also social locations
social isolation, see isolation
social justice, 56, 108-09, 201, 206, 319
social locations, 187, 207, 277, 322
    class, 198–200
    elements of, 200–201
    gender, 189–95
    intersectionality, 201–3
    impact of oppression, 188
    impact of privilege, 188
    race, 196–98
social media, 136, 138, 240, 289
social roles, 185–86
social self, 90, 91
social stratification, 238
solo time in nature, 274, 287–88, 302
somatic, See embodied/embodiment
Somé, Malidoma, 169, 215, 239
Somé, Sobonfu, 257
soul, 89–91, 181–85
spiritual bypass, 114, 213
spirituality, 2, 113, 115, 132, 134, 146, 219, 238, 348,
    land-based, 117
    science separated from, 234
spiritual technology, 258
Starhawk, 105, 105n, 106, 114

statement of intent, 208, 241, 248–50, 252
stereotypes, 83, 84, 163–64, 188
stories/storytelling, 65–67, 285
stress, 55, 56, **150**
student loan debt, 10
substance abuse, 9–10, 95, 152, 283
suicide, 9, 158, 283
support circle, building
    mentors, 68–71
    peers, 72–73
Surfing the Creative program, See Golden Bridge
symbolism, 258, 261

T

Tamera community, 163
Taylor, J. Miakoda, 104, 105n
technology/technological connectedness, 9, 34, 238, 287
ten essentials for rite of passage into adulthood, 34, 35. See also adulthood
therapy, 33n See also psychotherapy
threshold(s), 254, 256, 266, 273–76, 275, 284, 295–97
Thurman, Howard, 265
time, cultural conceptions of, 36, **37**, 39, **41**, 347–48
transformative justice, 216, 218, 329
trauma, 55–57, 132, 153, 171, 173, 215, 316, 319
    ancestral, 58, 59, 288
    childhood, 125, 322
    collective, 57–58, 97
Tribal Canoe Journeys, 119
Turtle Island, 22, 112, 117, 229, 250, 330

U

ubuntu, 206
unhealthy patterning of body, 174
United States culture. See American culture
Universe Story, The 234–39
unverified personal gnosis (UPG), 301n

V

van Gennep, Arnold, 12, 43–44, 44n
Viera, Steph, 115
Villanueva, Edgar, 320
virginity, 163–64
von Mendlesohn, Benjamin, 163
vulnerability, 87, 140, 182, 218, 246, 248–49, 322–23

W

Waggoner, Edith Hartshorne, 220
Western worldviews and cultures, 22, 22n, 39-42, 53, 65, 76–77, 79, 81–82, 90, 95–97, 134–35, 206–7, 326
white culture, 114, 182, 323
    whiteness, 224
    white nationalism/nationalist, 14, 187
    white settlers, 77n
    white supremacy, 120n
Whyte, David, 297
wholeness, 23, 54, 194
wild wandering, 253–57
wisdom, 21, 79, 134, 222, 301, 318
witch burning, 190–91, 229
Work that Reconnects, The (Macy), 311
Work Won't Love You Back (Jaffe), 318
Wounded Knee Massacre, 229

X

Xhosa, 218–19

Y

Yehuda, Rachel, 58, 250, 252
Yon, Laura, 247
Youth Passageways, 7, 279n, 284, 325, 326
    cross cultural protocols in rites of passage, 345–50
yuuyaraq (Yupik law), 33
Yuuyaraq, the Way of the Human Being (Napoleon), 31

Z

Zimbardo, Philip, 151, 151n

LINK TO ONLINE RESOURCES FOR FURTHER STUDY

Each section of this book is a world of exploration in its own right! Scan the QR Code to access an up-to-date database of resources: books, podcasts, websites, videos, and more. Some of these resources I drew on as I wrote this book, others I've learned about more recently.

SHARING YOUR STORY

As I shared at the beginning of Rites and Responsibilities, there are so many voices and perspectives missing from this book! My hope is that over time, more young people will share their stories and contribute to future iterations of this project. Do you have a story you'd like to share on any of the themes of this book? Scan the QR code to let me know!

This is also a great way to reach out to share any corrections to the book.

Printed by Amazon Italia Logistica S.r.l.
Torrazza Piemonte (TO), Italy

48775742R00238